AMERICA
ON THE RERUN

AMERICA

TV SHOWS

A CITADEL PRESS BOOK

ON THE RERUN

THAT NEVER DIE

David Story

Published by Carol Publishing Group

A Citadel Press Book
Published by Carol Publishing Group
Citadel Press is a registered trademark of Carol Communications,
Inc.
Editorial Offices: 600 Madison Avenue, New York, N.Y. 10022
Sales and Distribution Offices: 120 Enterprise Avenue, Secaucus,
N.J. 07094
In Canada: Canadian Manda Group, P.O. Box 920, Station U,
Toronto, Ontario M8Z 5P9
Queries regarding rights and permissions should be addressed to
Carol Publishing Group, 600 Madison Avenue, New York, N.Y.
10022

Carol Publishing Group books are available at special discounts for
bulk purchases, for sales promotions, fund-raising, or educational
purposes. Special editions can be created to specifications. For
details, contact Special Sales Department, Carol Publishing Group,
120 Enterprise Avenue, Secaucus, N.J. 07094

Designed by A. Christopher Simon
Manufactured in the United States of America

10 9 8 7 6 5 4 3 2 1

Library of Congress Cataloging-in-Publication Data

Story, David.
    America on the rerun / by David Story.
        p.   cm.
    "A Citadel Press Book."
    ISBN 0-8065-1410-8
    1. Television progress—United States—Anecdotes.
    2. Television actresses—United States—Interviews.
    3. Television actors and programs—United States—Miscellanea.
    I. Title.
PN1992.3.U5S76   1993
791.45′75′0973—dc20   92-37558
                                                            CIP

For Carol:
Thank you for being a friend

Acknowledgments

There are so many people who helped to make *America on the Rerun* possible, and going back to the very beginning I must thank my friend Ritch Colbert, whose enthusiasm over the years for the television industry has proven to be contagious. Thank also to Pat McFarland of the Arts and Entertainment Network, Lisa Schiraldi of Nick at Nite, Sara Lowe of the Family Channel, Keith Merryman of Orion, my sister Debbie Story, Grace Marsh and Diane Hunter of the University of North Carolina Center for Public Television, Lisa Mateas and Dick Connell of TNT, Ward McCarthy of TBS, and a very special thank you to TBS SuperStation's Kate McSweeney. And not to be overlooked is Karen Hatcher of Michael Parver and Associates in Atlanta.

I can't thank enough professional fan Tina Jakes, a respected *Gone With the Wind* collector among other things, who led me through the complex world of fandom, along with her cohorts, Fred Causey, Jack Townsend, David McGriff, and Margie Perry. And thanks to Robert Finocchio, who arranged my interview with the gracious Diana Millay, and to other generous individuals such as Eddie Albert, Patrick Macnee, Everett Greenbaum, Aaron Ruben, Norman Felton, Dick Gautier, Dave Ketchum, George Lindsey, Alan Young, Al Simon, Herb Browar, Bob Leeds, Donna Douglas, Vic Mizzy, John Schuck, Al Lewis, Lara Parker, Sherwood Schwartz, Connie Forlsund, Kasey Rogers, Dick Sargent, Bob May, Bill Mumy, Ray Walston, Michael Ansara, Leonard Stern, Yvonne Craig, Rene Auberjonois, and David Wilde, who was married to the late Joan Bennett.

I also extend my appreciation to various fan clubs (f.c.), festivals, and publications, such as those headed by Ann Teipen (*The Wild, Wild West*), Bob Hines (*Gilligan's Island*), Vicki Holt (the Robert Vaughn f.c.), Lynda Mendoza (the David McCallum f.c.), Jim Clark (*The Andy Griffith Show*), Jim Pierson (the *Dark Shadows* festival), "Big Bucks" Burnett (*Mr. Ed*), Diane Albert of *TV Collector*, Dave Campiti of Innovation, Ron Nastrum of Atlanta's "Dixie Trek" festival, Terry Crissman of Atlanta's "Fantasy Fair," and Blanche ("Trina") Trinajstick, whose *National Directory of Fan Clubs* provides a comprehensive listing of such organizations.

Thanks to Bill Tetreault, Farris Preston, and Richard Barnes for photos and videotapes, and to my fellow Atlantans for additional photos and feedback—Mark Wood, Rob McQuillan, Sam Patton, and Dr. James Bryant. I also salute my fellow authors Joey Green, Herbie Pilato, and Jon Heitland for their insight into *Get Smart*, *Bewitched*, and *The Man From U.N.C.L.E.*, respectively.

I appreciate the assistance of three dynamic Girl Fridays: Sherwood Schwartz's Darlene Schwartz (no relation), Leonard Stern's Jo McDaniel, and Dave Campiti's Pam Leitt. And many, many thanks to Clay and Renee Turner for their hospitality during my trip to Los Angeles. And last, though not least, a heartfelt thank you to my housemate Ginny Smartt, who for many months took messages, made phone calls, and lived daily with the chaos and hysteria that resulted in *America on the Rerun*.

Contents

AMERICA
ON THE RERUN

"We respond to these myth-imbued tales with our hearts, and we are caught up in the whirlwind of the life force. We feel a connection with all humanity throughout time, and we are enriched by that connection."

LARA PARKER

TRIBUTE TO DICK YORK

Dick York died on February 20, 1992, at the age of sixty-three, a victim of emphysema. While a patient at Blodgett Memorial Medical Center in Grand Rapids, Michigan, York suffered from heart and kidney complications, as well as pneumonia.

The father of five children and thirteen grandchildren, York found his health problems beginning back in 1969, when he exited *Bewitched,* due to an addiction to pain killers and chronic back problems. According to the late Harry Ackerman, who spoke candidly to *TV Collector* magazine prior to his own demise, York constantly missed work due to one of several illnesses, including his prescription drug addiction.

Ackerman told *TV Collector*'s Diane Albert that York once even collapsed on the set, causing the episode to be shot without him, as were twelve other episodes over the years. These shows, said Ackerman, were run consecutively the summer before Dick Sargent stepped into the role, so that by the time the new Darrin appeared, many viewers had forgotten what the old one looked like.

"[Liz] didn't like Dick [York] physically very much," confesses Sargent today. "[She and I] got along better—we did more 'kissy-kissy' stuff than they did. Fortunately no one thought that it was me who passed away. I always thought that Dick York was a marvelous actor and I greatly admired him."

"Dick York—I thought he was wonderful," concurs fellow *Bewitched* player Kasey Rogers, "God love him!"

Though York finally beat his drug addiction, he was washed up as an actor. He consequently supported his family with welfare, unemployment checks, and menial work such as janitorial jobs. York, who received no residuals from *Bewitched,* supplemented his meager income with a pension from the Screen Actors Guild.

In 1987 he was confined to his home in Rockford, Michigan, where he was hooked up to an oxygen tank. Yet the courageous York managed to found Acting for Life, an organization to feed the homeless.

INTRODUCTION

For all of us who grew up in 1960s America, television was a magical happening. Replacing the ideal TV families of the fifties, such as those of Donna Reed and Robert Young and Danny Thomas, was to be a mythical assortment of witches and warlocks, misfits and monsters, spies, talking animals (and cars), hillbillies, and aliens.

During those years my favorite show was ABC's daytime Gothic soap *Dark Shadows,* perhaps for no other reason than that it was available for daily viewer consumption, as opposed to the other fifteen shows in this book, which were broadcast weekly. Though today reruns of *Dark Shadows* seem almost primitive in the naiveté of the scripts and the performances it is to me the most phenomenal of the shows to come out of the 1960s. The failure of producer Dan Curtis's glossy prime-time reworking two decades later is evidence of the impossibility of recapturing what for America's youth was a magical moment in time, flubbed lines, Styrofoam props, and all.

Vampires and werewolves were not the only TV monsters in the 1960s. There was *The Munsters,* the most amusingly bizarre of the shows. I mean, what were these good folks? Who were they and where did they find that Marilyn chick? Even after researching the series, I am still not sure about any of the above. This I do know: they were delightful and fun to watch, with Herman's innocent, childlike demeanor, Lily's maternal instincts, Grandpa's amusing pranks, strange Eddie's youthful nastiness, and Marilyn's pseudo-Monroe sex appeal.

And of course, there was *The Addams Family,* the most timeless of all the shows, and a testament to the perverse art of Charles Addams, whose talents were so sublime that his ideal of the perfect American family has been perpetuated, ever more successfully, as evidenced by 1993's *Addams Family Values.*

And on the flip side of these ghouls and eccentrics were their comical cousins—the endearing pranksters of *Be-*

witched and the mischievous genie of *I Dream of Jeannie.* As the classiest of all the 1960s sitcoms, *Bewitched* is in a category by itself. How could a vehicle boasting of talents such as Agnes Moorehead, Maurice Evans, Paul Lynde, Alice Ghostley, Alice Pearce, Kasey Rogers, and Dick York (yes, he is my favorite Darrin) be anything less? And all the more reason for us to regret that the elegant Elizabeth Montgomery has put the whole thing behind her.

Then there's Barbara Eden as everybody's favorite Jeannie in what was the most escapist of the sixties shows. Indeed, technology met mythology face-to-face when astronaut Tony Nelson found that tawdry bottle on the beach. And to paraphrase Eden's former husband Michael Ansara, Barbara might not have been able to act her way out of a paper bag, but my! She was pleasing to look at and still is: a 1960s icon seemingly frozen in time.

Another series which sometimes bordered on the paranormal (or at least the abnormal) was *Gilligan's Island,* the silliest of all the shows. But after talking to creator Sherwood Schwartz, one understands that "silly" is actually a compliment. The shows were meant to be cartoonish—parodies, if you will, of everyone we've ever known metamorphosed into five colorful castaways. Now, that was some feat! And the longevity of the show in rerun heaven leaves no doubt as to the savvy, if not genious, of Schwartz.

It was also during the 1960s that we journeyed into space, and I'm not talking *Star Trek,* which took its space people too seriously—and as a youngster I did not. I am thinking of the most extraordinary of aliens, Uncle Martin, as portrayed by Ray Walston, now the judge on *Picket Fences.* Uncle Martin made space fun and safe and a far cry from all those nasty Klingons and Romulans. Yet fun as it was, it could not top that other TV space odyssey *Lost in Space,* the campiest of the shows from the 1960s. This one gave space adventure an edge, as the exploits of Will Robinson and Dr. Smith added an extra thrill. And best of all—young Will was just my age. Boy, could I relate to that one!

Fortunately sixties television was not all ghouls and aliens. No one can survive on a diet of just one genre, and our television menu was peppered with assorted hillbillies, oddballs in what were called the downhome sitcoms. The corniest and longest-running of these was a gem called *The Beverly Hillbillies.* Everybody loved Granny, despite her cantankerous ways; admired Jed for his wisdom and Jethro for his lack of same; and lost their heart to Elly May for her innocent, fresh beauty.

The Hillbillies and their ties to a mythical rural place called Hooterville eventually spawned another series, *Green Acres,* the most surreal of all the sitcoms. Eddie Albert and Eva Gabor headed a cast that exploded in a one-of-a-kind Warhol-like kaleidoscope of humor and zaniness perhaps unmatched until *Newhart* came along years later.

Filmways, which parented *The Addams Family, Green Acres,* and *The Beverly Hillbillies,* also nurtured another program, which may not have been set in the country, but boasted a cast of barnyard critters led by the most outrageous of the sixties stars, none other than Mr. Ed, the wondrous talking horse, who may have been the hooved "Garfield" of his day.

The last of the rural sitcoms may, at first glance, seem out of place, but the enduring *Andy Griffith Show* was not about a normal, nuclear family. It was about the Taylors, a motherless family and extended kin—townsfolk that included misfits and oddballs. The miracle was that this disparate group came together and it worked, resulting in more warmth, patience, humor, and tolerance than ever exhibited on any TV show. And in light of that assessment the Griffith show may have been even more fantastical than any of the others.

As an adult I admit that my love of television spies, born in the 1960s, has surpassed my love of ghouls, eccentrics, werewolves, and hicks. The legendary *Get Smart* was a TV first, debuting as what would become the first true satire on the tube. That it still runs on Nick at Nite is no surprise. The most futuristic of all the lighthearted 1960s shows, *The Wild, Wild West,* is something that still thrills me whenever I catch it in reruns, though Robert Conrad seems awfully short these days. *The Man From U.N.C.L.E.,* a road show James Bond send-up, may seem more campy than exciting today, but it remains, undisputedly, the sexiest of the sixties programs. We may not have completely understood what was going on between Napoleon Solo and all those lovely leading ladies back then but we knew they were up to something!

It's always appropriate to save the best for last, as is the case with *The Avengers,* my favorite show of yesterday today, and the kinkiest television show of them all, making even *Twin Peaks* and *Picket Fences* seem like children's fare. There never was or ever will be a lady as sophisticated, sassy, and seductive as Diana Rigg in her persona as Mrs. Emma Peel, partner to Patrick Macnee's debonair and dandy John Steed. When these two came together on screen, it was, in my mind, the height of sixties TV magic.

I believe that there will be something for everyone in *America on the Rerun.* These truly are TV shows that remain eternal—they have proven themselves time and time again. They're sixteen of my favorites and I offer them chronologically by their premiere dates, from my perspective and that of many of the participants. I extend a special thanks to publisher Steven Schragis who recognized the marketability of my vision when I first proposed it to him in 1991. Heartfelt thanks also to the lovely Lara Parker of *Dark Shadows,* who summed it up best when she uttered the phrase "myth-imbued tales," for all of these shows are such. And with a vision of Vietnam and social and sexual revolution on the homefront during the 1960s, we all had a need to escape into television: extraordinary, classy, satirical, phenomenal, enduring, campy, timeless, silly, outrageous, futuristic, sexy, kinky, surreal, corny, bizarre television. So, here's to television, to America, to reruns. Enjoy!

Andy Griffith, Ronny Howard, and Frances Bavier (*photo courtesy University of North Carolina Public Television*)

ONE

THE ANDY GRIFFITH SHOW

(October 3, 1960–September 16, 1968)

Enter low-key Sheriff Andy Taylor (Andy Griffith), father of the all-American youngster Opie (Ron Howard). Enter pop-eyed, hyperkinetic Barney Fife (Don Knotts), Taylor's fumbling deputy. Enter motherly Aunt Bee (Frances Bavier), housekeeper to widower Andy and son Opie.

Add a sprinkling of colorful townspeople—dense gas station attendant Gomer Pyle (Jim Nabors), fussy barber Floyd Smoot (Howard McNear), Barney's pining girlfriend Thelma Lou (Betty Lynn), drugstore proprietor Miss Elly (Elinor Donahue), town clerk Howard Sprague (Jack Dodson), ill-mannered illiterate Ernest T. Bass (Howard Morris), town drunk Otis Campbell (Hal Smith), Gomer's bumpkin cousin Goober (George Lindsey)—and you have all of the magical ingredients that immortalized the sleepy fictional hamlet of Mayberry,

North Carolina, and made *The Andy Griffith Show* the finest and most endearing of all the sixties sitcoms.

Launched from an episode of Danny Thomas's *Make Room for Daddy* in 1960, the Griffith show was another offering of CBS program chief James Aubrey.

During its first season (1960–61), *The Andy Griffith Show* was on Monday at 9:30 P.M. and placed number four in the ratings. The series dropped to number seven in season two, but steadily climbed after that being rated number six in season three, number five in season four, number four in season five, back to number six in season six. During its final two seasons it moved to number two and number one respectively. And though the show itself never won an Emmy, Don Knotts carried home five statuettes as Outstanding Featured Player in a comedy and Frances Bavier earned one, too, in 1967.

In the pilot, "Danny Meets Andy," Frances Bavier played a character named Henrietta Perkins. She would later be introduced as Aunt Bee Taylor in "The New Housekeep" episode of the new Griffith show on October 3, 1960, staying on in Mayberry even beyond the life of *The Andy Griffith Show* into its spin-off, *Mayberry, R.F.D.*

Its eight-year run found a virtual parade of lovable guest stars and semi-regulars in the streets of Mayberry: Mabel (*Bewitched*) Albertson as Howard's mother; Aneta Corsaut as schoolteacher Helen Crump, Andy's sweetheart (and later wife); Jack Burns as Deputy Warren Ferguson, Knotts's temporary replacement in 1965; Paul Hartman as Emmett, the fix-it handyman; Jack Prince as farmer and songbird Rafe Hollister; Peggy McCay as Andy's high school flame Sharon de Spain; Michael J. Pollard as Barney's insecure Cousin Virgil; Denver Pyle as mountain man Briscoe Darling; Maggie Peterson as Briscoe's buxom daughter Charlene; Keith Thibodeaux as Opie's pal Johnny Paul; Bernard Fox as the proper Englishman Malcolm Merriweather; Buddy Ebsen as Opie's hobo friend; Alan Hale Jr. as hot-to-trot farmer Jeff Pruitt; Sue Ane Langdon as perky county nurse Peggy Simpson; Bill Bixby as young playboy Ron Bailey; Gavin MacLeod as a sheriff-without-a-gun actor; Don Rickles as itinerant peddler Newton Monroe; Jerry Van Dyke as a destitute carnival banjo picker; Barbara Eden as Floyd's manicurist; George Kennedy as a big-city detective; Parley Baer as Mayor Stone; Ron's brother Clint Howard as Leon, the peanut butter kid; and Arlene Golonka as Millie, Howard's girl. Later she was the girlfriend of Sam Jones (Ken Berry) on *Mayberry, R.F.D.*

The series' directors ranged from Richard Crenna, Coby Ruskin, and Earl Bellamy to Jeffrey Hayden, Aaron Ruben, and Bob Sweeney, who directed the reunion movie *Return to Mayberry.* Howard ("Ernest T.") Morris, directed fifteen episodes.

The best of *The Andy Griffith Show* scripts were penned by Jack Elinson; Charles Stewart; Leo Soloman and Ben Gersham; John Whedon; Harvey Bullock and William Idelson; and Jim Fritzell and Everett Greenbaum, who wrote the *Return to Mayberry* script along with Bullock.

Betty Lynn comments on the 1986 reunion special, which brought together most of the original cast with the exception of Donahue, Burns, and Bavier: "It was just absolutely wonderful. And everything went so well. And we all enjoyed each other. It really was a marvelous time."

Return to Mayberry remains arguably the best of all the TV reunion movies to date. As Greenbaum and Bullock's script unfolds, Andy comes back to town with wife Helen after nearly twenty years and feels he wants to be sheriff again, but finds he must run against Barney, who's still engaged to Thelma Lou. Opie is now all grown up and is editor of the town newspaper. In all, sixteen stars returned, along with many of the original crew.

And the formula worked again, twenty-five years later for fifty-six million people tuned in to watch *Return to Mayberry,* which, in turn, led Turner's TBS SuperStation to produce in 1990 its own special on the Griffith Show entitled *Thirty Years of Andy,* with Knotts, Lindsey, Lynn, Smith, Morris, and Dodson.

"I thought it was very complimentary," says Aaron Ruben of the TBS special, "in paying respect to a show that we all felt deserved that kind of recognition. The show never won an Emmy." On the subject of the Turner special, Greenbaum suggests, "It had a quality that the people doing it didn't realize—it seems to have been made in Mayberry. It had a very overall small townishness about it that was nice. As [director] Bob Sweeney said, 'It showed why actors need writers.' "

As an example of good writing Greenbaum offers this: "I liked the show that Harvey Bullock wrote in which Opie kept a wild bird in a cage. I liked it so much that when I was asked to write *Return to Mayberry* I selected Harvey to write it with me. He's a wonderful fellow. He has a strength I lack in plot construction.

"The people who run the networks are more or less idiots," continues Greenbaum. "Before they came to me, they had spent a lot of money on scripts that were just awful—they were written about people you'd never seen before—the descendants of the original cast. And they were all going to analysts so Andy finally called me and said he was going to run away and hide.

"They didn't want anybody my age writing. I got a hold of Dick Linke, Andy's manager, and I said, 'We want everyone in this, anybody who played an interesting or memorable character.' We even wanted to get back the Darling Family. They are actually a group called The Dilliards.

"Dick Linke said the American public doesn't want to see anyone who's fat and has gray hair, and I said, 'You idiot, that's exactly what they want to see. They want to see how their old friends look now. That's what they want to see.' So finally they started coming and even Ronny [Howard] came, surrounded by secretaries."

"North Carolina looked just the way I thought it was gonna look," recalls Howard, "and the people were just wonderful."

But what has happened to some of those warm and humorous folks from Mayberry? As for Andy's gal pals, Peggy McCay of "High School Reunion" (February 4, 1963) has been on countless TV episodes. And Elinor Donahue moved on to *The Odd Couple* as Felix's girlfriend for a couple of seasons, *Mulligan's Stew,* Fox's *Get a Life,* and a half dozen or so other shows.

She recalls that *The Andy Griffith Show* "was fun. I was going through a bit of turmoil in my personal life [and] I really don't remember anything about it. My private life was foremost and I was sort of sleepwalking my way through it." She was first introduced in the episode "Ellie Comes to Town" October 24, 1960, playing a young pharmacist who moves to Mayberry to help her uncle at the local drugstore. Totally ethical, Ellie refuses to sell matronly Emma Watson medicine without a prescription and Sheriff Andy is pressured by Emma to intercede. He soon learns that Ellie's uncle has been selling Emma Watson sugar pills for years. As for Ellie, she learns a lesson in diplomacy.

"Irresistible Andy," airing the following week, solidified, at least temporarily, Ellie's relationship with the sheriff and her status on the show. After asking Ellie to be his date for the church picnic, Andy feels as if things are happening too fast, and in order to back off, he encourages Ellie's interest in three more of Mayberry's eligible bachelors. Discovering Andy's plan, she confronts him and they make up to the point where they are able to keep their date for the church social. This is the beginning of Andy's first real romance. But Ellie left Mayberry after that first season never to return.

Donahue has her fond memories of her days in North Carolina's mythical town. Her favorite episode is "The Christmas Story," which aired December 19, 1960. In this show, Andy and Barney discover the true Christmas spirit when they help a prisoner and his family celebrate the holiday in the Mayberry jail. As a result the town scrooge is touched by the joy of the season.

And as far as the real love of Ellie's life, towheaded Opie Taylor, Donahue says, "I've not worked with any child actor as talented as Ronny. We weren't acting in our scenes. Something lovely happened that can't be thought out." Whatever it was, she chalks it up to Mayberry's "warmth, humor and genuineness."

"I must say that in all fairness to Elinor, who's a fine actress and who has done a lot of wonderful things before and since," admits *The Andy Griffith Show* producer Aaron Ruben, "that whole first year [there was this] conventional notion that we had to get Andy a girlfriend—and Andy was very uncomfortable with the notion anyway to begin with because he didn't have the right approach to it by his own admission." (On Joanna Moore's guest appearances as the overtly sexual Peggy McMillan, Ruben adds, "That almost caught fire but Andy [kept] saying, 'I don't want to have a show with fights in the kitchen.'")

Ruben continues, "In the roles [Andy] had played previously in *No Time for Sergeants* and even *A Face in the Crowd* he had a peculiar and almost awkward attitude toward women. Even in *A Face in the Crowd* he was kind of awkward and heavy-handed in his attitude toward Lee Remick.

"He just didn't know how to deal with these women—he was uncomfortable and awkward—and to this day, if you ask him, he says he doesn't like to look at those first year's shows, particularly the ones [dealing] with women because he was being a comic and an awkward one at that, in terms of these women and it was Andy who first discovered that he could no longer play [a] comedian even though he started out with some very funny monologues and he was hilarious in *No Time for Sergeants*.

"But in the midst of this series, surrounded by Aunt Bee and Opie and the various townspeople, that he could no longer be the comic—he had to be the straight, he had to be the leading man, as he put it, and once he arrived at that conclusion that he was now a leading man, he could be more comfortable with women. He could deal with them on a straight forward basis and not behave like some goofy teenager."

"We got into a huge argument about women's rights the first day on the set," recalled Aneta Corsaut of Griffith in the book *Mayberry, My Hometown*. "We were out in the middle of the street on location screaming at each other and it ended up being very good [for] both of us and we became good friends. . . . We have been good friends for many years."

Things had settled down by the time of Corsaut's favorite episode, "Helen, the Authoress," which aired February 27, 1967. In this show Helen Crump's children's book is published, but Andy feels left out during a visit with Helen to her publisher in Raleigh. Andy is not sure if he can deal with Helen's newfound celebrity status, but she handles her fifteen minutes of fame very gracefully, and as they say, all's well that ends well.

And just as Andy Griffith made the transition from Rotary-circuit comic to TV leading man, so has his TV son Ron Howard make the transition from child star to respected director as an adult—with six years of *Happy Days* in between. Today he lives near Griffith show costar Aneta Corsaut's sister in Greenwich, Connecticut, far from the maddening crowds of Los Angeles.

"Ron Howard the director is certainly not the Opie we knew," says George Lindsey today. "He's not the guy we knew."

"Anybody's surprised at such a meteoric rise," says Aaron Ruben of Ron Howard's current fame, "because that's what it was. Very often someone who's played a supporting role in a series will go off and decide, 'Well, I think I want to be a director now,' and so they'll have a [moderate] success, but I mean, he took off like a rocket. And I guess I can't think of anybody more deserving.

"I think he was not quite six years old when he came on the show, and I don't remember working with anybody who was ever so thoroughly professional and so thoroughly involved with his work, and a great deal of that [credit] has to go to his parents because they kept a watchful eye. They were far from stage parents and he was a good kid to begin with, but who knew about all that hidden talent that he had?"

"I wasn't surprised [by Ronny's success]," insists Greenbaum. "He was the most wonderful little boy who ever lived and his parents were very sensible."

Ron Howard sums up his feelings on Mayberry in *Mayberry, My Hometown:* "If people live together and basically try to do the right thing and try to look out for each other—then life might not be too spectacular, but it can be rich and very rewarding."

Ron credits Andy with having taught him how to put humor and truth into a story, and costar Howard McNear with having taught him courage and determination: "He suffered a stroke—two strokes actually—during the course of the show, but he always came back. Each time he would have lost a little bit of his mobility, but not that wonderful sense of timing."

"Howard McNear was the funniest," Aneta Corsaut says today, "the most naturally funny man . . . and he came from mostly doing drama. He was just brilliant."

"Howard was darling," agrees Betty Lynn. "Howard had a great humor, a tremendous humor. Almost a pixielike quality."

"When I think of Howard McNear, I have such a longing for him," Aaron Ruben says. "I miss him so—he was such a delight. He was funny and he was also funny without really trying to be funny. We'd sit around the conference table and Andy would ask him a question—it was [Howard's] delivery and it was his complete innocence—and whatever he would say, Andy would slide down to the floor and pound the floor with his fists. If anybody could get Andy hysterical, it was Howard. He was a delight of a man, extremely modest, very retiring.

"I once told him I was planning to write a script for him in which he'd be the featured player. He got all flustered, 'Oh, I wish you wouldn't do that.' I said, 'You'll like this, you'll really like this, Howard. It's about mail-order matrimony and you get involved with a woman; and he just died a thousand deaths. That's the kind of guy he was. It came off well!"

The episode was "Floyd the Gay Deceiver" (November 26, 1962), in which Floyd through the classifieds misrepresents himself to a wealthy widow who's coming through town. Andy and Aunt Bee are recruited to help bail him out, only to discover that the widow herself has been less than honest. Andy covers for her to save face for Floyd.

"Howard was just great," Everett Greenbaum concurs. "He was that same person. He was Floyd the barber in real life as well. I remember that terrible suit Don [Knotts] wore as Barney. Howard always thought that was a beautiful suit. He kept saying, 'Where did you get that wonderful suit?' and he'd keep feeling it. He just loved that suit.

"He had been in movies—in the thirties he was a young leading man, a romantic lead, and the studio sent him down on Hollywood Boulevard to take ballet lessons and he was in this studio in his ballet clothes [doing his] knee bends at the bar and a plumber was there fixing the radiator, and the plumber looked up at Howard and said, 'Jesus Christ!' which strikes me as very funny."

"The funniest man I ever worked with!" exclaims George ("Goober") Lindsey when asked about McNear. "He was without question the fun person on the set. I never was. I was pretty grim, frankly."

But McNear and Griffith weren't the only two who helped to shape the young Ronny Howard. Another was his real-life dad, Rance Howard, who, along with Sid Morse, wrote Ron's favorite episode "The Ball Game" (October 3, 1966), in which Andy umpires a little league baseball game between Mayberry and Mt. Pilot. To prove his impartiality Andy calls Opie out in the final inning. Later a photo proves that, though the play was close, Opie was safe. Helen and Aunt Bee keep Andy from learning of this, though.

And what about Ron's little brother Clint? "Clint is so inventive and brings so much to every scene," says Ron, "that he's an absolute joy to work with."

Clint played Leon in five episodes of the Griffith show and in 1963 was in the film *The Courtship of Eddie's Father* (along with brother Ron and Shirley Jones). He was a regular as obnoxious Stanley on the short-lived *Baileys of Balboa* (1964–65) and also worked with brother Ron on *Happy Days* and in Ron's *Splash, Cocoon, Parenthood,* and *Backdraft.*

Interestingly, Howard Morris of the Griffith show was also involved with *Splash.* Having directed Ron on the Griffith show, Morris this time around was directed by Ron. "He did a terrific job," recalls Ron, "and we had a lot of fun that day."

"I worked with Howard [Morris] on *The Sid Caesar Show* as a writer and he's got this crazy Quixote-approach to humor," recalls producer Aaron Ruben, "and that wonderful character that was developed for him—Ernest T. Bass—it couldn't have been better."

"My Fair Ernest T. Bass," which aired on February 3, 1964, was an attempt to polish the unrefined manners of grungy Ernest T. Andy and Barney pass him off as a proper Bostonian at Mrs. Wiley's elegant dinner party. All goes according to plan until someone cuts in on Ernest T. and his dance partner, and Ernest T. hits the guy on the head with a vase. Another memorable episode starring Morris was "The Education of Ernest T. Bass" (October 12, 1964).

Everett Greenbaum also knew Howard Morris "from

Don Knotts as Deputy Barney Fife, on the lookout for jaywalkers

the *Sid Caesar* days in New York. Ernest T. Bass is another character Jim and I created; [Howard] brought a lot to it—the way he pronounced words and the way he behaved. He was just perfect for it. He brought a lot to the character that really made it go over the top, the same as Jim [Nabors] did with Gomer."

"In retrospect," adds Ruben, "the thing about the Griffith show was that each character, each role was so perfectly designed for that actor, like Barney for Don and even Sheriff Taylor for Andy and the barber for Howard [McNear] and Ernest T. Bass for Howard [Morris]. I'd never seen him play such a wild-eyed character but he was marvelous in it. He was just wonderful."

Over the years Morris has directed feature films and numerous TV sitcoms, including *The Dick Van Dyke Show, One Day at a Time, Laverne and Shirley, The Bob Newhart Show,* and *Get Smart* (which he cocreated with Mel Brooks and Buck Henry—Brooks was an old *Your Show of Shows* buddy).

Another Mayberry character with a custom-designed role was Gomer Pyle. "Andy and his wife came down to see me [at the Horn in Santa Monica]," recalls Nabors in *Mayberry, My Hometown,* "and afterwards he said, 'I really don't know what you do but you do it very well.' There was a part in an episode called 'Man in a Hurry'— the filling station kid—Andy asked me to read for it."

"He came into the series after Andy heard him sing at a place called the Horn in Santa Monica," confirms Betty Lynn. "Andy was very impressed with him."

"[George Lindsey] was almost the original gas station attendant," recalls Aaron Ruben. "He had come in and I had interviewed him. He had just come off of Broadway in the musical *All-American*. And I was already to sign him and Andy, after that day's shooting, came into my office and said, 'Have you already hired the guy who's going to do the gas station attendant?' and I said, 'No, but I'm about to because this fellow sounded very good.' He said, 'Well before you do that, would you listen to a young guy I saw the other night at some little club where he sang?' and it turned out to be Jim Nabors, who came in—and he was kind of nervous and ill at ease, but he more than made up for it with his freshness—and I said 'Let's give him a shot.' And that was that."

"How do you work through [that] kind of disappointment?" Lindsey asks today. "Life goes on. I was very, very upset because I just knew that Gomer role and I could do it and it was mine. And I could have done it [but] it probably wouldn't have been like [Jim] did it. Then I sort of had to go along with a Goober with a Gomerish tint to it. Jim was good but I approached [my] character a little differently. It took me about a year to find that character."

"And George Lindsey, as good as he was, he simply did not have [that] star quality that Jim had," adds Ruben. "He

was stepping into a tough spot. To begin with, there wasn't [another] character like Barney and even Gomer. The reason I left the show was that I had created *The Gomer Pyle Show* and I had to take over as executive producer. I had done both shows for one season and it was getting [to be] too much and that's why I left it and Gomer became the star of his own show. There was not that same attitude toward George Lindsey, good as he was."

Gomer left Mayberry for Camp Henderson to star in *Gomer Pyle, U.S.M.C.* (1964–70) with Frank Sutton and Ronnie Schell. "He was probably the nicest character you could ever play," says Nabors of the role who earned him his own show. "He was all good."

Nabors's series remained in the top ten through the sixties, although some critics blasted his countrified performance. Gomer's cry of "Shazam!" was taken from the Captain Marvel comics. "Surprise!" (in triplicate) was his own idea.

"I didn't care for [Gomer] being in the Marines particularly," contributes Greenbaum, "Jim [Fritzell] and I had created the character of Gomer [in 'Man in a Hurry'] and we were very fond of him and we enjoyed writing it. And, I was kind of disappointed when he left the Griffith show."

"Jim took off and became a big success after five years as Gomer," says Ruben of Nabors, who also enjoyed a successful singing career and today lives on a macadamia nut plantation in Hawaii. "He went out to do clubs and county fairs and became a wealthy man and lives in Hawaii. Jim enjoyed his stardom for as long as it lasted."

Nabors's favorite Griffith show episode remains "Citizen's Arrest" which aired on December 16, 1963. In it, Barney gives Gomer a ticket for making a U-turn and Gomer later gets even by making a citizen's arrest of Barney for the same offense. A feud erupts because Barney considers himself above the law, and Andy has to referee. "'Citizen's Arrest' sort of solidified me in the series," Nabors recalled in *Mayberry, My Hometown*. "And it was just very funny."

But apparently executive producer Danny Thomas and Andy Griffith did not have that same attitude toward Knotts as they did toward Nabors. It long was rumored of the Nabors spin-off that the real reason Knotts was leaving the show after the 1964–65 season was that he had not been offered his own program.

Around that time Griffith told *TV Guide:* "I don't deny Don's leaving left us with a problem, especially after Gomer going. Sheriff Taylor—he's too sensible, too sharp. Can't provoke the comedy. Can't be made a fool of. What he needs is a troublesome friend to get him into all those troublesome situations. Way last year Don talked to me about leaving. He had all kinds of offers, finally took the Universal deal because it offered him movies, as well as TV. After all, he'd spent nine busy years on TV. I would have done the same thing."

"I did get a call from the *New York Times* saying what's going to happen to the show now that you and Don are leaving," Ruben relates. "I said, 'Nothing.' Everybody is sorry to see Don go and he was replaced with Goober and a couple of other characters. I'm not going to make comparisons because Don was an original.

"There was nobody and there hasn't been anybody like Don, but if the show had fallen apart because either Don or I left," he continues, "it would have meant it was all built upon the ability of one person to make this thing work and it wasn't. It was built on a really solid premise and its principals—namely Andy—were responsible for making it work. He was the guy that carries the weight of this wonderful premise."

"I was stunned when I found out Don was leaving," recalls Lynn today. "I was one of the last to know. I knew they wouldn't need Thelma Lou anymore."

But was Knotts's decision to leave made out of haste and a desire to save face? "I don't know that Don ever got a role that fit him so comfortably and was so beautifully tailored for him as the role of Barney Fife," Ruben adds. "He's such a talented guy, a really inventive and original comedian, he did well. Certain roles come for certain actors and that's it—it's their most triumphant moment. They [just] go on after that."

On leaving the Griffith show, Knotts has said, "I had a series offer, the Universal deal, and others, but took Universal because it involved what I wanted to do most, comedy feature films." But Knotts would be back for a few guest appearances, as in the episodes "The Return of Barney Fife" (January 10, 1966), "The Legend of Barney Fife" (January 17, 1966), "A Visit to Barney Fife" (January 16, 1967), "Barney Comes to Mayberry" (January 23, 1967), and "Barney Hosts a Summit Meeting" (January 29, 1968).

Knotts's onetime agent, Sherwin Bash, once said that laughs were serious business for Don—for him comedy was a grim business.

"Some comedians are tight inside," Knotts has said before, perhaps speaking of himself, "But Andy is warm. You can get close to him."

Aneta Corsaut saw a different Don than she remembered at the time of the 1986 TV reunion: "He was quite the lady's man and he was funny. He was more fun when we did *Return to Mayberry* than during the series."

And a lot had changed for Knotts over the years. After making a number of big screen comedies, he returned to TV and starred during the 1970–71 season in *The Don Knotts Show*, which was rather lukewarm, and then did a stint as Ralph Furley in *Three's Company* (1979–84). In 1990, he rejoined old friend, Andy Griffith, in a recurring role in *Matlock*, as Ben Matlock's annoying next door neighbor.

Born July 21, 1924, Knotts is a native of Fidgety, West Virginia. In Don's infancy his father's illness forced the family to move to Morgantown. A graduate of the University of West Virginia, he began his show business career as a ventriloquist with a dummy named Danny. He unsuccessfully auditioned in his teens for *Major Bowes' Original Amateur Hour* and *Camel Caravan*.

Back in Morgantown he enrolled in the speech program of the university, intending to teach. During World War II, he was put into Special Services and he and Danny entertained the troops in the South Pacific. Finally Knotts "drowned" his dummy in the Pacific so he could get all the laughs himself. It seems he did, indeed, take his comedy seriously.

Following the war he hit the Big Apple again, landing a five-year run on a children's program, three years on *Search for Tomorrow* (as Wilbur Peabody, mute brother of Rose), and using his trademark nervous routine, found a regular spot on *The Steve Allen Show*.

Knotts's Broadway debut was with Andy Griffith in the Broadway smash *No Time for Sergeants* in 1955 followed by his first screen appearance in the 1958 film version.

Griffith had taken it upon himself to call playwright Mac Hyman's agent about Hyman's *No Time for Sergeants*, eventually landing the role of hillbilly G.I. Will Stockdale in the hit comedy and in the motion picture, as well. (He had also played the role in the 1955 TV version before Broadway.)

He was born Andrew Samuel Griffith, son of Carl and Geneva, in Mount Airy, North Carolina, on June 1, 1926, and was educated at the University of North Carolina where he considered going into the ministry before switching his attention to music and drama. (His father was a retired furniture factory foreman.) In his junior year, Griffith married singer Barbara Edwards. The couple joined the Carolina Playmakers, appearing together in Paul Green's annual historical pageant *The Lost Colony* on Roanoke Island. This part got Griffith an audition at the Paper Mill Playhouse in New Jersey. He soon began playing the Rotary circuit as a monologist, spinning his first down-home yarn in 1952 at the Raleigh Little Theater. Then Mr. and Mrs. Griffith hit the circuit together with him strumming guitar and her hoofing it. They often appeared on a bill with Jerry Van Dyke, Dick's brother.

One of Andy's routines of this tour was "What It Was, Was Football," an hilarious description of the game. A small record label in Chapel Hill put it on disk and this led to Andy's big break.

Dick Linke, a representative of Capitol Records, soon signed Griffith to a personal-management contract and

Aneta Corsaut as Helen Crump and Ronny Howard as Opie seem to be waiting for Andy to pop the big question

booked Andy on *The Ed Sullivan Show,* and then into the Blue Angel in New York, where his drawling, down-home routines bombed. As a result Linke geared him toward the Southern club circuit.

Two years after his successful Broadway debut in 1955, Griffith won rave reviews for his dramatic role in Elia Kazan's *A Face in the Crowd.*

Griffith's only comment on *A Face in the Crowd* is, "It was a bust at the box office."

And though Griffith's next film, the screen version of *No Time for Sergeants* a year later in 1958, was successful, *Onionhead* (1958), another service comedy, this time putting him into the coast guard, was not.

Griffith fared better in the 1959 Broadway musical *Destry Rides Again* and in a TV production of *The Male Animal.* His own television show was the next step along the way. Producers Sheldon Leonard and Danny Thomas both had heard Andy's football routine and the Griffith show was a natural.

"I was working in New York at the time and Sheldon Leonard [executive producer of the Griffith show] came to New York and sought me out," Aaron Ruben remembers, "and was asked if I would be interested in producing the new *Andy Griffith Show* because, as a result of [*The Danny Thomas Show*] spin-off, General Foods bought the show and what they were lacking was a producer. I had been a writer and a director—I had not been a producer [before]. And at that time this whole notion of the producer also being a writer was developed by Sheldon Leonard because he felt that if you are going to produce then you should have the knowledge necessary for changing the script. And so it came into being—writer/producer. And today I would say that just about every show on the air certainly comedies, the producers are writers as well."

As it had turned out, the Thomas pilot was so successful that it resulted in a five-year Griffith contract, a scheduled thirty-two episodes, and a $58,000 budget.

Though Griffith would leave the show in 1968 of his own accord, it was a move he would come to regret. For the next nine years there was nothing.

"I did five pilots that got nowhere, had two series [*The Headmaster* and *The New Andy Griffith Show*] that flopped," recalls Griffith. "I couldn't get arrested."

For awhile Griffith floundered along in such TV movies as *Strangers in 7A* (1972), *Winter Kill* (1974), *The Girl in the Empty Grave* and *Deadly Game* (1977), and *Crimes of Innocence* (1985). And he did some big screen movies—like *The Second Time Around, Angel in My Pocket,* and *Hearts of the West.* And then came TV success again, in the form of *Matlock* (premiering September 20, 1986), a series which has since featured Don Knotts, Betty Lynn, Aneta Corsaut, Arlene Golonka, and Everett Greenbaum (as Judge Katz).

"They were planning *Matlock,*" recalls Greenbaum, "when we were writing *Return to Mayberry,* and *Matlock* would not have gone on if *Return* had not brought in such tremendous numbers."

"We pretty much all learned from Andy," insists George Lindsey today. "I and all the rest of the cast a lot of the times when we weren't working would come to the set just to watch. All these people could be trusted to perform their parts so that would make your part [look] good. If you trust another actor to carry their load, then it's going to be fine."

"One of the things that makes recalling the Griffith show so nice [is] we really had no problems like a number of shows today," Ruben claims. "Maybe one of the reasons the show was such a success [is that the] people really liked each other. They enjoyed doing the show. At the end of the week actors would often come to me and say, 'I'm so sorry it's over—I had such a wonderful time.'

"Andy [created] an atmosphere and environment on the stage that people [responded] to. It was always fun and

Jim Nabors as Mayberry's favorite gas station attendant, Gomer Pyle

games. In between scenes he and Don would go off with their friend, Lee Greenway, our makeup man, and Lee played the banjo and Andy the guitar and they would sing these country songs [and] hymns and that's the kind of [set] it was.

"Andy had a good relationship with every member of the cast and crew and the writers, [even] Frances [who] was rather strange—she was a lonely woman and not too terribly happy a woman and it was not easy to warm up to her or get to know her because she didn't respond but she was a little bit aloof. I never questioned her about this—whether she felt this sort of thing she was doing [the show] was beneath her."

Aaron Ruben goes on: "I think she enjoyed it, but remember she had been an actress on Broadway and very often [they] look down their noses at television and are very condescending when it comes to television.

"She certainly didn't have a stronger [background] than Andy, who had been on Broadway several times and had done that remarkable role in *A Face in the Crowd*. I think she was well-schooled, I think she was a fine actress, really thoroughly professional but kind of strange and remote."

Ruben seems right on target in light of the fact that in December of 1989 when Bavier was buried in Oakwood Cemetery in Siler City, North Carolina, just a week before her eighty-seventh birthday, there were only twenty mourners in attendance, none of whom were Griffith show cast members. Though Bavier was cremated, the plain wooden box at the gravesite was positioned in front of Griffith's floral tribute: a large crucifix of carnation and roses.

"We who knew her will always remember her," said Andy Griffith at the time of her death. "We say goodbye with a great deal of sadness."

Greenbaum was less magnanimous: "She was a strange woman and she had always made it a point to tell me when I was on the set that the only thing wrong with the show was the writing, so I was never overly fond of her."

In Bavier's obituary a man named Steven Ray Farish, identified as a longtime companion, described the late actress as someone who stayed up all night reading and slept during the day. Farish had been Bavier's chauffeur, cook, and nurse until he was sentenced to prison in 1984 on a manslaughter conviction. He was sentenced to the Sanford Correctional Center for twenty years after killing a man in a domestic dispute.

Farish has said that he was only fifteen when he met Bavier and that, as his own mother had just died, she took him in. Despite Farish's conviction, Bavier continued to call him frequently at the prison.

A native New Yorker, Bavier had retired to Siler City in 1972. She had suffered from cancer, as well as heart problems. She was rarely seen in public in her later years

and seldom left her home at 503 West Elk Street. A veteran of *It's a Great Life* (1954–56) and *The Eve Arden Show* (1957–58) (she once had even played a villainess in an episode of *The Lone Ranger*), she continued in the role of Aunt Bee initially in *Mayberry, R.F.D.*, before being replaced by Alice Ghostley. Bavier had inadvertently discovered the quiet community of Siler City while dieting at the Duke University Medical Center.

Bavier's mother was forty and her father sixty when Frances was born (December 14, 1902). She'd had a much older half-sister for whom she had cared during the woman's later years. From 1928 to 1933 Frances was married to a businessman who decided finally that her career was more important to her than her marriage.

"He knew I had this goal," she recalled in an interview before her death. "With me it's always been a fight to prove something. That's why I became an actress in the first place. One day I ran into a friend of mine. She told me she was going to be an actress. I thought, 'I'm a better actress than she is,' and that's when I decided to go to the Academy [but] I never wanted to be a star."

Bavier studied drama at the American Academy of Dramatic Arts in Manhattan, and made her Broadway debut on April 27, 1925, following graduation. The show, *The Poor Nut*, was a hit and lasted for three hundred performances. Then she toured in stock companies, returning to the Great White Way in 1931 with the Children's Players' *The Little Princess* at the Princess Theatre and in *Racketty Placketty House* at the Hecksher Theatre.

During the mid-thirties, Bavier performed with the Theatre Union at the Circle Repertory Theatre off Union Square in a series of politically relevant dramas—*The Black Pit, Mother*, and *Bitter Scream*—that some critics described as leftist.

Following a successful stint in *Bitter Scream*, Bavier in 1937 moved up in the world—as did the Theatre Union—from Union Square to the Nora Bayes Theatre on Broadway, opening in the production *Marching Song*, and two seasons later, replaced Dorothy Stickney under the direction of Joshua Logan in *On Borrowed Time*.

By 1941 Bavier was ready to take on the role of Peggy in the Orson Welles-John Houseman production of *Native Son*.

She was also in the 1943 comedy *Kiss and Tell*, followed by *Little A, Jenny Kissed Me*, and *Magnolia Alley*.

Of *Little A*, the *New York Morning Telegraph*'s George Freedley wrote, "Miss Bavier is practically a vaudeville show in a restrained way. It is [she] who brings[s] the comedy which is necessary to relieve the tension of [Hugh] White's drama."

Bavier's last days on Broadway were spent in *Point of No Return*, starring Henry Fonda. In California she then found work in a string of films.

"I suddenly switched from ingenues to old ladies," she once told *TV Guide*. "I didn't have to keep trying to look young. There must have been a psychological letdown [though] when I began playing character parts—that must be why I gained weight."

As far as the Griffith show went, Bavier once said, "I've had to take a back seat and watch others get the laughs, and it hasn't been easy. Sometimes I think that I live in a narrow world—to the studio in the morning and then back again at night. I know that our house at the studio—the set, with the kitchen and living room—isn't home, but . . . I came out in 1950 to do a picture, and I've always been planning to go back.

"You hear people say that they dread getting to be sixty-five, but now I want what everyone else takes for granted—a house and a garden." She ended up with six thousand square feet in Siler City.

"She was always a kind of reclusive lady," remembers Ron Howard, who was unable to make contact with her in her later years. "Wonderful and charming to be around, but when she went home—that was her own world. She didn't socialize."

"It was a tragic blow to all of us," said George Lindsey at the time of her demise. "It's like losing a member of the family because she was like a member of my family for a good period of my life. We all loved Frances very much."

Today he talks more freely about her. "[She was] certainly an enigma. She liked me, she liked working with me, she had trust in my acting. When we worked together we were pals but I never saw her socially at anything, but I do know that she thought I was a good actor. And as she got older, and crankier, she was a little harder to work with but she admired my abilities and I know that, so we got along real good."

"She was always one of my favorite people," said Jim Nabors in December 1989. "I am a better person for having known her. [She was] very, very good to me when I first started out and I was totally inexperienced in the business."

"I feel like I should have made every effort to contact Frances," says Betty Lynn, "because I truly love[d] her—I loved working with her and I admire[d] her so much. I wish I could be the kind of actress Frances was; I wish she [had known] I was thinking of her."

"Andy told me that he had gone to see her one day," recalls Aneta Corsaut, who was the last cast member to have contact with Bavier, spending a week with her months before she died, "and she wouldn't let him in."

Perhaps the best epitaph for Bavier comes in Hal ("Otis Campbell") Smith's choice of his favorite episode, "Aunt Bee, the Warden" (March 12, 1962), in which Aunt Bee figures prominently when Andy runs out of jail space and takes Otis home, naming Aunt Bee warden. She conse-quently convinces Otis that it would be better to reform than serve any more time in her cellblock.

"It was the case of giving a guy a role that just seemed to fit him beautifully," Aaron Ruben says of Smith and his Otis Campbell. "He was a very jolly guy."

"American mores have changed," says Everett Greenbaum today in agreement, "and we don't think drunks are funny anymore so we had to change him in *Return* from being a drunk. We made him an ice cream salesman."

"Hal was on the radio in Buffalo—my hometown," remembers Greenbaum today, "And I never realized it was the same Hal Smith until we drove back together from [being on] location for *Return to Mayberry,* and that's when I found out he was the same fellow."

Born in Petoskey, Michigan, and raised in Wilmington, North Carolina, and Suffolk, Virginia, Smith spent his teens working vaudeville with his brother, billed as Trade and Mark.

A veteran performer, as was Bavier, Smith began his acting career at the age of six, appearing in *Peck's Bad Boy* with Jackie Coogan in 1921. He worked as a band vocalist (1933–41) and as announcer/actor and disk jockey/writer between 1937 and 1950 at radio stations across New York before ending up in Hollywood. A World War II veteran, Smith appeared in a number of Eddie Dean westerns, the Ma and Pa Kettle series, the Francis the Talking Mule series, and many other movies, including *The Ghost and Mr. Chicken,* with Don Knotts.

On television he appeared as a regular in *The Ruggles, I Married Joan, Fair Exchange, Jefferson Drum, The Redd Foxx Variety Show,* and *Saints and Sinners.* He appeared in twenty-two episodes of *Ozzie and Harriet* in one season but never in the same role. He has also been a popular character voice in *The Flintstones, Winnie the Pooh, Popeye, Huckleberry Hound, Quickdraw McGraw, Top Cat,* and other cartoons.

His association with Disney led to work as the voices of Goofy, Jiminy Cricket, and Winnie the Pooh. On the stage he has appeared in *Show Boat, The Man Who Came to Dinner,* and *You Can't Take It With You.* He also makes appearances on the nationwide *Focus on the Family* radio show.

And though Smith's favorite episode of the Griffith show paired him with Frances Bavier, George Lindsey's own favorite pairs him with a dog: "A Man's Best Friend," which aired November 29, 1965. It zeroes in on Opie and a buddy planting a walkie-talkie under the collar of Goober's new dog. In this *Mr. Ed* scenario Goober's dreams of stardom are crushed when his talking dog refuses to speak to anyone other than him. Andy catches on and helps Goober plot his revenge against the boys.

Goober was actually introduced in the "Fun Girls" episode which aired April 13, 1964, though that was not the first time his character had been mentioned. This

Jack Dodson who played town clerk Howard Sprague (*photo courtesy Jack Dodson*)

episode found Barney and Andy canceling their dates with Thelma Lou and Helen so that they could work late at the sheriff's office, but they are soon interrupted by two good-time girls from neighboring Mt. Pilot. Thelma Lou and Helen drop by the office in time to see the two escorting the girls out to the squad car in attempt to get them out of the Mayberry jail and back to Mt. Pilot, and they jump to the wrong conclusion.

The next evening after the party girls dump Andy and Barney for Gomer and his cousin Goober, the sheriff and

his deputy talk their way out of the situation and back into Helen and Thelma Lou's good graces. Goober stayed on in town and the two bawdy broads returned in "The Arrest of the Fun Girls" on April 5, 1965.

"We created [Goober] by talking about him in that script, 'Man in a Hurry,'" explains Greenbaum, back-tracking for a moment. "And that's where Goober came from and I thought [Lindsey] did it very well."

A graduate of the American Theatre Wing in New York, Lindsey had roles in musicals such as *All-American*

Andy Griffith with the show's head writer, Everett Greenbaum (on banjo), and frequent
director Bob Sweeney (*photo courtesy Everett Greenbaum*)

and *Wonderful Town.* A native of Jasper, Alabama, he headed for Hollywood in 1962, where he found a role in the film *Ensign Pulver,* and within the next two years he appeared in over forty television shows.

"We all came from the theater," says Lindsey today. "Frances and Jack and me and Andy, Don, we all came from the New York theater. It's a great thrill to open on Broadway—that's a tremendous thrill that a lot of actors don't have and I got to do that. I always figured that if you went to New York and got on Broadway, they'd bring you to Hollywood and it worked for me.

"I get asked so many times—whatever funny happened on the set—nothing funny happened on the set. We didn't think each other were funny. We, as the characters which we became every day, did not think each were funny or unique. I [Goober] didn't particularly like Floyd, but I went over there.

"A lot of people in town didn't particularly like Goober. I hung around Andy because he was my idol. Howard Sprague and I didn't like each other, but we hung out so in the context of the characters [though] we didn't think we were unique or different [and] certainly not funny. That's one of the things that made the show—the honesty. We sort of became those people every day.

"I don't think that they understood that [Goober was one of the things that helped hold the show together]," complains Lindsey today, "but I think that possibly I took up the slack [in later episodes] because you have to have comedic relief, you know—you've got to have the town buffoon.

"And I've said this a million times, and been quoted a million times that I asked Andy about Goober and he said, 'He's the kind of guy that would to into a restaurant and say: Hey, this is great salt!'"

Griffith was once quoted in *TV Guide:* "At one point Goober was considered a possibility as second banana. A number of others, including nightclub comic Don Rickles and British actor Bernard Fox, were in the running. The decision was to forgo a replacement for Knotts [in 1965]."

"I trained [Fox] to fight Ernest T.," recalls Lindsey of an episode called "Malcolm at the Crossroads" that aired September 27, 1965. "I trained him in the back of the filling station." (Andy assigns Englishman Malcolm Merriweather, veteran of two previous episodes, to replace Ernest T. Bass as school crossing guard. Ernest T. goes off the deep end, threatening to fight Malcolm.)

In the end though, Lindsey is quick to defend Jack Burns, who was dropped from the show after only one season: "I think it's pretty hard for anybody to step in and be Don Knotts's replacement. I think he had an impossible task.

"I think whoever did that—it wouldn't have worked, so they shouldn't have tried to replace Don, they should have just basically, I think, gone on and let me do it cause I was

already there and identified, but they didn't. I [myself] loved the interplay between Don and Andy—it [was] sheer brilliance [but] I don't think Jack had a chance when it started."

Lindsey continued on as Goober in *Mayberry, R.F.D.* until 1971, before joining Nashville's *Hee Haw,* and has been with the show until its cancellation in 1993.

On a philanthropic level, for seventeen years Lindsey took part in the George Lindsey Celebrity Golf Tournament in Montgomery, Alabama, serving as an honorary coach for the Alabama Special Olympics.

"I still own a lot of property in Jasper, Alabama, a couple of farms—I still have tremendous ties to Alabama. We all had a life before Andy Griffith," points out Lindsey, who has been taking his one-man show *A Day With Goober* on the road. "I do good stand-up—people don't know that [and] I guest starred on about sixty television shows. But I haven't done enough in my life to feel like I've given it the full shot yet and I've been very blessed.

"When Andy did *Matlock* he didn't want to do anymore Andy Taylor stuff," says Lindsey. "I've never seen *Matlock*—I think everybody in the [*Mayberry*] cast has been on [it] except me [and] I would love not to be Goober but that ain't in the cards right now. I would love to be remembered as a very fine actor and a very fine comedian. [But] it wouldn't bother me to be remembered as Goober. That's what's going to happen. That's a critique of the show and that's a critique of [my] work. When they say 'Hey, Goober,' what they're saying is 'We like you,' otherwise they wouldn't speak to you."

Lindsey also speaks of life after *The Andy Griffith Show:* "I was the costar of *Mayberry, R.F.D.* It starred Ken Berry and myself and that's a fact that nobody remembers. [CBS executive] Fred Silverman canceled everything that was really [rural] oriented in one day—*Petticoat Junction, Green Acres, Jim Nabors, Mayberry, R.F.D.* We were number seven when we got canceled. I thought the money and all was going to go together, but most people think that I was just a cast member of *Mayberry* but I was the costar."

One of the highlights of *Mayberry, R.F.D.* was Arlene Golonka, whose role as Millie in the Griffith show was beefed up when she was paired with Ken Berry this time around, rather than with Jack Dodson.

Her character had been established firmly in the "Howard and Millie" episode of the Griffith show, November 27, 1967. Howard Sprague, played by Dodson, proposes to Millie and she accepts. The happy couple plan a trip to her native West Virginia but enroute begin to quarrel, finally deciding to put the engagement on hold. Golonka also figured prominently in the Griffith episode "Howard's Main Event" (October 16, 1967).

But the best Jack Dodson performance, according to

Frances Bavier as dear old Aunt Bee herself (*photo courtesy University of North Carolina Public Television*)

"Mayberry had people that were warm and funny and yet had depth and cared about each other," says Betty Lynn in *Mayberry, My Hometown,* offering her own thoughts on the continued popularity of the series."

Though recognized everywhere as Barney's main squeeze, Thelma Lou, Lynn has also appeared in films going back to the late forties.

"Betty Lynn was Barney's girlfriend and she played it very well," attests Greenbaum. "[In the reunion] Andy ran into her in the graveyard and she was in town visiting and he knew that Barney was coming back and was still single and we had them get married."

"I thought it was a one-shot thing," Lynn told an interviewer. "Then they asked me to be a regular. I told them I was under contract with the Disney studio. . . . [But] it was wonderful to be a part of [*The Andy Griffith Show*]. I loved the humor of it. It was a very special place in all our hearts. I loved the characters. All the actors and actresses were quite talented. I still love it."

Lynn was born Elizabeth Ann Teresa Lynn in Kansas City, Missouri, the daughter of a professional singer. As

Aneta Corsaut, whose own credits include *The Blob* (1958) opposite Steve McQueen, was not in a Griffith episode, but in a movie, "I loved [Jack] in Ray Bradbury's *Something Wicked This Way Comes.*" (Today, for the most part, Dodson does voiceovers for commercials, ranging from Campbell's Soup to Perkins's Restaurants, and is in the David Lynch film *Row of Crows*.)

A stage-trained actress, Golonka had studied for three years at the Goodman Theatre School of Drama in Chicago before moving to New York, where she appeared in *I Won't Dance, Take Me Along* (with Jackie Gleason), *Come Blow Your Horn,* and *Second City,* with Alan Arkin, among others, along with a great many movies in Hollywood.

"I love theater with my heart and soul," she says. "I came from humble beginnings and feel it was my love for theater as a child that gave me the dream—which later became a reality—and afforded me a beautiful, fruitful life in a career I love."

Hal Smith as Otis the town drunk (*photo courtesy Transtar Entertainment*)

29

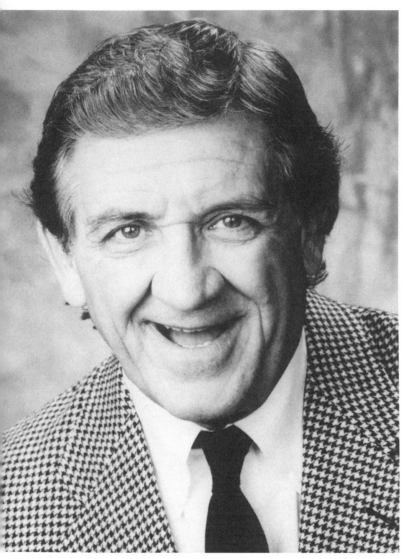

George Lindsey, who was Goober Pyle, Gomer's equally hayseed cousin (*photo courtesy Bobby Roberts Entertainment Corporation*)

young adult Lynn soon graduated from supper clubs to a Broadway show. Catching the eyes of several talent scouts, she was given a screen test at Fox, and was soon an ingenue in movies like *Sitting Pretty, Apartment for Peggy,* and *Mother Is a Freshman.*

Post Griffith show she played Brian Keith's secretary in *Family Affair* (1966–71) and Fred MacMurray's secretary in *My Three Sons* (1971–72). She was even temporarily reunited with Ron Howard in *The Smith Family.* In recent years, Andy Griffith had her back several times (along with other Mayberry denizens) on *Matlock.*

Her favorite Griffith episode is "Up in Barney's Room" (December 2, 1963), chronicling Barney's eviction from his boarding house for cooking in his room. He sets up housekeeping in the back of the jail. Andy has difficulty coping but is saved from confronting his homeless deputy

when the dishonesty of a new tenant prompts Barney's former landlady to invite him back.

"Sweet Betty, very innocent—the perfect companion for Barney," says Ruben today. "You couldn't have found anybody better and she [was] just as sweet and wholesome in her offscreen life as on."

Betty Lynn sums up the appeal of the Griffith show: "It's some slapstick and some gentle comedy and some craziness that somehow is all made believable—we had great writers and producers on that show. And we had fine directors."

And one of those directors was Bob Sweeney, who also helmed *Return to Mayberry.* "To many sophisticated people, it appeared at first that we were in cornball country," Sweeney figures. "Then they begin to see past the rural façade. Mayberry is definitely the star of the show, this nice town with its semi-nutty, lovable people, where nobody hurries. Viewers feel warm and comfortable in a dreamtown."

"The idea was such a sound one and that relationship between Andy and Opie and Aunt Bee and the rest of the townfolk—it was so solid," stresses Ruben today, "[but] the media looked down upon [the show] and categorized it

Clint Howard, Ron's brother who, as a youngster, was a frequent *Andy Griffith Show* guest (*photo courtesy Clint Howard*)

Andy and Barney confronting Otis over his mode of transportation

as just another country bumpkin, hillbilly show. They put it in the same category as *Green Acres* and *The Beverly Hillbillies*. It [had] the kind of premise that has a lasting value. I'm taking nothing away from *Hillbillies* and *Green Acres,* which were highly successful, but I just don't think they had the lasting value that the Griffith show had.

"It's taken almost thirty years for a lot of people to see [the quality]. I run into people and they say, 'I've been watching those reruns—that was really a good show, wasn't it?' And we knew we had a good show, something different, something rather special. But the fact that [it took place in] a small town and people talked the way they did—especially Andy and Opie—[people] said, 'It's just another country show,' and they never really got beyond that and that's too bad. I know that Andy was really kind of offended by that because he himself is a very sophisticated person—his taste in music, his taste in decor—he's really a sophisticated guy."

Ruben has been asked about his favorite episode. "It would be very hard to pick because I was on the show for five years and in those days we did thirty shows a season. There was one in particular in which we started our season with a story featuring Opie. The one I remember in particular was one with Opie in which he kills a mother bird with a new slingshot that's been given to him. It had its moments of comedy with Don and of course, its poignant moments with Opie and what he learns from this unfortunate accident. He didn't really mean to kill the bird—he was just shooting aimlessly."

"Opie the Birdman" aired on September 30, 1963, and in this episode the youngster must take on the responsibility of being a foster parent to the three offspring of the mother bird he accidentally kills. He's faced with the tough decision as to whether or not to free them when they learn how to fly.

"The writers more or less took that approach where you developed a story in which you featured one of the cast," says Ruben. "There are a couple [of others] that stand out—the ones in which Don Knotts was featured. He was always so wonderful. The most compelling reason for being successful [in a series] is your characters' relationships, and *Roseanne* is certainly successful for that is high in the ratings but not highly thought of by the media—*Married . . . With Children*—you have relationships there that work. I don't know that you have a show today nor do I think that you could have one with the warm type of relationships that we had on the Griffith show. There's an acidity, [they're] not as soft, not nearly as sentimental as the Griffith show. It worked at that time."

"Jim Fritzell and I may have left the show but I never left Don and Andy," Greenbaum stresses. "I continued working with them until now. I've been acting with Andy on *Matlock* whenever they invite me.

"After we left the Griffith show we did movies. We did a picture called *Good Neighbor Sam* with Jack Lemmon. Then we did three films with Don—*The Ghost and Mr. Chicken, The Shakiest Gun in the West,* and *The Reluctant Astronaut*—and one with Andy called *Angel in My Pocket.*"

"Jim and I were always employed and during the two years we were separated I was working out here so I never had to go through the terrible unemployment insecurities that ninety percent of actors go through and for that reason I'm very delighted to have [been a writer]."

Greenbaum also admits: "I'm very grateful to the Griffith show because it's been like a small annuity for me all these years. And when we did it we thought maybe they would run each episode, maybe two or three times.

"I started out in '50–'51 [with] a radio show of my own in Buffalo and I went to New York where I had bit parts in shows and I was on a Yiddish radio show and that was canceled and then I started writing *Mr. Peepers* and I acted twice on [it]. The first time was when someone was fired in the dress rehearsal, and the second time we wrote an enormous part for me—that was when Alice Ghostley was my [TV] wife—and I went on and drew a blank. I never said anything. That concluded the acting until after I retired from writing.

Does he have a favorite Griffith episode? "I was always fond of a show called 'Man in a Hurry,' and that was always a very nice show, a very philosophical show that had a point of view, and 'Barney's First Car' and 'Class Reunion' I liked very much."

"Class Reunion" (February 4, 1963) had Andy and Barney meeting up with their high school sweethearts at a reunion of the class of '45. Barney's old heartthrob hardly recognizes him but Andy's recalls him vividly. Recognition of their differences makes their second parting more manageable.

"Barney's First Car" aired on April 1, 1963, with Deputy Sheriff Fife setting out to buy a car of his own. Unfortunately his choice turns out to be a real lemon, so Andy prepares a trap for the little old lady (guest star Ellen Corby) who took Barney for a ride, so to speak.

"There are only two people in my whole history in this business that I liked having fiddle with the script—make little changes," says Greenbaum, "and one was Aaron Ruben." And though it may not be everyone's personal favorite, most of the cast and many of the fans agree that the best written episode of the Griffith show was "Man in a Hurry," scripted by Greenbaum and first aired on January 14, 1963.

This show deals with a high-powered businessman forced to remain in Mayberry because his car breaks down. He moves from anger to a more relaxed state of mind, managing to prolong his stay after learning that there is more to life than just being in a hurry.

Arlene Golonka, Millie Swanson toward the end of the series and on the spin-off, *Mayberry U.S.A.* (*photo courtesy Arlene Golonka*)

Frances Bavier's house and library in Siler City, North Carolina, and her vintage auto, auctioned off after her death (*photos courtesy University of North Carolina Public Television*)

"[Mayberry is] a place where people are safe, where they are surrounded by people they're fond of," offers Greenbaum, when asked to explain the show's longevity, "and who are usually amusing, and it's the way we imagine things used to be and, in a large part, were. The world is a much rougher place than it was fifty years ago. [Mayberry] was the times and the chemistry of the people who got together. We never dreamt that thirty years later it would be bigger than ever."

Perhaps *TV Guide* once summed it up best when quoting Griffith: "So much of Mayberry is like it used to be, there are overtones of a past era. . . . I like those scenes where we just sit and talk. Barney talks about his big plans for the evening—a stroll past the hardware store window display, a bottle of pop at the filling station, and I tell him if I got big plans too—going down to the church choir practice—and vote on the new choir robes. Folks may have their troubles in that town, but no one ever has any big problems in Mayberry. . . . It's the sense of nostalgia that we create—it's the feeling that Mayberry is timeless."

Mayberry mania lives on—there are all kind of memorabilia: Mayberry figurines (Andy and Opie goin' fishin' and Aunt Bee crochetin'); the Andy and Opie mug; the Andy and Opie plaque; *The Andy Griffith Show* trading cards; the Mayberry Collection Lollipops (assorted flavors); and Aunt Bee's *Mayberry Cookbook* from Rutledge Hill Press.

They still joke in Griffith's hometown of Mt. Airy, North Carolina, that he never left, he just took it with him. In July 1991 Mt. Airy brought it back when it spent $2,000 to renovate the old city jail so that it would look exactly like the interior of the Mayberry one.

"It's a great idea," said Jim Clark, president of the Andy Griffith Rerun Watchers Club, at the time. "They've got a replica of the squad car already. I guess they needed a jail to go with it."

And with the run of *Matlock* it seems that homeboy Griffith has once again achieved what Pat (*Green Acres*) Buttram called "a Southern accent with a Northern income."

On the 1993 reunion show, Andy is surrounded by Ron Howard, Jim Nabors, Jack Dodson, George Lindsey, and Don Knotts (*photo courtesy CBS*)

Alan Young and the title star © *copyright Orion Television Entertainment (photo courtesy Orion Television)*

MR. ED

(January 5, 1961–September 8, 1965)

"Mr. Ed was a remarkable horse," says Herb Browar, associate producer of the sixties series. "As you know, horses are supposed to be dumb, and he was far from it and the trainer loved the horse. He said [once], 'There are two ways people treat horses—they love them or they hate them.' If you love the horse and you're kind to him and good to him, then he'll do what you want him to do."

And in the mind of the viewing public, Ed was a cantankerous and ornery character, with a soft heart. He was a hypochondriacal equine who loved books, music, television, loafing, and fillies. The series was based upon stories by Walter Brooks which originally appeared in *Esquire, Liberty, Argosy,* and the *Saturday Evening Post.*

Mr. Ed remains so popular thirty years later that cable's *Nick at Nite* has orchestrated several promos for the show, including one that never really got off the ground: a scented magazine ad that invited readers to sample the fragrance of Mr. Ed's aftershave. Initially it couldn't be decided whether or not the scent should be offensive or pleasant. They ended up going for a realistic hay smell.

"[*Mr. Ed*] has had a renaissance to such a tremendous degree," says Alan Young, who portrayed architect Wilbur Post. "I own a piece of it, so I know. I go out now and again for *Nick at Nite* to do [public] appearances and there are at least three generations who come to the shopping malls and they are all so dear—the grandparents, the parents who were raised with [*Mr. Ed*] and now their children who are seeing it [for the first time]."

The series at first was syndicated in 1961, but picked up by CBS for the 1962–63 season and remained with the network until 1965, with Young portraying the owner of the talkative Mr. Ed, who was abandoned in the stables by

[his] previous master. Mr. Ed turned out, of course, to be a talking horse but Wilbur was the only person worthy of Ed's reparteé.

"The networks didn't seem to want it [in the beginning]," says Young, "They showed me a pilot with different actors and I thought, this is funny. So, I said fine."

"The [original pilot] was owned by George Burns and Arthur Lubin," notes Al Simon, executive producer of the series and former president of Filmways TV Productions. "If that [pilot] did not sell, then there was something wrong with it. It [didn't star] Alan Young—they used somebody else [Scott KcKay] although Rocky Lane did Ed's voice. As a matter of fact I wasn't even involved in that. I'd set up the three camera system for *I Love Lucy,* and as a result of that, George Burns came to me [about doing *Mr. Ed*], and Filmways came into the picture and we got together. There were good writers—that was the real key. But George Burns retained his interest in the show."

"We were not directly involved with the original pilot," Herb Browar says. "With George, you've always got something interesting. George owned the show to begin with. He made the pilot before I was connected with it, but it wasn't that good of a pilot and it didn't sell. Al Simon and I were running a little enterprise and we were producing some shows while we were with McCadden Productions [the Burns outfit]. We were doing a show at that time called *Panic.*

"What we were asked to do was [edit down the original *Mr. Ed* pilot] to a twelve-minute presentation film for Studebaker [preceded by a three-minute short] with the new cast, because we felt that the cast in the pilot was kind of weak, and of course we had access to all of Burns's writers and we had a couple of other writers and we did this twelve- to fifteen-minute presentation film with Alan Young."

"[The show] was purchased by Studebaker," continues Simon "and in an effort to put it on the air, Steve Mudge [who handled the Studebaker account with the D'Arcy Agency in New York] went around and [raised] sufficient money to do it and of course [Studebaker] bought the show."

"So [it] was sold to different regional groups of these Studebaker [dealers]," Alan Young recalls, "and they all bought it and [paid for] time on their local stations and put it on. [Studebaker had initially been approached by Martin Ransohoff, chairman and CEO of Filmways.] So we had a network bigger than any we could have had if we'd been signed by one of the three [big ones]. That was the first year. And it did so well that CBS grabbed it up the next year [Studebaker did not want to fully finance another year]."

"We made the [presentation] film," states Browar, "and based on that Studebaker went ahead with it. They had been looking for a show that had a personality that could be identified with [their product]. And they were able to do that with Alan. The last shot [in the presentation film] was of Alan rolling out from under a Studebaker with a rag in hand and he's polishing the side of the car and the camera is focused on him and he says, 'I certainly hope that you buy the show because I really need a job!' As a result they accepted it and none of the networks were interested so we went into syndication. From then on it, more or less, had a life of its own. *Mr. Ed* is the only show in the history of syndication that started out in syndication and was [then] picked up by a network."

As Herb Browar remembers it, "Al and I were running the Burns and Allen outfit, and they liquidated, and Al and I were placed with having to make another connection and we were contemplating going to Fox. So we started Filmways TV Productions, Incorporated, as a subsidiary of Filmways, Incorporated. I was the vice-president in charge of production for Filmways.

"[When] we formed Filmways TV, Al and I discussed [the fact] that now we have a company, what do we do with it? Well, we had to start making shows. Both of us felt that *Mr. Ed* always had a great deal of possibilities and it was unfortunate that the pilot had not sold. Burns owned it because he had financed the pilot [at a cost of $75,000], so one day George Nasser [who owned General Service Studios] said, 'You know, you now have this company—if you could do something with the *Mr. Ed* project [we] think that has a great deal of possibilities.' So all of our thoughts were pointed in the right direction. As a result of that conversation one thing led to another and a company was started [with Burns] called the Mr. Ed Company, and that consisted of Burns, Simon, and Arthur Lubin."

Lubin, a graduate of Carnegie Tech (also Browar's alma mater), began his career as an actor at the Pasadena Playhouse during the twenties before getting into films in the twenties. He became a house director at Universal, doing things like Abbott and Costello's *In the Navy* and the Maria Montez-Jon Hall *Ali Baba and the Forty Thieves,* as well as the prestigious forties version of *The Phantom of the Opera.* Later he directed the first six "Francis the Talking Mule" pictures, which could be considered the basis for *Mr. Ed.* Lubin's television credits range from episodes of *Maverick* and *Bonanza* to *77 Sunset Strip.* And only once was he reprimanded by George Burns during his stint on *Mr. Ed,* and that was for inadvertently shooting the horse's private parts on film.

But a slip of the tongue on Lubin's part almost nixed *Mr. Ed* before the series ever got off the ground. "The chairman of the board of Studebaker had a meeting," relates Browar, "and showed this presentation film, [and] Lubin had given an interview to a syndicated entertainment reporter, and had mentioned that a pilot had been made which had not sold. [The chairman], reading the newspaper [back] in Indiana, came across this item and said, 'By God, this show we're buying has been refused by the networks!' So he called up and said, 'You're selling me your soiled goods! I want a fresh show!' So the deal is off. About ten days go by and they're showing him ideas and such and at the end of it all, everybody decided that *Mr. Ed* was still the best idea for [Studebaker]. The show was on again."

In the meantime, according to Browar, the trainer had sold Mr. Ed under the misconception that the deal was off.

Browar continues: "[So] I'm trying to get a hold of [horse wrangler] Les Hilton, and he's in the wilds of Tennessee on location. Finally he calls me and tells me who he sold the horse to, and I said, 'You've got to get back here to get another [horse]. We've got to find a horse. We don't have the luxury of time. Don't go back on location. You're on salary with [Filmways] as of now. Get out here and start looking for a horse!'"

And a horse was exactly what Wilbur Post found in the barn of his new home on the day that he and wife Carol took up residence.

"The first episode was my favorite," Young recalls of the one written by William Burns, Bob O'Brien, Irving Elinson, and Phil Shuken and directed by Rod Amateau. "It was the first time that Mr. Ed spoke. I went out to see the old barn and in the barn was a horse. I said I wanted to keep [him] and the horse said, 'Thank you very much.' That was what I liked about it."

"Al had a different concept," stresses Browar, "and George [Burns] was very happy with Al's concept, so much so that George insisted on staging the first three months of the show. He would stage and Arthur Lubin would shoot it and direct it for television, but those first three months were quite a hoot. Of course, we did all the rewrites. We did that in George's office, which was on the lot. And every now and again George would come in and make comments."

Connie Hines was Post's wife Carol, and the happy couple resided at 17230 Valley Spring Lane, next to neighbors Larry Keating and Edna Skinner (1961–64) and Leon Ames and Florence McMichael (1964–66). The voice of Ed, the show's real star, was that of veteran western star Allan "Rocky" Lane.

"We looked at a lot of girls," Browar remembers, "and Connie was one of them. She had just moved [to L.A.] and she had an apartment beyond the Strip. At the bottom of the hill was a pay phone on a corner and she didn't have a phone [yet] in her apartment so I got a hold of her—she would call in periodically after we interviewed her—

when it came down to choosing between this girl and Connie, I said, 'Connie, from ten A.M. on you're just going to have to stay on that corner and wait until [you] get a call.' Well, she dropped everything and she stationed herself on that corner until about four in the afternoon. Finally we decided on her and I was glad [because] I ran around with Connie that first year while I was single. We didn't even test her because we didn't have the money. So I told her over the phone and she was at a busy intersection on the Sunset Strip and she was dancing around yelling, 'I got it! I got it!'

"When we did that presentation film, the camera caught all that energy—all that bubbliness—and she couldn't act too damn well. I was in Japan one time and whoever dubbed her voice matched [her persona] to such a degree that it made Connie seem like a hell of an actress, but I don't mean to take anything away from Connie. She was a great personality. She was just terrific."

Hines was born in Dedham, Massachusetts, where her father managed a stock company. She grew up in the dressing rooms of stars such as Margaret Sullavan and Jeff Donnell, later moving to Boston where she pursued acting. Hines then relocated to Florida where she hosted a morning and evening TV show for a local station, and also appeared in regional theater. On to New York, she joined the Helen Hayes Equity Group, and later, in 1959 after arriving in Hollywood, she was signed by CBS for role in a movie for its *Rheingold Theater*.

"Connie was delightful and attractive," attests Simon, "and served a purpose with the audience." Her favorite *Mr. Ed* is episode number two, "Ventriloquist" (January 12, 1961), written by Lou Derman and Phil Davis and directed by Rod Amateau.

Versatile veteran actor Larry Keating, who had portrayed Roger Addison, was a native of St. Paul, Minnesota, and got into show business when noted star John Gilbert gave him a job as assistant stage manager in a stock company he (Gilbert) was running. Larry soon became an actor in stock, then Broadway, radio, and films. (His movie debut was in *Song of the Sarong* in 1945.) He appeared on radio in *This Is Your F.B.I.* for seven years. In 1953 he became George Burns and Gracie Allen's next-door neighbor, Harry Morton, on their television show for the next six years. Then along came *Mr. Ed*. In 1963 Keating learned that he had leukemia, though he continued to play Roger Addison on the show. He died on August 26, 1963, at age sixty-four. The last episode in which he appeared was "Patter of Little Hooves" (October 20, 1963). It guest starred Leo Fuchs.

Broward relates a tale about Keating and the talkative Mr. Ed: "Now [once] in a show when Keating is thrown out of his house, he comes over and Wilbur lets him use the barn and there's an iron cot in there, but Ed has the

Connie Hines and Alan Young as Carol and Wilbur Post © *copyright Orion Television Entertainment* (*photo courtesy Orion Television*)

blanket. So Keating [takes] the blanket and lays down on the bed and Ed comes and takes it off of him and goes back into his stall. And Keating goes back and gets the blanket and comes back—he was always fighting with [Ed]—and Ed comes back to take the blanket again, and as he is turning around his [back] end is right over Keating's head. So [Keating] raises up and Les [Hilton] screams: 'Don't move, Larry!' and the cameras are going and you can imagine what happens next. Keating is frozen in position and it's on film [somewhere]."

Keating's replacement was another veteran actor Leon Ames, who came in to play Gordon Kirkwood. Born Leon Waycoff in Portland, Indiana, he made the first of literally dozens of films (the 1932 *Murders in the Rue Morgue*) before changing his last name to Ames in 1935. Prior to joining *Mr. Ed* during the 1963–64 season, Ames was the star of the TV versions of both *Life With Father* (1953–55) and *Father of the Bride* (1961–62). Aside from

acting, he at one time owned a Ford dealership in Studio City.

"Edna Skinner is in Oregon," says Young of the actress who portrayed Kay Addison. "Nobody seems to know [exactly] where she is—she's an avid fisherwoman. She was disappointed when she was dismissed from the show [following Keating's death]—it was unfortunate and I don't blame her; anyone would have been disappointed, but, I guess there was really no other way to go. [The Posts] had to have neighbors—a man and wife, and that was it."

Skinner was cast in the beginning only after actress Constance Miller had been dropped. (She looked too much like Hines on film.) A native of Washington, D.C., Skinner attended the American Academy of Dramatic Arts in New York, along with the likes of Kirk Douglas, Lauren Bacall, and Jennifer Jones. On Broadway, Skinner, who had served as a commander during World War II in the American Women's Voluntary Services, replaced Celeste Holm in *Oklahoma!* before going on to become Maggie the cook in the TV sitcom of *Topper* during the 1954–55 season. *Mr. Ed* was her next series. She filled a transitional void, remaining for nine episodes without Keating, as Jack Albertson came in briefly to portray her brother, Paul Fenton. Skinner's favorite episode of *Mr. Ed* is "Stable for Three," the third in which she appeared as Kay Addison.

"Larry was in the Burns and Allen show and he was marvelous in what he did," praises Simon. "He was a very, very good comedian. It's very, very difficult to replace someone, especially if the show has been on for quite a while because the audience [has expectations] but that doesn't mean that it can't be done. [After Larry's death] we wanted to add something new to the show because we were losing so many [viewers] and we thought letting Skinner go was the thing to do. She went to live up north [in Oregon].

"Florence [McMichael] was fine—there was nothing wrong with her, but I can't say that [she and Leon] brought in a new audience. They were just there and they did a very good job."

"Florence was a real quiet one," Young reveals of the actress who played Winnie Kirkwood. "She divorced and married someone else. She was a dear heart, but she didn't mix very much. She lived in Pasadena and had been a housewife in those days, was married to a postman, and was a dear, sweet gal."

McMichael got her start on Broadway, later performing on radio in New York with Phil Silvers and Jackie Gleason. During 1960–61 she played the Douglas family's neighbor, Florence Pearson, on *My Three Sons*.

Allan "Rocky" Lane was the man behind the scenes, and literally at times, the man behind Ed. Lane was born Harry Albershart on September 22, sometime between 1901 and 1907. He hailed from Mishawaka, Indiana, and was an athlete at Notre Dame at South Bend. He was discovered by Fox agents in the late twenties, after being a male model. With limited Broadway experience, Lane made his screen debut in 1929 as the lead in Louise Dresser's *Not Quite Decent*.

"[Rocky] was the only one we could find [who wanted to do it]," Al Simon says. "It was very, very difficult. He was a star in his own [right] to some degree and he asked us not to put his name on it, which was absolutely wonderful as far as I was concerned because then I could say that Mr. Ed [played] himself."

Lane played in numerous films in the thirties before becoming one of Republic's leading cowboy stars in the forties and fifties, with his "wonder" horse Black Jack. Lane was twice among the top ten Western money-makers (1951 and 1953).

His first Western, *Law West of Tombstone,* premiered in 1938, though he didn't sign with Republic until 1940.

In the forties, Allan Lane portrayed Red Ryder in eight pictures, and later became "Rocky" in *The Wild Frontier* (1947). He had his last starring role in a 1953 Western. A couple of years later he made a Red Ryder TV pilot called *Gun Trouble Valley.* By the late fifties, his career in films was more or less finished although on television he appeared on *Gunsmoke, Colt .45, Bonanza,* and other shows. Following *Mr. Ed,* he retired, spent his last years at the Motion Picture Country Home in Woodland Hills, California, where he died on October 27, 1973, of bone marrow disease.

"Rocky was very straight," Alan Young recalls, "just the way the voice was. He was not much on comedy, which made it even better. I left right after the show [ended]. I went to Broadway, so I lost touch with just about everybody. Rocky passed on [after] I had just gotten back [from New York] and talked to him once on the phone."

Herb Browar states: "[Rocky] had been a star and was more or less unemployed. I have a feeling that it was Arthur or Al who came up with Rocky, and he always wore an off-white cowboy outfit and he wore a hat. And, he was a handsome man, tall and well-built. He would hardly ever talk about himself but I found out that he had played professional football in Notre Dame many years [before]. Rocky, I think, became extremely important for the show, because he was an actor and had been a star. We built a folding screen [at eye level] and behind that we put a mike and we moved that around [accordingly] so that Rocky could see the horse when Les Hilton tickled Ed's mouth. He did his homework. He knew the script, he knew his lines, and he liked [the screen] around him because it gave him sanctity and privacy and that's how we would do it. And Rocky started to give the horse a personality because, first of all, the horse was very [rebellious]. The voice made the horse really alive. Rocky became the horse [in his own mind]. He contributed a tremendous amount to the believability of the horse. He made the horse alive. And over a period of time he started to think he was the most important person in the company.

"He was a very shy guy and I think that he loved horses. I remember one day he was out back smoking a cigarette and the horse was in the stall [doing his business] and the [excrement] had an odor. So I kind of looked [at Rocky] and he said to me, 'Listen, Herb, I don't believe anybody telling me that he doesn't like [that] smell!' But Rocky got to believe that he was [irreplaceable]. An incident took place which was intolerable, and we did not have a backup for [Rocky] so the way to settle [that] was to interview a lot of voices and I found a country singer and he wrote songs and he had a voice very similar to Rocky's. We needed somebody. So I asked Rocky to meet me at a certain time. I arranged to make a tape of [this singer] with a script and we did a scene and I had one of the editors [look out] for Rocky, and he was on time so we rolled [the audio] and I had everybody standing around and it was timed [for when] Rocky came in and he was quiet and I'm looking at him and he's listening and all of a sudden he realizes that this voice is not his, but it's saying Ed's lines, and when it was over he said, 'What's going on?' He thought we were going to replace him. That's the first thing that went through his mind. I said, 'No, Rocky, we don't have a backup voice.' And, that solved the problem with Rocky. He was a very important part of that show."

"[Rocky] was excellent and the value of his voice contributed a lot to [the show's success], a great deal to it. He actually made it sound that if there was such a thing as a talking horse it would sound like [him]," Al Simon adds.

The real star of the show, of course, was Mr. Ed. George Burns told *TV Guide,* during the show's original run, "We don't treat him like an animal but like an actor. And it comes out funny."

"Everybody loved Ed. He was an actor, just like everybody else," Browar said. "They didn't make a fuss over him. Les made it a hard and fast rule that nobody fed him—that nobody gave him anything. He would get furious if anybody did. One of his controls was in feeding [Ed]. He wanted [the horse] to depend on him [for meals]. One day I remember talking to Les. 'Gee, you know, usually when you look in a horse's mouth the teeth look lousy [but Ed's] look terrific; what do you do?' and he said 'I brush them with toothpaste—I use Pepsodent.'"

"I never regarded [Ed] as a horse," admits Young, who rode Ed every morning they weren't working and continued to ride him after the show ended. "Lane was the voice—he'd stand on the side of the set [and] the trainer would have the horse move his lips at the same time [Lane] was talking. Mr. Ed could turn a mean phrase and he knew it—he was like an Army buddy—only if you [were] real stuck [would] he get you out. Ed's real name was Bamboo Harvester. I learned to ride on Ed. [He] lived with his trainer, and I became very friendly [with him], as friendly as you can be with an old cowpoke. They're pretty secretive people, but he was so kind. He really did give me my first riding lesson on Ed. [He] was an animal lover. We had the Humane Society down the first day of shooting and I never saw them again."

"Most people don't know about it," Browar admits, about Mr. Ed's "talking." "We kept it a secret for years, but the trick was very simple—Ed wore a bridle and Les would run a very thin nylon fish line [through] the bridle and up under Ed's upper lip and then stand off about ten feet and when he wanted the horse to talk he would jerk that line and it would irritate Ed's upper lip and he would make those motions with his mouth.

"Les told me one day that Ed knew anywhere between twenty-five and thirty word commands. His feeling about horses was that they were really not that dumb. The other thing about Ed was we built a special stall on the outside of the stage and at the back wall there happened to be a very large door that would open and close, and in back of that was a row of dressing rooms. At the end there was an area in which we built a stall for Ed and we put a big gold star over it and we always had a lot of hay. Les always had a wrangler with him who would take care of the horse and we had a special blanket made for [Ed], and Ed really realized that he was something because of all the attention and the way that he was handled. Les had a small ranch in the Valley and he kept [Ed] there."

Browar goes on to reminisce: "There was one word Ed got to know very well. At the end of a day's shooting if he was in the last shot, and the assistant director said, 'That's a wrap!' Ed took off—he would drag that wrangler right to that back door because it was six o'clock [and] he knew he was going to go home and get fed—he'd run over people [if they were in the way]. We had a trailer—Studebaker gave us a truck—and we bought a trailer and we had it painted up [to read]: I'M MR. ED, WATCH ME ON CBS. Les would put him in the trailer and then he would wait for the wrangler to clock out. And Ed would start kicking the [inside] of the trailer—he wanted to get the hell home. And when they would stop in traffic, at the long stop lights, Ed would start kicking again until he got home. He felt that he was a star. He was very aware of everything that was going on around him."

Mr. Ed, a.k.a. Bamboo Harvester, had no greater fan than Alan Young.

"Alan was very good," stresses Al Simon. "What was right about him was his relationship with the horse was such that no one watching the show would question it."

Brower insists that "Alan Young has never really been given the credit that is due him, because [he] also made that horse real. You never felt that he felt as if Ed were a horse."

And George Burns agrees: "The most important thing about *Mr. Ed* [was] that there's a man who everyone thinks is crazy—[the horse would] only talk to one person, the man, who everyone thinks is nuts. The horse isn't the star of the show, the man is."

Browar adds, "In my initial discussions with Alan [about Ed], Alan said, 'Well, I'll just treat him as another character and not as a horse,' and if you study anyone of the shows you will see that Alan plays with him as if he's another human being. It takes a talent, which Alan had, to be able to converse and recognize and treat the horse as another person. Alan made you believe."

Alan was born Angus Young in Northern England on November 18, 1924, to Scottish parents. The family moved to Vancouver when Alan was five. At age thirteen

Florence McMichael and Leon Ames as Winnie and Gordon Kirkwood, the Posts' bewildered neighbors © *copyright Orion Television Entertainment (photo courtesy Orion Television)*

Mr. Ed having a heart-to-heart with guest star Mae West © *copyright Orion Television Entertainment*

Alan Young and Mr. Ed (*photo courtesy Alan Young*)

Young started in show business as a stand-up comic in Canada, earning $2 for his first public appearance, delivering a monologue before the Caledonian Society of Vancouver.

He was on a local radio station by the age of fifteen, and a couple of years later, he was discovered by Frank Cooper, who overheard him clowning on the air. Cooper promptly wired Young traveling expenses to come to New York as a summer replacement for Eddie Cantor.

During World War II Young served in the Canadian Navy; after a stint in New York City, he went on to Hollywood, where he made his film debut in 1946 in *Margie*. He subsequently starred in *Androcles and the Lion,* and *Aaron Slick From Punkin Crick,* and later *Tom Thumb* and *The Time Machine*.

"I was born in England," says Young, "but I went to school in Canada [where] I was in radio and then brought [here] to do radio, and then I signed to do movies with Fox and I worked for Howard Hughes for two years. I only did one picture for him. He was always eccentric."

He hosted *The Alan Young Show* on television from 1950 to 1953. (Earlier he had starred in the radio version.) In between *The Alan Young Show* and *Mr. Ed,* Young attained American citizenship and performed in London.

"When I first heard about [*Mr. Ed*]," he confesses, "I did not want to do it. I was offered [the show] by Arthur Lubin while I was doing [*Alan Young*] in 1953 and turned it down. I said, 'Oh gosh, I wouldn't talk to a horse. I [was doing] a review show, a stand-up monologue, and sketches and that sort of thing. *The Alan Young Show* won three Emmies—I won one [myself]. It was a big switch [going to *Mr. Ed*].' Six years later, when I hadn't worked in a while, they approached me again and I was ready to talk. I was happy to talk to anybody [who'd pay me]."

Aside from writing and performing on his Emmy Award-winning first series, Young also directed several episodes of *Mr. Ed,* such as "TV or Not TV," "The Horse and the Pussycat," "Ed and the Bridegroom," "Don't Skin That Bear," and "Ed and the Motorcycle."

After *Mr. Ed* left network television, Alan Young left Hollywood for a number of years. First he starred on Broadway in 1967 in *The Girl in The Freudian Slip* and then he moved on to Boston to work for the Christian Science Church. In the late seventies, he resumed his show business career, this time mainly doing character voice for animated series like *The Smurfs, Mr. T., Spiderman,* and *The Chipmunks.*

More significantly, he became the voice of Disney's "Scrooge McDuck" and has worked primarily on the *DuckTales* series and in *DuckTales—the Movie.* Young's *Mickey's Christmas Carol* (1983) was nominated for an Academy Award, and he has appeared in the HBO pilot *Sitcom* (1983) and the very short-lived (three episodes) CBS series *Coming of Age* in 1988.

"[Recently] I came in for opening night [of *Show Boat* in Pasadena]," adds Young, "and went on for Van Johnson [when] he became ill, and finished the run. I [also] do Scrooge McDuck (in *Duck Tales*). I wrote *Mickey's Christmas Carol* about ten years ago—I wrote it as a record first and it was rewritten as a movie."

On the topic of guest stars, Al Simon explains: "What we didn't want to do was present [somebody] who wasn't any good [for the show], and a lot of people could not understand *Mr. Ed* because when it first came out [they] said, 'What are they going to do with a horse that talks?' and a lot of people thought that it was a kid's show. But it never was."

Barry Kelley played a recurring role as Carol's father, Mr. Higgins, during several episodes through the years, beginning with the first season on CBS. He had first worked under the direction of Lubin in *Francis Goes to the Races.* Jack Albertson also appeared in several episodes, including "Mister Ed's Blues" and "Ed the Songwriter," as Roger Addison's brother-in-law, Paul Fenton.

Clint Eastwood guest starred in "Clint Eastwood Meets Mr. Ed" (April 22, 1962), written by Lou Derman and Sonia Chernus. Donna Douglas of *The Beverly Hillbillies* costarred. "Clint was good," Young recalls. "He played himself. We were doing a Western benefit and he came over to direct the show."

Mae West appeared in "Mae West Meets Mr. Ed" on March 22, 1964. She was then seventy-one, and confessed to the press, "It is unusual for me to do this kind of show, but I'm doing it to please my fans." The script was penned by Lou Derman and Bill Davenport. "Mae West—you couldn't get close to her," admits Young. "She [lived] in her own world. *Mr. Ed* was her first and only television appearance."

Donna Douglas also was in "Busy Wife" on January 19, 1961, in a script by Lou Derman and Ben Star, with Justus Addiss directing.

Eleanor Audley played Wilbur's Aunt Martha for the first time in "The Aunt" (March 2, 1961), written by Derman and Star and directed by Arthur Lubin. She returned in the role in "Animal Jury" on January 13, 1965.

Elvia Allman appeared in "A Man for Velma" (April 27, 1961), also written by Derman and Star and directed by Lubin. Nancy (*The Beverly Hillbillies*) Kulp showed up in "Pine Lake Lodge" (June 25, 1961), written by Derman and Davenport and directed by John Rich.

Donna Douglas returned, this time with Alan Hale Jr. (The Skipper on *Gilligan's Island*) for "Ed the Jumper," written by Derman and Bill Crewson and directed by Lubin. Raymond Bailey, also of *The Beverly Hillbillies,* appeared in "Ed the Beneficiary" (January 21, 1962), written by Derman and Robert O'Brien, with Lubin directing. In an episode scripted by Derman, entitled "George Burns Meets Mr. Ed," a.k.a. "Ed Finally Talks" (February 18, 1962), the boss himself turned up. Lubin, as usual, directed. Zsa Zsa Gabor was the guest of honor in "Zsa Zsa" (January 28, 1962), written by Derman and Crewson and directed by Lubin.

On September 29, 1963, Dodgers catcher Johnny Roseboro joined the legendary Durocher and Sandy Koufax in "Leo Durocher Meets Mr. Ed," written by Derman and Michael Fessier.

Sharon Tate guested first in "Ed Discovers America" (September 13, 1963), an episode written by Derman and Larry Rhine, and later in "Love Thy Neighbor" (December 15, 1963) in a script by Derman and Davenport. Butch Patrick of *The Munsters* surfaced in "Don't Laugh at Horse" (November 3, 1963) in a script by Derman and Rhine. Both of these episodes were directed by Arthur Lubin. Will Green choreographed the latter.

Alan Young today (*photo courtesy Alan Young*)

Abigail van Buren, "Dear Abby" herself, visited the *Mr. Ed* set on October 18, 1964. The episode was scripted by Derman and Larry Rhine.

Johnny Crawford of *The Rifleman* was the featured player in "Ed-a-Go-Go" on September 19, 1965, written by Derman and Rhine. "Love and the Single Horse" brought Raymond Bailey back to the *Mr. Ed* set, this time with Irene Ryan in a cameo as Granny Clampett. Derman and Rhine again teamed to turn out this script.

Victor (*Get Smart*) French and Sandra (*Bewitched*) Gould were paired in the October 17, 1965, episode entitled "Anybody Got a Zebra?" It was scripted by the team of Derman and Rhine.

Other guest stars over the years included Jack Bailey, Jacqueline Beer, William Bendix, Sebastian Cabot, Hans Conreid, Thomas Gomez, Harold Gould, Jack Kruschen, Jack LaLanne, Charles Lane, Marc Lawrence, Mike Mazurki, Jon Provost, Benny Rubin, Vin Scully, Moose Skowran, Hazel Shermet, Ricky Starr, and Miyoshi Umeki.

"None of us ever thought [*Mr. Ed*] would be popular to this degree," confesses Al Simon. "We all liked the show. We thought it was a good show. [Our writers] came up with some very good ideas and we treated the horse as if he were [a person] and the horse just felt that he was better than most people—he thought that he knew more than everybody else. The thing that made it good was that it was sophisticated and [Mr. Ed] would ask Alan to do things that would make Alan look like a fool. The audience liked that."

Mr. Ed lives on in reruns and memorabilia. Collectors covet such marketable items as Mr. Ed Halloween Costumes, circa 1962; the Mr. Ed Board Game (1962); the Mr. Ed Talking Plush Hand Puppet (1962); and the Mr.

Mr. Ed's behind the scenes team (from left) Herb Browar, Lou Derman, and Al Simon (*photo courtesy Herb Browar*)

Ed Record Album. These items range in price from $50 for the board game to $125 for the Halloween costume. Mr. Ed comic books, dating as far back as 1962, range in price from $2 to $45. The Mr. Ed Coloring Book goes for $35, while the *Mr. Ed Little Golden Book* fetches $18.

In addition, *Mr. Ed* spawned a *TV Guide* cover story (March 31, 1962), the issue going today for as much as $25. The Mr. Ed Fan Club, operated by Texan entrepreneur Big Bucks Burnett, offers the 45 RPM single "Tiny Tim Sings Mr. Ed." There is also the Bantam paperback book *The Original Mr. Ed* by Walter Brooks, containing a collection of stories published in 1964.

"The show went off the air," Browar remembers, "because they eventually put it on at 5:30 P.M. on Sundays since they wanted to schedule double-bill football. When they moved *Mr. Ed* around after *Lassie* started to lose ratings, they put *Ed* in as a lead-in [to *Lassie*] and that kept *Lassie* on for another couple of years because the lead-in [held] the audience."

But *Mr. Ed* is still with us, as attests Young, at least on *Nick at Nite:* "Everything helps your career, and [*Mr. Ed*] certainly gave me a chance to stay home with my family. I was so happy to have a show which was so family-oriented. And today, I'm grateful for it because it keeps going on and on [in reruns]. I wouldn't mind being remembered as the man who talked to a horse."

And what of the equestrian thespian with the Pepsodent smile? It has been generally believed that the Patsy Award-winning Mr. Ed died on February 28, 1979, at the age of thirty-three, but that was a stand-in horse, once used in a publicity shot. Actually, in 1968 the nineteen-year-old Mr. Ed developed kidney problems and arthritis and was put down.

What was the underlying secret of Mr. Ed's appeal and the longevity of this series?

"If you're going to have an animal talk, you must consider him as a human being," explains Arthur Lubin. "You must positively believe the horse talks. He was not a horse. He was Mr. Ed."

Rest in peace, Bamboo Harvester.

THREE

THE BEVERLY HILLBILLIES

(September 26, 1962–September 7, 1971)

Imagine a tall country bumpkin behaving oddly in front of Buckingham Palace and shouting nonsense about Sir Walter Raleigh. Imagine his companion—a blond, sugary Southern girl.

And this is exactly what creator and producer Paul Henning imagined for the premiere of the sixth season of the popular *Beverly Hillbillies,* calling it a shot in the arm for his beloved Filmways sitcom.

"I thought to myself," writer-producer Paul Henning told *TV Guide* at the time, "what if Jed Clampett inherits a castle? We needed something new . . . and here it was. From that sprang a whole series of situations."

Earlier on location at a pharmacy near London's Heathrow Airport, hundreds gathered when Jed, Granny, and Elly May arrived in costume. The crowds, who had not seen *The Beverly Hillbillies* on the tube in over two years,

shouted things like, "Granny, where's your jug?" and "Did you bring your shotgun with you?"

The castle of residence was none other than six-hundred-year-old Penhurst, where Henry VIII had dined and later beheaded his host. This was a far cry from the Clampetts' Beverly Hills mansion, which was actually the Bel-Air home of the widow of hotel magnate Arnold Kirkeby. Mrs. K. had been only too happy to oblige when Paul Henning asked for the use of her premises.

She donated the remuneration for the use of her estate to her favorite charity. The interiors of the Clampett abode were back in Hollywood's General Service Studios; cost: $65,000. The cast and crew only visited the real mansion about half a dozen times. The pool alone, though only twenty-six inches deep and twenty feet by twenty feet, cost $20,000 to build.

45

And though the hillbillies and their crew were warned never to divulge the identity of the real owner of the Beverly Hills estate, of which only exterior shots were used, sightseers and gawkers were soon cruising past the Kirkeby estate, whereupon one bold stargazer had the audacity, according to Irene ("Granny") Ryan, to verbally accost the lovely widow Kirkeby, who was picking flowers on the lawn: "Hey, Granny, give us your autograph."

What made this offbeat and unlikely show so popular—all the way from the Ozarks to Great Britain—is that three decades later its four main characters are still beloved by the American public.

At the start, Filmways executive Herb Browar said, "TV runs in cycles. We felt the cycle was right for fun. Our hillbillies are charming, delightful, wonderful, clean, wholesome people. The word 'hillbilly' will ultimately have a new meaning as a result of our show."

And he was right. *The Beverly Hillbillies* was one of the most successful of the rural comedies from the sixties. The brainchild of CBS president James Aubrey, the series was initially blasted by critics, but climbed to number one and remained there until 1964, spawning other sitcoms like *Petticoat Junction* and *Green Acres*.

"The series aimed low and hit its target," said Rick DuBrow, TV critic for UPI, on the show's premiere though it was at the top of the heap by the 1962–63 season. It would remain in first place for the following season, dropping to number eight by 1965–66 and number nine by 1966–67. The show would come in at number ten in 1968–69.

Henning, known for his work on *The Bob Cummings Show* as well as on *Fibber McGee and Molly,* had collaborated with Stanley Shapiro on the screenplay of the Doris Day-Rock Hudson movie, *Lover Come Back,* earning himself an Academy Award nomination. He would later go on to compose the *Beverly Hillbillies* theme song, which Lester Flatt and Earl Scruggs performed over the credits and recorded for Columbia Records. The title of the series was borrowed from a Depression-era country-music band.

With only Henning's verbal outline, Filmways chairman Martin Ransohoff negotiated a deal, selling James Aubrey on the idea and talking CBS into financing the project on the strength of a handshake.

Despite network backing, the show could easily have faded into oblivion because of its Wednesday night slot opposite Perry Como's successful show. Filmways, at its own expense, mounted a media campaign consisting of twenty-to-sixty-second filmed promos, reaching 35 million viewers in eighty-five cities starting six weeks before the series' debut.

By the time the second episode aired, the show was already climbing to the top of the ratings. The network promptly cashed in with a $500,000 merchandising campaign: *Hillbillies* board games, comic books, and other items such as jigsaw puzzles and Elly May paper dolls.

In this series which was taking the country by storm, veteran performers Buddy Ebsen portrayed widowed patriarch Jed Clampett and Irene Ryan was his cantankerous mother-in-law, Daisy Moses, better known as Granny. Newcomer Donna Douglas portrayed the curvaceous but oh-so-innocent daughter Elly May, and Max Baer Jr. both goofy nephew Jethro Bodine and sister Jethrine. Raymond Bailey had the role of exasperated Milburn Drysdale, president of the Commerce Bank of Beverly Hills, and Nancy Kulp was prim, plain-Jane secretary Jane Hathaway.

To make these backwoods characters even more believable, a ban was placed by CBS on any publicity showing the performers out of character. That meant that no one saw Ebsen on board his yacht or a tuxedo-attired Baer club-hopping with starlets, like Cheryl Crane, daughter of Lana Turner.

Perhaps the best loved member of the Clampett family was Granny, and it was ironic that Ryan had not been Henning's first choice for the part. On the contrary, he had not even considered her at all. She stood five-foot-two and weighed only ninety-eight pounds. Henning thought she was too thin, too short, and too young (she was fifty-nine at the time). Her retort was that if he got anyone older, the crone wouldn't last through the run of the series. Undaunted Ryan paid Henning a visit and reminisced about the dialogue he had once written her for *The Dennis Day Show.* Impressed, Henning gave in and arranged a screen test as he had for thirty-six other contenders.

"I wasn't sure how I could make myself look like the character," Ryan told *TV Guide* after the series aired, "because Granny was . . . seventy-two years old. When I got to the set the morning of the test, I took the prop man aside and said, 'Gimme a real old pair of glasses—and don't give them to anyone else.'"

In the test Ryan admonishes Jed (Ebsen) for not doing anything about the way young Elly May Clampett dresses. Jed's response is that Elly May always stands proud and tall with her shoulders thrown back—to which Granny replies "It ain't her shoulders bustin' them buttons on the front of her blouse," peering over the rim of those wire-framed glasses, which have dropped down her nose, ever so slightly.

"I knew I was in," boasted Ryan afterward, in triumph. And wire-rimmed glasses were not Granny's only trademark. One day the sound man told Ryan that the army boots would have to go because they were too noisy. The actress tried another pair but the switch was short-lived.

Those old boots had become as much a part of Ryan's interpretation of Granny, as were those old-fashioned glasses.

And indeed, Ryan made the perfect costar for Broadway and film veteran Buddy Ebsen. "I played with Buddy Ebsen in summer stock in 1940," recalls Herb Browar, "in a play called *The Poor Nut*. So we were old buddies when he came on the show."

Buddy's real name is Christian L. Ebsen Jr., a song and dance man who was a big star in films in the thirties. Already burned-out on playing hillbillies, he insisted that Jed be the straight man, the responsible one, in control of the family fortune. Henning agreed.

But the real Buddy Ebsen was a far cry from Jed Clampett. He and his family lived at Newport Beach and kept horses at Agoura, California. He enjoyed sailing and once raced his Lapworth 36 in the Tri-Island Race off the coast of California and owned a thirty-six-foot sloop called "Turquoise."

Ebsen, who was fifty-four at the time *The Beverly Hillbillies* premiered, was best known to the TV generation as George Russel, sidekick to Davy Crockett in the Disney series with Fess Parker, but what attracted Henning to Ebsen were his portrayals of Audrey Hepburn's forsaken much-older husband in *Breakfast at Tiffany's* and of a hospital den father in *The Interns,* with Stefanie Powers.

Donna Douglas has her own special memories of working with Ebsen, as is apparent when she recalls her favorite episode. "The one sitting on the front steps and my Paw said to me that I was growing up and I was getting older and that I was beginning to pop my buttons. That was probably one of the cutest. Most of my scenes were with Buddy Ebsen. [I] was probably closest to him, my Paw."

Handsome Max Baer, a motorcycle enthusiast and connoisseur of stripteasers, was the son of the former heavyweight champ, and at six-foot-four, he weighed in at two hundred pounds. Only twenty-five when the series began, he solemnly remarked on his cross-dressed characterizaton of Jethrine, "I have never understood Jethrine."

"When we were looking for a Jethro for some reason or the other the casting people were always sending us former football players that played end," recalls Herb Browar. "They were tall and athletic looking. One day a fellow comes in, a blond fellow, tall, and he reads for us and we like him. Before he leaves he says, 'By the way, my car wouldn't start'—he said that he couldn't get his car started in the morning and he asked his neighbor to bring him down who was also an actor—would we mind if he [read] for us as well. We had no appointment with him. We didn't know him, [but] we said, 'No, we don't

mind.' So I went out to give him a script and he had already talked the secretary into getting [him] a script and he was already reading Jethro's lines, so we gave him a few minutes and we told him the scene we wanted him to read. And he came in and he said his name was Max Baer Jr. and here's this big, good-looking guy, and he reads for us.

"And here's the thing that stuck out in my mind," continues Browar, "and I'm sure that everybody else thought the same thing. In his reading, he was the only one—and we read a lot of people—and we decided to test three of them—he was the only one who gave a little bit of substance to the character. So we decided we'd test him. Well, he was the last one who came on the screen when we were watching the tests. And, hell, when he came on the screen that screen just exploded. And that's what the camera does. It'll either kill you or it'll make you."

"Max [was] a pain in the neck sometimes," recalls director Bob Leeds. "He was very capable and he knew his lines and he was very professional on the set. He was the youngest one of the bunch and he'd go off in his own direction sometimes. He didn't like people meeting him on the street and calling him Jethro, and Jethro wasn't exactly the brainy on the series. He resented that and even when the series was finished people would call him Jethro all the time and he had a tough time getting away from being Jethro. He'd go in for [auditions] for pictures and they'd see Jethro all the time."

"This role has given me the opportunity and the money to play golf," Baer remarked flippantly to *TV Guide* during the run of the show, "[and] the golf is my job . . . the show is my hobby . . . I learn from Irene and Buddy and [director] Dick [Whorf]. I can take direction but I'm no comedian."

As for the supporting players, Henning had once had an unpleasant experience with a banker in Arkansas and in belated revenge he breathed as much as he could of his monetary nemesis into the life of stuffy Milburn Drysdale.

"Ray [Bailey] plays him for pure outrage, like a funny Scrooge," Henning told *TV Guide* at the time. "He's an amazingly good actor . . . and he just has that wonderful look of distinguished larceny."

And on the topic of Bailey's audition in 1962, Henning added, "That's the best cold reading I've ever heard."

"The big thing this show has brought me is prestige," stressed Nancy Kulp (who played Drysdale's sexually repressed girl Friday) in a late sixties *TV Guide* interview. "For years I was just a good character actress. I don't consider myself a comedienne, I'm just an actress. I may make people laugh but this is a gift."

Kulp previously had been a regular on *The Bob Cummings Show* (a.k.a. *Love That Bob*) from 1955 to 1959.

On Kulp's longstanding political feud with Ebsen, Leeds explains, "A Democrat [Nancy] and a Republican [Buddy]—they argued once and a while about it [but] everybody was very congenial." (Following the show's departure from prime time, Nancy Kulp went on to *The Brian Keith Show* during the 1973–74 season as Mrs. Gruber, wealthy owner of the free clinic in Hawaii where "Doctor" Keith practiced. The actress then retired from show business, moved to Pennsylvania, and took an active interest in politics. She ran for congress in the early eighties but lost, according to *Variety* in its 1991 obituary on her, in great part because Buddy Ebsen publicly opposed her.)

But despite the refinement of the supporting players and the rowdiness of Baer, the distinctiveness of Ebsen, and the lovability of Ryan, the show's starlet was, undeniably, Donna Douglas.

Browar recalls: "[One day] in the late fifties my secretary said to me, 'There's a young lady out here who would like to speak to you—she says she's an actress.' I always had an open door policy—I used to wing it all the time. She comes in and she was wearing gloves and she was wearing a hat, one of these big summer hats, and I knew immediately—here's a beautiful girl, a really beautiful girl, and she had a portfolio with her. And I didn't ask her to open the portfolio, so we chatted for a while and she was very charming, and I said, 'Why don't you go down and see [my partner] Al Simon?'

"So I called and said, 'Al, there's a girl here I think you ought to meet . . . great personality.' So that's how she got to know Al and myself. The thing was, she used to drop in every once in a while. She didn't make a pest of herself. And every time that she came in, it was delightful to be able to take a few minutes off to chat with her and everything else. Now you could never find out anything about her. She never talked about herself, never talked about her history, would change the subject immediately. You never knew anything about her.

"We were doing a [detective] show at that time called *21 Beacon Street* and one day she happened to come into the office. Her figure was not that great and she didn't give off any sexuality whatsoever, but she was very beautiful. I always remember her hands—[they] were like a child's hands, so she comes in one day and I happen to be reading a script we're gonna do on *21 Beacon Street,* and it required a secretary to try and get in touch with her boss and when she can't, she gets up, opens the door, and he's lying dead on the floor in his office. So I called Al and I said, 'Guess who's here?' He knew. You couldn't help but like her and you weren't annoyed by her. But she was a delightful break in [our] routine. And I said, 'Al, in the next episode, why don't we let Donna play the secretary?' He said, 'Fine.' So I called the casting people and that's what she did. That was the first thing she did for us.

"About a year or so later she still comes dropping in once and a while. We're now doing *Mr. Ed.* She happens to come in one day when I'm reading the episode where Wilbur wants to become an artist and he wants to use Ed to [pose with] Lady Godiva. And she happened to come in at the time I was reading it—talk about timing—so I called Al and I said, 'Hey, why don't we let Donna be Lady Godiva?' and he said, 'Fine.' So I called casting and they put her in a body stocking. She had a couple of lines—she couldn't hurt the scene."

Alan Young recalls, "I remember the episode where Donna was a model and she sat on Ed's back. I remember she was one of the most gorgeous girls and very ladylike and very Southern and very aloof. We just loved her and we all thought, 'Boy, she's going on to do something else!' and Filmways signed her for *Hillbillies* after that."

And the loveliness of Douglas was the perfect contrast to other less-than-gorgeous components of the Clampett household. One of those was Duke, played by Stretch, a twelve-year-old bloodhound and another was the infamous truck, a 1921 flatbed, for which the owner was paid $25 a day for shuttling it to and from the studio. It was not uncommon to find the old truck parked on the curb outside the hillbillies' Beverly Hills mansion or to find old Duke snoozing on the sidewalk.

Thanks to Paul Henning, Bea Benaderet was brought to the show as Jethro's ma—Cousin Pearl Bodine. Benaderet would later go on to play Kate Bradley in Henning's *Petticoat Junction,* starting in 1963. Earlier, the veteran radio actress (she was switchboard operator Gladys Gearshift on the old *Jack Benny Show*) had been neighbor Blanche Morton on *The George Burns and Gracie Allen Show* (1950–58).

Not to be overlooked were Harriet MacGibbon as Drysdale's wife Margaret, Charlie Ruggles as her father, Daddy Farquar, and Louis Nye, as her dippy son from a previous marriage. In later episodes Shug Fisher was the backwoods rube, Shorty (1965–67) and Roger Torrey was Mark Templeton (1970–71). Lester Flatt and Earl Scruggs, who strummed and sang the show's theme song, periodically turned up as themselves.

Beverly Hillbillies triviates will recall that, during the 1963–64 season, starlet Sharon Tate appeared as secretary Janet Trego. This was several years before her marriage to Roman Polanski and, later, the infamous Manson murders.

But despite her sexpot image and the later publicity that surrounded her tragic death, Tate never came close to replacing Douglas as the public's favorite hillbilly gal.

From the very beginning Douglas had told producer Henning that playing Elly May would be just like reliving her own past:

The erstwhile Doris Smith (she would later use the stage names Tina Baron and Dot Bourgeois) was born in

48

Pride, Louisiana, on September 26, 1939. Doris/Donna would make her *Hillbillies* debut exactly twenty-three years later, after beating out one hundred other girls for the part.

"Elly was sixteen [and I was] a little bit older," Douglas told Joan Rivers in November 1991. "Actually I didn't know too much about acting. It was all pretty new to me and we were working with Irene and Buddy who'd had lots of experience. So I never knew [about not being able to] follow the dog act or the kid. When I started to work with animals it gave me the opportunity to do something [new], so the more I did the more I got to do, the more they added on.

"We were both born in the country, real poor little girls,

Irene Ryan (Granny) and Buddy Ebsen (Jed Clampett), surrounded by Max Baer Jr. (Jethro), Nancy Kulp (Jane Hathaway), Raymond Bailey (Milton Drysdale), and Donna Douglas (Elly Mae Clampett) (*photo courtesy Donna Douglas*)

Buddy Ebsen in his best Jed Clampett pose (*photo courtesy Buddy Ebsen*)

that kind of thing. Basically I tried to keep it simple. After *The Beverly Hillbillies* I went to night school and got my real estate license, and I did that for a little while but I kept making personal appearances and all that kind of stuff. In time I did a country album and a gospel album and I did some singing and some [more] personal appearances."

Herb Browar recalls: "Donna was a delight to work with and she was just a terrific, terrific gal [but she had] a very strange, interesting history. She comes from Louisiana, she comes off a farm. She became Miss Baton Rouge [and] she got married young, had a child—she's got a son who's got to be in his forties—I don't know what happened with the marriage, the kid, I guess was raised by

her parents—she went to New York to become a model and she became very successful as a model.

"Hal Wallis was in New York one time and happened to see her. He had a production unit at Paramount, and he signed her to a six-month contract because that's the way [the studios] worked. And he brought her out here and she made one picture for him, and he knew right away that she couldn't act, so he didn't pick up the option. And she hung on for a while. I understand she even pitched for [Paramount's] softball team. Anyway she couldn't make a go of it and therefore and she went back to New York to model."

Douglas had indeed moved with her family to Baywood

and at age seventeen married local boy Roland Bourgeois, bearing him a son named Danny. The marriage soon fell apart and Douglas hit the beauty pageant trail, being named Miss New Orleans in 1957 and Miss Baton Rouge in 1958.

"Some people think its strange that I don't have my son with me," Douglas once commented to the press, "but he's with people he loves and who love him. He lives with my folks. What could I give him, working all day?"

After leaving Louisiana she had gone to New York, where she modeled and did some television variety shows. Hal Wallis spotted her and signed her. Her best remembered film appearance would be opposite Elvis in *Frankie and Johnny* (1966).

Her big television break finally came as Elly May, despite the critical panning of *The Beverly Hillibillies*, although *TV Guide* soon proclaimed that Douglas had done "more for bluejeans in seven months than cowboys did in 110 years."

And later Henning would comment himself on the tomboyish appeal of the Clampett daughter, such as when Elly used her bra as a slingshot: "I was a little red-faced about that bit. I just thought it was a little overboard. I still wish we hadn't done it."

Donna Douglas minimizes Elly's provactive attire: "I wore long jeans—everybody comes [up] to me, a lot of times, and they say, 'Hey, I remember when you wore those little cutoff jeans,' [and I say] 'No,' but everybody thinks I did."

During the series' original run, Donna had told *TV Guide,* "I'm not thinking of getting married again, but if I found somebody I was interested in, I'd adjust. But I don't socialize a lot. I don't go out a lot. I still get a little shy."

Douglas, who appeared in 215 *Beverly Hillbillies,* has since admitted that after the show was canceled she felt let down and didn't know what to do. For nine years the series had been a big part of her life. But by then she was married to director Bob Leeds and took off in a new direction—real estate and singing.

In 1978, she attempted a country music singing career that didn't jell, before reprising the role of Elly May in the 1981 TV reunion movie, *Return of the Beverly Hillbillies,* directed by Leeds, from whom she was then separated.

According to Douglas, Max Baer did not want to do the reunion movie, though she, Ebsen, Nancy Kulp, and Earl Scruggs returned, joined by Linda Henning (Paul's actress daughter) as Linda, Ray Young as Jethro, Werner Klemperer as Miss Jane's reluctant fiancé, King Donovan as Andy Heller, Lurene Tuttle as Mollie Heller, Shug Fisher as Judge Gillum, Imogene Coca as Granny's 100-year-old maw, and a young Heather Locklear as Heather.

"Yes, I did *Return of the Beverly Hillbillies,*" Leeds confesses. "I hate to say it, but I [did]. It was a little heavy-handed but that was the way it had to be. Ray Young had a tough situation—you really can't replace anybody. That was Heather Locklear's first part, her first little part. Imogene was great. The only problem she had was she didn't want people to think she was that old. We did put an awful lot of makeup on her. And she said, 'People haven't seen me in so long they're gonna think I look like this.' We had to convince her that, no, they wouldn't think she was that old and bad-looking."

Despite her estrangement from Leeds, perhaps Donna Douglas finally found closure in returning with Ebsen and Kulp to the *Hillbillies* set once again. In any case, it brought back memories of the show's cancellation years before: "In our case we were on a seesaw—they kept saying we'll keep it on [but] they finally let us know. We were all disappointed, I think. Maybe not Maxie, but I was real sad."

And now the Clampetts and friends will live yet again on the big screen in *The Beverly Hillbillies,* which went into production in early 1993. Jim Varney is playing Jed, Cloris Leachman is Granny, Erika Eleniak is Elly May, and Diedrich Bader is Jethro. As Drysdale, there is Dabney Coleman, and Lily Tomlin plays Miss Jane. Rob Schneider and Lea Thompson also are aboard, all under the direction of Penelope Spheeris.

Jethro and Elly Mae find themselves in Merrie Olde England (*photo courtesy Donna Douglas*)

"I'm coproducing two movies—a comedy adventure and a children's animated that's in development," says Douglas today. "I got my 'Donna Douglas' doll and I do arts and crafts fairs—I do quite a bit of that work with young people a lot."

The new Donna Douglas Doll wears jeans (not cutoffs) but the original Elly Mae Clampett Doll wore a yellow dress, bloomers, and white shoes and sells today for as much as $78.

Leeds replaced actor-turned-director-painter-sculptor-scenic designer Richard Whorf, who had once described *Hillbillies* as "a very good comic strip—most of all we have going for us the complete wonder, amazement, and incredulity of the Clampetts at this world they never knew existed. They never wholly adapt themselves to it."

"Well, I was the film editor there for three years," explains Leeds today. "One of the directors had emphysema and he had to bow out and then I took over. I had directed [other things] long, long before that. [It wasn't any] problem at all because I knew all the characters and I knew the actors. There wasn't any problem. I had already been on the set for three years.

"I did several shows with Phil Silvers and I did the shows with Shug Fisher, and I can tell you one thing, Phil was a very serious man . . . and between what he played and what he was personally was quite a contrast. And he was very serious about everything that he did but very, very funny with his gift of gab and he would make things up as he went along—he really enhanced what was written, but he was a very funny man when you were working with him." (One of Leeds's favorite episodes is the one in which Phil Silvers sold Central Park to the Clampetts.)

As for life after the *Hillibillies,* Leeds says, "I did a series called *Sam,* I did *Project: U.F.O.,* including the episodes in which Donna appeared. But more people saw *Beverly Hillbillies* than any of the others."

Remembering his most memorable episode, Leeds recounts, "Donna got bit by a chimp [Cousin Bessie]. We were shooting a scene and she had Cousin Bessie in her arms and we got through shooting and Donna didn't move and she said, 'Don't anybody move because she's got my thumb in her mouth and she's clamped down on it.' I guess if you try to pull it away they'll tear it, so Bessie put a pretty good hole in her and they took Donna to the hospital to make sure she'd get a shot. That was the only accident, but once we had the bear on the set and Drysdale was in the kitchen and the bear was supposed to come up behind him. Well, the bear took off and everybody took off—this was a big bear, he stood about seven feet tall.

"We all took off. I went up a ladder. I don't know why I went up a ladder because it was only a four-foot ladder and the bear was bigger than that. Everybody started going up the steps. The trainer had a cane in his hand and

kept beating the bear on the nose and the bear started screaming bloody murder and we thought—Oh, God, what's going to happen now—but he finally subdued the bear and they put him back in his cage."

Herb Browar relates: "We had an episode of the *Hillbillies* where a baby hippo escaped from the zoo and wanders around on the estate, and Jethro says, 'That's the biggest [hog] I ever saw in my life!' And that was the joke. The point was that this baby hippo—we got it out at Thousand Oaks, there was a compound out there—made friends with a baby elephant and they were inseparable. Wherever the hippo moved, the elephant moved, so when [the handlers] brought it in, they had to have the baby elephant on the stage. When they would finally get the hippo to the point where they could shoot a scene, the elephant would move and the hippo would drop everything and move—he knocked the set down, the lights down, just to get over next to this elephant."

"The hippo wouldn't work without the elephant—they were pals," insists Leeds, recalling the same episode. "The hippo wouldn't do anything without the elephant."

And who was always on Elly's case about her critters? None other than Irene (Granny) Ryan.

Whorf once told *TV Guide:* "Because of Irene's years of vaudeville training, when she constantly had to study human nature in order to make people laugh, she has brought to this role a little bit of what every grandmother is. Although she's a hillbilly granny—it's the identifiable universality of her character which makes her so great. She's the roots—conniving, superstitious, guarding her kitchen like a she-wolf, using every trick to get her own way, even self-pity."

"People love Irene for exactly the same reasons they admire Granny," Paul Henning says. "She's got spirit. She's tough, intractable, spunky. Nobody can push her around. . . . She's independent. She personifies the pioneer American. Whenever you read about these mountain areas you always find a granny woman who is arbitrator, midwife, and herb doctor."

"Irene was very funny and a very nice person and would do anything you said," says Leeds, "and she was very complimentary. She had red hair and she was tiny and she was very vivacious and a very outgoing person. When she got sick she was doing *Pippin* in New York."

"Granny's a fighter of the American pioneering tradition—and so's Irene," Ebsen told *TV Guide* while the series was still going strong. "She has discipline, strength of character. She's the kind of woman who used to load rifles, hand them to the men, and shoot them herself. Irene's tough. A very strong sense of right and wrong. She's completely self-reliant. There's a kinship between Irene and me. We both went to the school of hard knocks. The school that teaches you to rely on your own resources."

As formal a portrait one can expect of the Clampetts

Donna Douglas as Elly Mae Clampett (*photo courtesy Donna Douglas*)

"I think whatever happens to our lives we've done ourselves," Ryan once commented in another *TV Guide* interview, "I think your thinking has everything to do with you and your life. . . . I've been bounced down and I've had to come back with my own strength. . . . I can take those jolts that life dishes out and come up again. . . . That's what I admire most in other people, too—inner strength. It's Buddy Ebsen and I who have the discipline. Max Baer and Donna Douglas, they're the ones who are late and seldom apologize for it, seldom call. I wouldn't think of coming in late." But in other ways Ryan was nothing like her hillbilly counterpart: "I'm a conservative, really. . . . I'm devoted to Reagan. His whole thinking is congenial to me."

"When I was a kid," she told *TV Guide* in still another of numerous interviews, "I worked through the Ozarks, where our characters are supposed to be from. They are terribly funny, warm people, but up to now, nobody ever really got them down on paper. Our show did."

Born in El Paso, Irene moved with her family to California when she was an infant. She won an amateur contest in San Francisco at age eleven and when she was thirteen—pretending to be sixteen—her agent told her mother that little Irene was awkward. Always a trooper, she cashed in on the sullen gaze and shaky chin, incorporating those assets into a vaudeville routine.

In her teens, she ended up at Joyland Park in Sacramento on a bill with Arthur "Dagwood" Lake and his sister, Florence. Her mother was against her touring but feisty Irene's response was to quit school, take off, and never look back. Her first husband was her vaudeville partner, Tim Ryan.

In 1932 the Ryans went on radio as a team and were later used as a summer replacement for Jack Benny. After her divorce from Tim, Irene became part of Bob Hope's radio family and appeared in the forties with up-and-coming Doris Day. Years later when accepting the Distinguished Service Award from the National Association of Broadcasters, Hope would quip that FCC chairman Newton Minow's meddlings have led the industry up the path to *The Beverly Hillbillies*. Never at a loss for words, Ryan, on the strength of the show's ratings would snap, "Millions of folks have brought that outhouse inside their homes."

"I never portrayed a dumb wife," Ryan once said in her own defense. "I was the wisecracking type." She would often tease Hope about the possibility (and often probability) of a lukewarm audience response. "Just wait till you feel that flop-sweat," she'd warn, as Hope howled with laughter.

In Vegas in 1961 she laid eyes for the second time on Paul Henning, the man who would propel her to belated stardom. They had first met earlier when she had appeared on *The Dennis Day Show,* for which he was a writer.

At the time that Henning's *Beverly Hillbillies* idea stuck with her, Ryan was still recovering from divorce from second husband, Harold E. Knox, a motion picture production manager.

Like Ryan and Ebsen, supporting player Raymond Bailey was a veteran performer, who had made his mark in *Secret Service of the Air* (with young Ronald Reagan) and dozens of other films.

"Raymond was wonderful," Leeds recalls. "He was a great guy to work with. He was very intense and he'd get really upset if he flubbed his lines and he worked very hard and he was a joy to be with—they all were."

"Ray always seems to be mad at something," costar Nancy Kulp once remarked of her television boss to *TV Guide*, "but he isn't really. He's a fumer, tough, unapproachable, and sensitive. He blusters and tries to pretend that he doesn't like to be liked, but he does and I don't know anyone [who] doesn't like him."

Bailey was born in San Francisco on May 6, 1905, the son of poor Irish parents. Along with his three sisters, he grew up in Oakland. Dropping out of school at fifteen, he got a job as a messenger boy in a Bay Area bank and ended up working at Yosemite National Park by age nineteen.

During the Depression he had shouldered a pick and shovel on the WPA and had rode the rails and slept in hobo jungles, toiled in Hawaiian pineapple fields, ending up working in a movie studio as a $4-a-day laborer before moving on to sing in Tinseltown's sleazy nightclubs for as little as sixty cents a night.

His brief tenure as a studio laborer motivated him to seek in New York the riches Hollywood had not yielded. After bumming his way across country, he found not stardom on the Great White Way but another series of menial jobs which carried him around the world.

When he came back to Hollywood in 1934, it was as a cabaret singer, with an occasional jaunt in a road show. In 1938, at age thirty-three, he won his first movie role after much perseverance. With his newly-grown mustache, he found periodic work in Warner gangster films.

He spent the war with the Merchant Marines as a deck officer. He would later tour with *Mister Roberts,* spend eighteen months in Australia doing *Oklahoma!* and understudy Lloyd Nolan in *The Caine Mutiny Court-Martial* on Broadway and on tour. By the time *The Beverly Hillbillies* came along he already had over three hundred television appearances to his credit.

"Producers have forgotten about me," Bailey told *TV Guide* during the run of *The Beverly Hillbillies,* "I could play somebody's eccentric father in a Doris Day picture, I could do a tough dramatic role. I can do more than play a comedy but nobody asks me. I'm happy playing Drysdale . . . but I'm still an actor and there are other things I'd like to sink my fangs into."

"I wish [*Hillbillies*] had gone another five years,"

muses Leeds today. "It was a very nice set to work on. The people all got along and they all did what they were supposed to do. Occasionally there were little quibbles about lines and different things and why we'd have to do it over again but that's normal on a set. [Paul] was very smart, very creative, and very intelligent, and he knew exactly what he was doing. I think it was written very well and I think it was very humorous, really—you know, times have changed a little since *The Beverly Hillbillies* but, nevertheless, in those days it was a very humorous show."

Perhaps the one individual to suffer in the end has been Douglas. "I think Donna was like Max in a way, she was typecast as Elly May," Leeds feels, "and at that particular time when the show was canceled, there were a lot of public appearances for Elly May. There would have been for Jethro, too, but [Max] didn't want to do them. And Donna took them. And she traveled around the country for several years playing Elly May at fairs and different places and she stuck with Elly May. She did a few pictures in between. She did two *Project: U.F.O.* [shows] and she did *Adam 12* but she stuck with the Elly May thing and I think she wore herself out with it."

And indeed when CBS aired a retrospective called *The Legend of the Beverly Hillbillies* on May 24, 1993, a grandmotherly Donna Douglas was still sporting those golden locks that were Elly May's trademark. She was reunited with a somewhat frail (but still spry enough to do several dance steps) Buddy Ebsen, natty Max Baer, Louis Nye, and Roy Clark (Cousin Roy in the series). The special, which got amazingly good ratings, was hosted by singer Mac Davis and produced and directed by Jay Levey.

"Things happen in their own good time," Douglas says, "I don't fight life, but go with it, one step at a time." But even during the time of the show's original run, she had commented: "I used to do all sorts of parts, but when Elly came along I sort of fell into it. The character is not too far away from me. There's part of Elly May with me all the time. But I did have to forget a heap of living and learning to do this part. Elly's taken over quite a bit of my life—there's not much time left for Donna Douglas."

And perhaps that remains true. Douglas may have done well to have taken the advice of actress Bette Midler, who commented in the December 1991 *Vanity Fair* on her own struggle with the character that propelled her to stardom: "I'm glad I had a chance to live it . . . but I could see it was a path to Nowheresville. It was something that took constant maintenance, I just couldn't do it."

From country girl to Miss New Orleans to model to starlet to Elly May Clampett, Douglas has come full circle, all the way back to her Southern roots, immortalized in the public's mind as Jed Clampett's hillbilly daughter. It seems that, as ex-husband Leeds points out, she's stuck with the Elly May thing and has, in the end, been consumed by it.

Max Baer (no longer junior) of recent vintage (*photo courtesy Max Baer*)

56

Uncle Martin, with his silly antennae, contemplates earthling
Tim O'Hara who contemplates his next chess moves

FOUR

MY FAVORITE MARTIAN

(September 29, 1963—May 1, 1966)

Ranking in the top ten during the 1963–64 television season, *My Favorite Martian* was an extraordinary comedy about an extraterrestrial (played by veteran actor Ray Walston) marooned on planet Earth after his space ship crashes. The Martian moves in with *Los Angeles Sun* reporter Tim O'Hara (Bill Bixby) and assumes the name of Martin O'Hara, passing himself off as Tim's uncle.

Produced by Jack Chertok, the pilot was written by creator John L. Greene and directed by Sheldon Leonard. Harry Poppe was production assistant and George Greeley scored the music. In it, Tim O'Hara is assigned to cover the launching of the rocket-plane X-15 by his editor, Harry Burns (J. Pat O'Malley), and witnesses the crash of a UFO. He finds an alien from Mars with the disabled spaceship, following a run-in with military brass. An intergalactic anthropologist, here to study the

primitive planet Earth, the Martian convinces Tim to give him a place to stay while repairing his crippled ship, and he moves into the newspaperman's garage apartment at pretty landlady Lorelei Brown's (Pamela Britton) house.

Though everyone including Burns is skeptical of Tim's flying saucer story, it is published in the *Sun,* after which the police come to the garage apartment and cart the reporter away.

But despite Tim's unexplained antics, "Uncle" Martin remained the real mystery. Though it was cold and very dry on Mars he never complained about Earth being too damp. The air on Mars is less than one hundredth the density of Earth's and contains no oxygen, yet Martin was not bothered by our air. Mars' surface gravity is only two-fifths as strong as Earth's yet Martin was not weighted down on this planet.

"I read the script," says Walston, who before becoming an actor worked as a linotype operator at the *New Orleans Item-Tribune* during the Depression for $10 a week, "and I must say that I did not think it would get off the ground. I didn't think that it had a chance. . . . I must have been the most surprised person in Hollywood when it got on [the air]. I had forsaken New York in 1961. I had moved lock, stock and barrel [to L.A.] and I had been doing movies and television. I was with the William Morris Agency and they had the writer John Greene and the director Sheldon Leonard and the producer Jack Chertok and [he] put it together, getting money from Milton Berle, Danny Thomas, Andy Griffith [who] put up half of the money it only cost $80,000 to make the pilot.

"There were a lot of people who cautioned me against doing it, saying it won't go—it's a fantasy and it won't go at all. When we did go on the air the following year, *I Dream of Jeannie* went on and at the same time *Bewitched* went on. *Bewitched* lasted eight years and *I Dream of Jeannie* lasted five years and we lasted three [107 episodes]. But I suppose it was about four weeks into shooting that I realized I had put myself in a jam playing a character like this, it was going to hurt me, and I felt that there was nothing I could do about it at that time. I spoke to the producer and he said, 'Nothing like that is going to happen.'

"It's all that ridiculous business of being typed. The Martian [was] kindly, whimsical and basically good. But people like to put you into a mold. Why, in New York, I lost a number of parts because of the *Damn Yankees* role—there's such a thing as doing a part too well, you know. The only thing [*Martian*] has done for me really is to give me practically worldwide recognition."

And it did indeed bring television fame to Walston, a veteran of the stage and screen. Born Harry Schippers in New Orleans, he began his acting career in 1939 with the Margo Jones Community Players in a Houston production of Maxwell Anderson's *High Tor*.

In a short six months he had graduated to *The Taming of the Shrew*, while keeping his day job at the newspaper in New Orleans, as he would for the next six years. Though he was in the spotlight on stage each night, life was not always easy as he took care of a bedridden mother, while living with his married brother. The family, for the most part, ignored his stage endeavors.

"My brother's interest in my acting," says Walston, "went only so far as a sarcastic slur or two about my masculinity when I grew long hair for the part of Romeo."

Striking out in 1943 with new bride Ruth Calvert, he was soon performing at the Cleveland Playhouse in Tennessee Williams's *You Touched Me*, under the direction of Margo Jones. More than twenty other productions would follow before he arrived in New York in 1945 as understudy to Maurice Evans in *Hamlet*.

Three years later, appearing in *Summer and Smoke*, Walston won the Clarence Derwent Award as the Best Supporting Actor of that season, and was selected the most promising young actor in the *Variety* Drama Critics Poll. In early 1949 he appeared in *Richard III*, followed the same year by George Abbott's *Mrs. Gibbons' Boys*, and Garson Kanin's *The Rat Race*. It was at this point that producer Leland Heyward realized that Walston would be perfect for Luther Billis, the braggart seabee, in *South Pacific*, a role he played to great acclaim for several years first in the national company and then in London—and later in the film version. It was somewhere into the run that a young comic sought Walston's advice on acting and that was James Komack; their paths would again cross on the set of *My Favorite Martian*.

Returning to the States in 1952, Walston soon found himself back on Broadway in another Rodgers and Hammerstein show, *Me and Juliet*, directed by George Abbott. This was followed by two more musicals, Truman Capote's *House of Flowers* and then, with Abbott again, *Damn Yankees*, earning Walston a Tony Award in 1955. His Hollywood film debut was in *Kiss Them for Me* (1957), with Jayne Mansfield, after which he went on to do the film versions of both *South Pacific* and *Damn Yankees*. He later did two Billy Wilder movies, *The Apartment* and *Kiss Me, Stupid*, the latter off-center comedy dismissed as smut at the time and not considered much better now. Walston is a songster who tries to sell his material to Dean Martin who is out to seduce Kim Novak, his (Walston's) wife.

"A very exciting thing happened [for me]," remembers Walston, "when [Billy Wilder] called for me to come in after Peter Sellers, who was making *Kiss Me, Stupid* had a heart attack after four and a half weeks of shooting. It was impossible to pass up [the film] though now, in retrospect, I wish that I had because it turned out to be the first flop that Wilder ever had. The picture was a real bomb."

And along came the phenomenal success of *My Favorite Martian*.

"I don't think that there's any question about the special effects attracting a great many people," says Walston. "[But] once they got the pilot made they didn't deal too much in space at all thereafter—I was very disappointed about that. Had they followed the line of *Star Trek* it might have been a different story.

"The acting in it was good—good actors were in the leading roles. Pamela Britton had the body of an eighteen-year-old—she kept herself very well. She didn't smoke, she didn't drink or anything like that. She was a very wonderful specimen of a woman and [her death in 1974] was a shame—it was a real tragedy."

"[She] was doing a play in Chicago with Don Knotts and she began to have headaches. They persisted, she went to a doctor. They went through a lot of procedures and after a while told her she was fine and she went back to work and [the headaches] started again and she died from a brain tumor. It was sad because she was over forty when we did *Martian* but she spent more time [at] a gym I had them put up for me on stage than I did.

"How they arrived at a detective who was enamored of Mrs. Brown, and who was very suspicious of the Martian I don't know," adds Walston on the subject of Alan Hewitt's Detective Brennen. "The Martian could have put him away really fast [but] show after show the detective [was] pitted against a man who supposedly had all kinds of powers and it just didn't make sense. I disagreed with the producer about that character—I felt that the Martian who had demonstrated all kinds of powers during that first year was [wrongly] pitted against this arch-detective. Alan [too] has died since. He spent fifty-two years in the theater, movies, and television."

Walston goes on: "Aside from the special effects, aside from some of the silly situations, the approach to the work by Bixby and myself and Pamela and eventually Alan Hewitt was exceptional. But what took precedence over everything that happened in the three years that we shot was the attack by the chimpanzee. [In] the usual animal story line, the animal would speak to me in my ear and

Ray Walston, two decades after *My Favorite Martian* (*photo courtesy Ray Walston*)

then I would relay what he had told me to Bixby. It was a gag, of sorts."

"[This chimp] went berserk and he attacked me and chewed me up very badly. He chewed my face up, my neck, my ears. I thought maybe one eye was gone. We were down for eight weeks. It looked like we were going to fade right out [but] fortunately we had eight [episodes] already in the can. After that I requested that we not work with any more animals."

Walston also muses, "The thing about *Martian* was that it was hard to do. Chertok would do eight segments before we would get a little break and it [really] got tough. It was long hours and there were lots of special effects. And we had no rehearsals except for the [one] you'd have just before we shot a scene. Generally speaking, all the half-hour sitcoms at that time were all being done with one camera and most of them would meet on Monday to read the script. Tuesday the director would block it. Then on Wednesday, Thursday, and Friday they would rehearse and were way ahead when they started shooting.

"Now we did not have that luxury, simply because the producer was a pennypincher. He had [gotten away with] such things on *The Lone Ranger* and that kind of crap. So we had only three days and it was tough, really tough. I recall the last segment of the first year [we did thirty-eight or thirty-nine shows]—a couple of times they had to put speeches on a board for me [to read] because I was so exhausted I couldn't remember anything.

"Finally after we went into the third year when they went into color, it took a little bit more time to do it, but it was still tough. Both Bixby and myself used to walk out of there dragging ass on Friday. I never went near [*Martian*] in reruns but one time when I was doing a guest shot on *The Hulk* with Bixby, he was in my dressing room and we turned on the television set and one of the [episodes] was on and I was really surprised at the good acting in it. I haven't seen Bixby in quite a long time."

And what of the man who rescued the Martian from the spaceship back in September of 1963?

Bill Bixby was born in San Francisco on January 22, 1934, attended the University of California in Berkeley, started out modeling and appearing in industrial films and television commercials, and was later discovered in an actors' workshop, going on to do several guest spots on weekly series. His first regular role was on *The Joey Bishop Show* during the 1962 season. During the *Martian* run he found time for stage work in L.A., doing *Under the Yum Yum Tree,* and *The Fantastiks,* among others, and on Broadway he was in *The Paisley Convertible.*

Feature film roles came next, including costarring ones with good friend Elvis Presley in both *Clambake* and *Speedway.* He also starred in Disney's *The Apple Dumpling Gang* with Don Knotts and Harry Morgan. Directed by Norman Tokar, it had Bixby as a notorious gambler

Pamela Britton, Ray Walston, and Bill Bixby

who inherits three children. Knotts is predictable as his sidekick.

Bixby followed *Martians* with his role as widowed magazine editor Tom Corbett in *The Courtship of Eddie's Father* (1969–72), for which he received an Emmy nomination. The series costarred Brandon Cruz (Eddie, his six-year-old son who plays matchmaker for his dad), Miyoshi Umeki (Mrs. Livingston, their housekeeper), and James Komack (Norman Tinker, his art director). Tippi Hedren, Jodie Foster, Karen Wolfe, and Kristina Holland also had recurring roles during the show's three-season run.

Following his two hit sitcoms, Bixby, who also happened to be a professional magician, starred in the first of his two successful dramatic series, *The Magician* (1973–74), playing stage magician Tony Blake who dabbles in crime solving. Then he took the role of David Banner in *The Incredible Hulk*, for four seasons. One more series followed, the short-lived *Goodnight Beantown*, which aired sporadically during 1983 and 1984 on CBS.

Increasingly, Bixby was getting into TV directing. Not only did he direct two of the three *Incredible Hulk* TV movies in the 1980s, but he also worked regularly on series like *Ferris Bueller, Sons and Daughters, Man of the People,* and most recently, *Blossom.*

Affable Bill Bixby also found his career dogged by tragedy. In 1981, he and actress wife Brenda Benet of *Days of Our Lives* lost their young son to a rare disease, and the following year, Benet took her own life. Bixby subsequently rewed but the marriage lasted only two years. Late in 1992, Bixby himself confirmed supermarket tabloid reports that he was suffering from cancer and was undergoing experimental drug therapy.

As for post-*Martian* Walston, he returned to Broadway in 1966 with *Agatha Sue, I Love You,* again directed by George Abbott; then it was back to Hollywood for *Caprice* with Doris Day.

"I happened to be acting for a director named Frank Tashlin, whom I admired," recalls Walston, "I had done a couple of pictures with him before. But one morning I was surprised [by] Doris Day. I always thought she was such a pleasant [person] and I had a great admiration for the fact that she had the ability to show in her eyes what was happening in her mind as a character. But one morning I said, 'How are you?' and discovered that her general idea was [that people] should assume [without asking] that she was fine, that everything was perfect, the whole world was glowing, everything was rosy."

Caprice was followed by the movie musical *Paint Your Wagon* with Clint Eastwood, in which Walston played Mad Jack Duncan; Robert Altman's *Popeye,* and on to touring companies of *Canterbury Tales, The Odd Couple, Oliver!* and others.

"I've made some films [since]: *The Sting,* was an interesting film," says Walston. "*Paint Your Wagon*—I enjoyed that very much. I've done several road tours, but I no longer do theater."

In a late 1960s interview with *TV Guide,* James Komack, who wrote a number of *Martian* scripts, described a different Walston, one who was more thorough than he cares to admit: "One Sunday night, very late, I get an urgent, emergency message to get in touch with Ray. He says to me, 'What's glinkoil?' And I say 'What's what?' and what difference does it make at this hour of the night anyway?" It seems Ray was studying my script and one line says something about the flying saucer needing glinkoil and he wanted to know what was glinkoil. Only Ray would insist on knowing that."

At the time Walston defended his compulsive behavior: "The only way I can make the Martian believable and not just a magician is to absorb the character, to feel it. Then when you have to read lines that were rewritten two minutes before, it comes out perfectly in character."

And part of Walston's own technique was to read his lines into a recorder in a flat monotone, enabling him to learn the script with no inflection so that he would sound spontaneous when the camera finally rolled.

Between two Robert Altman films, *Popeye* and *The Player,* Walston starred as sarcastic school principal Arnold Hand in *Fast Times at Ridgemont High,* a role he recreated in the subsequent TV series. "[One day, Altman] called me and he asked me if I would do one day's work as an extra in *The Player,*" explains Walston. "That he was getting a lot of people around town to do the same thing, so I agreed to do it. He wanted me to play a priest. And I agreed to do it and when I showed up on June 30 [1991], here are some of the names that were involved with the scene that I did: Bruce Willis, Julia Roberts, Susan Sarandon, Peter Falk . . . and a lot of other people who are well known. And then I learned that two weeks before Altman had called upon Jack Lemmon, Robert Wagner [and others].

"So when I showed up, the scene that I [was in depicted] the execution of a woman in the gas chamber in San Quentin—Julia Roberts played that role. And the sequence consisted of shots of the chair, her coming down the hall with the priest, [her] being strapped in the chair. And in the background was a glass enclosure [where] you could see a lot of these celebrities. Then at the last moment as the gas is being released Willis in a real Hollywood ending saves her. It's a movie-within-a-movie."

Of late, Walston got terrific notices for the 1991 version of *Of Mice and Men* and has been seen in the recurring role of the acerbic justice of the peace in *Picket Fences* on TV.

Walston says of *My Favorite Martian,* "I was very disappointed that the series did not last longer than three years. The people at the top didn't know how to keep it alive. I watched [the show] on Sunday nights when we were shooting. Thereafter I never looked at it again because of problems I had with the producer. I just had a bad taste in my mouth about the whole thing.

"*Bewitched* lasted because they were hiring excellent people—Maurice Evans, the famous Shakespearean actor, Agnes Moorehead—that's the caliber of the people they [had]. In *I Dream of Jeannie* I don't know [but] I do know about us—we had a lot of barnyard characters playing in our show—a lot of dogs, cats, cows and, squirrels."

And though many of the guest stars on *My Favorite Martian* would go on to bigger things, at the time they were, for the most part, relatively unknown, familiar-faced journeyman actors.

Howard (*The Munsters Today*) Morton appeared in "Raffles Number Two" (December 8, 1963), written by Elroy Schwartz and Austin Kalish and directed by Oscar Rudolph. In this episode Martin is unable to get a driver's license because he has no fingerprints so he borrows some—those of a jewel thief.

O'Malley was in several episodes following the pilot. The first was "The Awful Truth" (November 17, 1963), written by Arnold and Lois Peyser and directed by Rudolph, and dealt with Martin's making it possible for Tim to be a mind reader for twenty-four hours.

"My Nephew the Artist" (February 16, 1964), written by Ben Starr and directed by Rudolph, brings the return of J. Pat O'Malley as Burns with the unemployable Martin selling his unusual paintings in order to earn enough money to cover his personal expenses.

O'Malley was back again in "The Disastro-Nauts" (June 7, 1964) with Alan Hale Jr. in a segment written by Bill Freedman and Ben Gersham and directed by Leslie Goodwins. In this show Martin learns of an inventor's experimental missile and plans to borrow it to return to Mars.

In "Who's Got a Secret?" (December 26, 1965), written by Marty Roth, and directed by John Erman, Gavin MacLeod was Mrs. Brown's brother Alvin, a schemer who convinces a general that he and Martin are building a spaceship. Alvin was brought back in "Man From Uncle Martin" (January 30, 1966), written by James Allardice and Tom Adair, and directed by Erman. This time he buys a worthless toy and Martin goes in search of the crook who sold it to him.

"Martian of the Movies" (September 26, 1965), written by Albert E. Lewin and Burt Styler and directed by Erman, spotlights Howard Morton in a tale of wedding bells for Tim. The episode also featured John Carradine and Arlene Martel.

"The O'Hara Caper" (December 19, 1965), also written by Lewin and Styler and directed by Erman, brings Morton back in a story about thieves. This one has Tim arriving at the scene of robberies in Martin's time machine.

Sharon Farrell was in "There Is No Cure for the Common Martian" (October 13, 1963), written by James Komack and directed by Sidney Miller. Uncle Martin catches the common cold in this one. The only problem is every time he sneezes, he disappears.

Butch Patrick of *The Munsters* appeared in "How to Be a Hero Without Really Trying" (December 29, 1963), written by Ed James and Seamon Jacobs and directed by Sidney Miller. Tim scales a mountain during a picnic to save a young boy (Patrick), while Martin searches the woods for a rare material he needs to repair his spaceship.

Henry Gibson was in "Danger! High Voltage" (April 19, 1964), written by Ben Gersham and Bill Freedman and directed by Leslie Goodwins. Martin is overexposed to an electric charge, which adversely affects all the household appliances.

Elvia Allman guest starred in "The Sinkable Mrs. Brown" (April 12, 1964). Written by Al Martin and Bill Lesley and directed by Oscar Rudolph, it had her as a pushy real estate agent persuading Mrs. Brown to put her home on the market, much to Tim and Martin's dismay.

David White of *Bewitched* turned up in "A Nose for News" (June 21, 1964), written by William Blinn and Michael Gleason and directed by Alan Rafkin, in which Martin is stiff competition for Tim at the newspaper after being offered a job on the merit of a free-lance story he submitted.

Pat (*The Munsters*) Priest appeared in "My Uncle the Folk Singer" (November 2, 1964), written by Lee Karson and directed by Oscar Rudolph. Martin's brain malfunctions and he becomes a hit songster on the coffee house circuit.

Linda (*Dynasty*) Evans was in "Martin's Favorite Martian" (May 16, 1965), written by Phyliss and Robert White and directed by James V. Kern. Tim is mistaken for a Martian when a family sees him wearing Martin's space-suit.

Marlo Thomas was in "Miss Jekyll and Hyde" (May 17, 1964) with Tom Skerritt. Tim falls in love and plans to marry but his betrothed (Thomas) learns of Martin's identity and plans to blow his cover, so the Martian sees that Tim's romance is scuttled.

Bernie (*Get Smart*) Kopell appeared in "Poor Little Rich Cat" (January 12, 1964), written and directed by James Komack, in which Martin, dumbfounded that a cat has inherited over a half million dollars, contacts the feline's attorney about turning the money over to a good cause.

Kopell returns in "El Señor From Mars" (June 13,

[even] some talk of trying to do a movie. If [Fries] had done a first-run syndicated show he couldn't have gotten Bixby. If they had done a movie, [Bixby] had voiced an interest in doing [that]."

In retrospect, Walston admits that *My Favorite Martian* was as difficult to write as it was, at times, to perform. Once in a script Komack had a character say, "I don't believe in little green men from Mars anymore than I believe in Santa Claus." Within days, according to Walston, Komack was called on the carpet, following an executive board meeting, to be told, rather tersely, "It [is] CBS's official position that there is a Santa Claus and what's more, one of the [our] executives confessed that he believed in Santa until the age of ten."

Summing up, Walston says, "You know, the most rewarding letter I ever got was from a third-grade girl who said that she could now sleep at night because she knew that, instead of horrible monsters, nice people came from the vast, scary reaches of space.

"And she was right you know. [On Mars] the trees are pink and when the boats go up through our canals there, why the spray makes enormous rainbows."

How extraordinary! But it would be too Pollyannaish to suggest that, yes Virginia, there really is an Uncle Martin, for when asked today if he would do it all over, given the chance, Walston replies honestly.

"No, no," he insists simply, "I wouldn't do it again."

Bill Bixby, now one of the most requested sitcom directors (*photo courtesy Bill Bixby*)

1965), written by Ben Gersham and Bill Freedman and directed by Oscar Rudolph. It finds Martin's antennae jammed, forcing him to postpone his trip to South America.

There was even a two-parter called "Go West, Young Martian" (September 12 and 19, 1965) in which Detective Brennen (Alan Hewitt) activates Martin's time machine. Inadvertently Tim and Martin are sent back to 1849 St. Louis, where they get into trouble with riverboat thieves. This episode featured Hal Baylor, Ken Mayer and Jeff DeBenning.

"Charles Fries took an option on *Martian* a few years ago," Walston observes. "The producer [Chertok] came up with a script called 'My Favorite Martians.' It didn't get off the ground and Fries's option ran out. They were trying to interest Lorimar and got nowhere. There was

Gavin MacLeod, who had a number of *My Favorite Martian* guest shots (*photo courtesy Gavin MacLeod*)

Elizabeth Montgomery in a glamour shot during the heyday of *Bewitched*

FIVE

BEWITCHED

(September 17, 1964–July 1, 1972)

One of the most adored, imaginative situation comedies from the sixties more often than not left its viewers bewitched, bothered, and bewildered as a lovely sorceress named Samantha navigated her way through marriage to an ordinary and bemused mortal.

Bewitched, headed by Elizabeth Montgomery, chronicled the exploits of Mrs. Darrin Stevens, a Donna Reed-like holdover and sweet-tempered all-American wife and mother with strange, nose-twitching powers, who never seemed able to liberate herself from her demanding mortal husband, the breadwinner who was played by Dick York for five seasons and later by Dick Sargent.

"The show made the audience care more about the characters than about the magic," says Herbie J. Pilato, author of the comprehensive *Bewitched* book. "Just like *Star Trek* was not about space people but about people

who happened to be in space, *Bewitched* is not about a witch but about a woman who happens to be a witch. They always respected their audience [as] there was always a sense of logic even within the illogic."

Darrin worked for an ad agency, headed by exasperated Larry Tate, played by David White.

"I loved David White," says Dick Sargent today. "His whole last few years were sad. His son was killed in a plane crash—the one that was blown up in Scotland [in 1989]. The mother died in childbirth by the doctor's mistake. She hemorrhaged to death, [and] then twenty-nine years later the kid was killed and I don't think David ever got over it—he was in pain all the time—a lovely man, God, he was a sweetheart."

The wonderful *Bewitched* cast included Agnes Moorehead as Endora, the perfect witch of a mother-in-law to

64

Elizabeth Montgomery bewitched by the show's comic book

Darrin; the incomparable Paul Lynde as practical-joking Uncle Arthur, the impish warlock with a sense of humor; Alice Ghostley as Esmerelda, the sweetly witchy but incompetent housekeeper/baby-sitter; Shakespearean veteran Maurice Evans as Maurice, the refined warlock who was Samantha's father and Endora's nemesis; daffy Alice Pearce (and then Sandra Gould) as snoopy Gladys Kravitz, the Stevens's nosy neighbor; George Tobias as Abner, Gladys's long-suffering husband; Erin and Diane Murphy alternating as Tabitha, daughter and witch-in-training; Mabel Albertson and Robert F. Simon as Mr. and Mrs. Stevens, Darrin's confused parents; and fluttery Marion Lorne as Samantha's Aunt Clara, a befuddled witch who had trouble getting her witchcraft right.

"Paul [Lynde] was fun but could be difficult at times," recalls Sargent of the late comedian, "But he was hysterical. God, he was funny. I remember one day we were sitting around—we were talking about the fact that Agnes was building her mother a farmhouse and Paul reared up out of his chair and said 'Her mother? Well, she'd better hurry!' "

Lynde, long a regular acerbic cutup on *Hollywood Squares,* costarred with Alice Ghostley on Broadway in *New Faces of 1952.* Their styles and facial expressions were so similar that it was often said that one was doing the other in drag.

"Alice—I love," continues Sargent. "She and I are still friends." She played Bernice, the Sugarbakers' daffy friend, on *Designing Women* in a recurring guest role.

"[Maurice] was a doll," reminisces Sargent. "I loved Maurice. He was a sweet man and it was just a thrill to work with him. As a famous Shakespearean actor, I kept looking up to him. He was a very, very nice man. We kept up for a little while and I kind of lost track of him. George Tobias—I never really got to know. I don't know why. He was kind of unreachable."

"Agnes Moorehead was the most professional actress in the world. But she didn't have that many friends—I felt that was a sad commentary on her life. She was a tough old bird. I made it a point to make her like me and she did."

Talent and dedication led Moorehead to stardom in radio, motion pictures, stage, and television. A five-time Oscar nominee, Moorehead then earned five Emmy nominations for *Bewitched.* She was born in Clinton, Massachusetts, the daughter of Presbyterian minister John R. Moorehead and his wife.

As a child, the one-day actress moved with her family to St. Louis, where she was educated. At ten she began to perform in summer theater and later was with the St. Louis Municipal Opera Company for four years. Graduating from Muskingham College in Ohio, Moorehead later earned a master's degree in English and public speaking at the University of Wisconsin. Then came her tenure at the American Academy of Dramatic Arts in New York. As one of radio's most active performers, she appeared on thousands of broadcasts, including *March of Time, Cavalcade of America,* and *Mayor of the Town.* She was a charter member of Orson Welles's famous Mercury Theatre Players and was cast as his mother in *Citizen Kane* and as Fanny Minafer in his *Magnificent Ambersons,* a role which earned her the New York Critics Award for Best Actress and her first Academy Award nomination. Late in the forties, she gained radio immortality for her tour-de-force performance in *Sorry, Wrong Number.*

With Charles Boyer, Sir Cedric Hardwicke, and Charles Laughton, Moorehead also appeared in a concert recital of George Bernard Shaw's *Don Juan in Hell* on Broadway and in Europe.

Her philanthropic efforts led her to a hospital where she came upon twins—a boy and a girl. The boy was cross-eyed and malnourished, and Moorehead took him back to California, but in the course of rearing him became a strict disciplinarian. When the boy came of age, he rebelled. Once he ran away, only to eventually return. Finally Moorehead found a gun under his bed and asked him to leave for good. He did and they were never reconciled.

While doing *Gigi* in New York after the run of *Bewitched,* Moorehead became ill. She'd already survived hip surgery in California. According to pal Debbie Reynolds in *Debbie: My Life,* Moorehead eventually ended up at the Mayo Clinic, where she was diagnosed with cancer and given chemotherapy treatments, to no avail. She was buried next to her father on a farm in Ohio. Her ninety-four-year-old mother came to Los Angeles for the reading of the will, only to discover that her actress daughter's lawyer was the beneficiary. All she got was a portrait of her daughter and all of her furniture. Liz Montgomery got a brooch. Mrs. Moorehead chose not to contest the will.

"Agnes had this wonderful dressing room off stage and it had these gold-gilded tables and she had these marvelous gowns," says Kasey Rogers, who portrayed Darrin's boss's wife, Louise Tate, on *Bewitched,* "and [she] would say, 'I love the illusion'—offstage she was the same as she was on. Just a very dramatic and interesting woman, and very talented. A serious actress."

"Kasey Rogers was very sweet—I haven't seen her in a long time—but she's a very nice lady," Sargent notes. "There were no personality conflicts ever on the show."

Kasey Rogers came to *Betwiched* right from 252 episodes of *Peyton Place* "and I tell you, the first couple of episodes I was like stiff as a board and finally Bill Asher [producer of *Bewitched*] said, 'Kasey, loosen up a bit,' and anyway it sunk in [that] this was comedy and as soon as my head clicked into the right place it was fine.

Elizabeth Montgomery and Dick York as Samantha and Darrin Stevens

Comedy is harder to play. I have to analyze it so much more thoroughly because it's too easy to just read through a script and miss the jokes and miss the laughs. A few things stand out but it's the overall feeling that you don't forget—you don't forget that. It's so strange because it's been a long time and I really don't remember the *Bewitched* episodes unless I see one on television, and then I go, 'Oh, yeah, I remember that now,' but it's difficult. It was a different feeling than *Peyton Place*."

Rogers won't name her favorite Darrin—York or Sargent—but her favorite episode of *Bewitched* was the one in which "Darrin was turned into this painter and he was doing these marvelous portraits and Louise wanted one and he started this lovely portrait [of her] and Endora put a spell on him and it came out with crossed eyes, a huge nose. I have both of those paintings—I did ask for those—I want to frame them back to back and put the nice one in front of the bar and we'll have a nice party and everybody'll have a couple of glasses of wine and then I'll switch it around."

"During the run of *Bewitched* I started racing motorcycles," recalls Rogers, who for awhile ran an actors' studio called Hollywood Underground Network. "I started riding in 1971 and *Bewitched* was not over for another year . . . then after the series stopped I started the women's nationals and had competitors from all over the United States and I raced for seven years—I loved it. I raced with Steve McQueen. His children and mine were racing minicycles and that's how I got into motorcycling.

"I got a divorce [after the series ended] and my kids have gotten married, but I guess the most exciting thing was opening my studio. I had a blast."

Since closing her studio Rogers has written a script for a *Bewitched* reunion with former student Mark Wood. Dick Sargent, Alice Ghostley, and Sandra Gould have committed to the project, and Wood wants to be cast as the Stevens's grown-up son Adam, in hopes that the reunion would evolve into a new series.

Kasey Rogers fondly remembers Marion Lorne, with whom (as Laura Elliot) she acted in Hitchcock's *Strang-*

Elizabeth with Agnes Moorehead, Erin Murphy, and Dick York (Darrin #1)

Elizabeth with Maurice Evans, Agnes Moorehead, Erin Murphy, and Dick Sargent (Darrin #2)

ers on a Train.

"I wished that I had worked with Marion Lorne," confesses Sargent. "I just loved her."

And Rogers concurs: "Marion was brought over here in the very beginning of her career—as we know her—by Alfred Hitchcock for *Strangers* her very first picture over here. I played a real bitch [in it] and I loved it and she was the dithery little person and just wonderful, and then to be with her on *Bewitched* was wonderful and she was even more dithery at that point. Sometimes she would dither around while she was trying to remember the dialogue and [she] was just adorable. We did work together a lot because she would pop in [though] not in my presence because Louise Tate [my character] never knew what was going on."

Lorne went on to win an Emmy for *Bewitched* during the 1967–68 season, as Alice Pearce had done during 1965–66.

Aside from Lorne, who first made a TV splash as Mrs. Gurney, the flustered English teacher in *Mr. Peepers,* and then was a hit on *The Garry Moore Show,* and the aforementioned Alice Pearce/Sandra Gould as busybody Gladys Kravitz, other *Bewitched* characters were Bernie Kopell as the apothecary, Reta Shaw as Aunt Agatha, Hal England as Waldo the Warlock, Greg and David Lawrence as Samantha and Darrin's son, Adam, and veteran actress Estelle Winwood as Aunt Enchantra.

"Sandra [Gould] and I have done plays together," says Kasey Rogers. "We'd known each other for years before we were on *Bewitched.* We normally did not work on the same date or the same set—maybe once or twice I worked with Maurice Evans because when they were there it was another story line and when Larry and Louise [Tate] were there, something else was happening so sometimes I didn't have the opportunity to work with some of these wonderful people."

"Sandy [Gould] is marvelous—she's full of energy," adds Sargent. "She's had a sad life [though]. Two of her husbands have died."

But the real star of *Bewitched* was, of course, Elizabeth Montgomery, who, coincidentally, was also married to the boss, William Asher. Even today Rogers praises the talent and skill of the actress who was equally at home playing comedy and drama, especially her knack for pulling off the role of Serena, Samantha's saucy cousin. Blonde Montgomery played her in a brunette wig.

"Samantha was closer to the real Elizabeth. To create a whole new way of speaking, an attitude, physical gestures, the voice—it was not just a wig and makeup," insists Rogers. "She created a different character and had she not done it so well, people would have just said, 'That's Elizabeth,' but many people did not realize it was her."

"Liz is a damned good actress," contributes Sargent,

"and [doing Serena] was such fun for her because she could get out of the Samantha character and do whatever she felt like. She loved that—she loved doing it. When you're doing the same character all the time it can get to be a bore."

"One day they were doing a special effects involving a big poof of fire and smoke," Rogers recalls, "and Elizabeth was alone on camera and the fire started and there were draperies—those were old, brittle sound stages— and the whole thing started burning and she stood her ground and stood there and stayed in character and we're all watching the fire get bigger and finally they said 'cut' and she walked out and they put out the fire, but it was way above and beyond the call of duty."

Aside from the talent of Montgomery, Rogers credits the ultimate success of the show with fine writing and fine directing.

"I'll tell you this, these past few years, interest in *Bewitched* has really surfaced. For a number of years, no one mentioned *Bewitched,* and then I had two young guys write me from Australia and eventually come over here to meet with me and bring me a big bouquet of roses and [take] me to tea. There are a couple of guys who have every episode of *Bewitched* on tape. *Bewitched* was such a fun series. I told [author] Herbie Pilato—'You are a *Bewitched* trekkie' [and] they're just all over the place— it's just amazing."

Yet despite all the accolades, today Montgomery says that she has reached other plateaus in the type of work that she does, but that's not in anyway a putdown of *Bewitched*—just that what she does today is simply what she does best now. (Interestingly, after *Bewitched* she has not done another comedy on TV to date—only dramatic telefilms.)

"I know there have been lots of offers for a reunion movie," explains Sargent, "but Liz doesn't want to be known as just the girl who did *Bewitched.* She wants to be known as an actress so she's put it behind her and that's it. [Liz and I] are very good friends but she doesn't care about reviving *Bewitched.*"

From the very beginning Elizabeth was out to prove herself. Her father, actor Robert Montgomery, never encouraged her to follow in his footsteps. Born in Hollywood on April 15, 1933, young Liz attended the Westlake School for Girls, and ultimately became a society debutante. Then the family moved to New York where her father had become a major figure in live television. Her education was completed at the Spence School for Girls in the East.

She then spent two years at the American Academy of Dramatic Arts. She made her television debut on December 3, 1951, on *Robert Montgomery Presents* in an episode called "Top Secret." Ironically, he didn't learn that she had been cast until after rehearsals started. She

Dick York as Darrin Stevens

soon became part of the anthology show's stock company and proved she was more than just the boss's daughter. Her stage debut followed in 1953 in *Late Love* with Arlene Francis, which won her a Theater World Award. Ironically she never again played on Broadway.

She married New York TV casting director Fred Cammann in the spring of 1955. They were divorced by August. This same year marked her first film role—*The Court-Martial of Billy Mitchell.* She would star in only two other movies.

After moving back to Hollywood, she married actor Gig Young, a union which lasted for six years. During this time she made two hundred TV appearances and was nominated for an Emmy for "The Rusty Heller Story" episode of *The Untouchables.*

Though it was not love at first sight when she first encountered William Asher on the set of her second movie, *Johnny Cool* (they were both wed to other people at the time), by October of that year each had divorced their respective spouses and had gotten married in Mexico.

From the Montgomery–Asher union came *Bewitched.* The pilot, loosely based on *Bell, Book and Candle,* was shown in November of 1963.

And as Montgomery pointed out, "When people normally think of witches they imagine either funny old crones with long noses or someone kind of dark sultry. The fact that I don't look exotic and witchlike is an enormous boost for the show's humor."

Montgomery, incidentally, was not even the first candidate for Samantha—Broadway's Tammy Grimes

Agnes Moorehead, who played Samantha's meddling witch of a mother, Endora (*photo courtesy Ann Teipen*)

was—but as fate would have it, Grimes had returned to New York by the time the final draft of the first script was written by Sol Saks (who never did another *Bewitched* script).

And Montgomery and Asher were getting set to do their own series for Screen Gems called *The Fun Couple,* based on the novel and short-lived play of the same name. Oddly enough while she was married to Gig Young, Screen Gems vice president in charge of West Coast production William Dozier had been hot after the couple to star in their own TV series.

But as Asher returned from his stint in New York with *The Patty Duke Show* to direct another project, the final "no" came from Grimes in New York. So Dozier contacted Elizabeth and Asher about *Bewitched* and then called Harry Ackerman, husband of television star Elinor (*Father Knows Best*) Donahue and the eventual executive producer of *Bewitched.*

"He was a lovely man," says Sargent of the late Ackerman. "One of the few real gentlemen—an old-time producer. He was good for his word."

As for Asher, he had arrived in Hollywood from his native Manhattan penniless and jobless prior to World War II and had obtained a mailroom job at Universal. This was interrupted by his service in the army, four years as a photographer in the Signal Corps in Astoria, New York.

He also served as photographer at Cushing General Hospital. Afterward, Asher returned to Universal first as an assistant film editor, then assistant cameraman. From behind the camera, Asher wrote a screenplay, *Leather Gloves,* with actor Richard Quine. Together they produced and directed it for Columbia Pictures in 1948.

Choosing the relatively young field of television as his medium, Asher directed shows such as *Racket Squad* (for which he also wrote), *Big Town, Our Miss Brooks, I Love Lucy,* and *The Danny Thomas Show.* He ultimately won two Emmys: for *I Love Lucy* and *Bewitched.*

"Bill always felt that he had to explain the character to

Kasey Rogers and David White as Louise and Larry Tate (*photo courtesy Kasey Rogers*)

Dick Sargent as the later Darrin Stevens (*photo courtesy Dick Sargent*)

me [in depth] like it was Proust or something," recalls Sargent today, "so he'd put his arm around me and walk me around the set while the crew was waiting for me and it was uncomfortable, but generally he loved my work and we laughed so much on the set—it was just a joy. I looked forward to work every day."

"Bill Asher [is] dynamite," exclaims Kasey Rogers. "I love Bill. He's one of the most talented people I can imagine. He knew comedy—he turned out these wonderful things."

Through it all Asher saw through the witchery: "Samantha . . . represents the true values in life. Materialism . . . means nothing to her. She can have anything she wants . . . yet she'd rather scrub floors . . . for the man she loves. It's emotional satisfaction she craves."

Elizabeth was pregnant when *Bewitched* sold so the first five episodes were shot around her; nonetheless, she had to report back to work three weeks after giving birth, filming twelve episodes in a hectic, fourteen-hour day frenzy. Two days after giving birth, she was propped up in bed learning lines.

She would later tell *TV Guide:* "The pressure has been just awful. It's something that I will never go through again. It gets to a point where I'm ready to scream. I never seem to be able to catch up. I look around and think it's kind of ridiculous for grown-up people to be playing these games."

But the reviewers were particularly pleased, labeling the show "beguiling" and "devilishly fun," and the series went on to run for 254 episodes. That first year it was the runaway surprise hit of the season.

Finally hitting its peak in 1965, the show continued to remain in the top ten through 1967. *Bewitched* was number two during the 1964–65 season, number seven in 1965–66, and number eight 1966–67. After 1970 the series dropped out of the top twenty when Dick York left due to back problems and an addiction to painkillers.

York, who was Darrin in the first 170 episodes, was making $120,000 per year during his time on *Bewitched*. He lived with his wife Joan and their five children in a home in the Hollywood Hills. But emphysema caught up with him. He ended up recording inspirational tapes to

Kasey Rogers with Richard Nixon (*photo courtesy Kasey Rogers*)

raise money for the homeless, aided by celebrities such as Jack Lemmon and the late Tony Perkins.

"The two witches are by far more spectacular than I am," York said in a *TV Guide* interview during the show's original run. "I'm just a human being and I'm identified by the critics as being just exactly like themselves. I, too, am watching the witch from the sidelines. I guess it's a lot more exciting to identify with someone superhuman than with someone normal. Maybe it's me. I don't think so, but the only way to tell if it's me or not is to kill me off in one show, give the witch another husband, and see if I'm missed."

Montgomery came to his defense, "I don't believe anyone underestimates Dick as an actor because I believe anyone who watches him work appreciates his talent."

Producer Danny Arnold also felt that "Dick is underrated and underestimated as an actor."

"I thought Dick York was wonderful," admits Rogers today. "He was quite a wonderful person."

York's background included a stint in radio serials such as *Jack Armstrong, the All-American Boy* (he played Billy Fairfield, Jack's best friend) and *Michael Shayne*. Soon Elia Kazan had discovered him and he was appearing in *Tea and Sympathy* on Broadway by 1953. Though he was nominated by the Drama Critics for best supporting actor, he did not win.

Other peaks in his career included a subsequent Broadway production, *Bus Stop,* the films *My Sister Eileen* and *Inherit the Wind,* and the TV series *Going My Way.*

In 1988, at the age of sixty, he said in a taped interview: "Look at me. I have a hose up my nose and haven't been out of the house for a year. The fact that I'm dying doesn't stop me from feeling very much alive."

Dick Sargent, who portrayed Darrin in episodes 171–254, recalls, "I was supposed to do *Bewitched* originally and I had an interview for it, but by the time they got back to me I had signed to a series called *Broadside*.

"Liz had always wanted me. We got along better than [she and York] and we did a lot more kissy-kissy stuff than they did. Every time I would try to do something different, they would shoot me down. I was watching some shows [recently] and I still think I was right—I feel I was much too strong, much too mad. It really looked like I was about to punch her and I still think that was wrong [but] as they kept explaining to me—if Darrin wasn't [there] then she'd be free to do her magic all the time."

Sargent is a veteran of more than three hundred TV appearances and numerous theatrical productions and films. Like Montgomery, he was born (April 19, 1930) into a show business family. His mother, Ruth McNaughton, who was the daughter of John McNaughton (the founder of the famous Los Angeles Union Stockyards), had, as Ruth Powell, important roles in such screen classics as *Four Horsemen of the Apocalypse* with Valentino and *Hearts and Trumps* with Nazimova.

"My mother was in a couple of silent pictures and my father was a location manager for Douglas Fairbanks Sr. and Erich Von Stroheim," recalls Sargent, "so they had a lot of theatrical friends. In those days it was a sin to be an actress, so [my mother] didn't stay in the business."

Sargent's father was Colonel Elmer Cox, a war hero, land developer, world traveler, boxing promoter, and investor, manager of San Francisco's plush Palace Hotel and manager of L.A.'s infamous gambling casino, the Colony Club.

"The only thing my father never did was [act]—he did everything else I can think of so that's probably the reason that I went into [the business]. My father died when I was eleven." Sargent would later confide to *People* magazine in November 1991: "I kept reaching out for him, but he always kept me at arm's length. I wanted him to love me and I'm quite sure he didn't. His funeral was like a B movie—shady guys wearing dark glasses . . . with big, busty blondes at their sides."

Sargent hails from Carmel, California, and his parents had already retired from show business at the time of his arrival. "I attended San Raphael Military Academy for almost two years and then I got tuberculosis and had to be taken out and went to Menlo School after that."

Though he survived a couple of suicide attempts while studying at Stanford University, Sargent starred in twenty-five plays with the Stanford Studio Players Theatre. Upon his graduation, he was in Joan Davis's TV sitcom, *I Married Joan,* and had a bit part in MGM's *Prisoner of War,* with Ronald Reagan. It was at this point that he changed his name from Cox to Sargent.

From digging ditches and selling in a department store, Sargent persevered, traveling to the Mexican city of San Miguel Allende to enter the import-export business. But the business folded and he returned to Hollywood and assorted TV roles.

His first major motion picture role for Fox was heralded by Louella Parsons: "The talk of the town is a young actor named Dick Sargent, a heretofore unknown, in Pat Boone's picture *Bernardine*. He's going far!" And Sargent did cop a Laurel Award from the nation's film exhibitors as one of the ten most promising newcomers of the year.

"I tried [to live up to Parsons's prophecy]," says Sargent, "but quite often I didn't work because I wasn't a leading man and I wasn't really a character actor so it was kind of hard to fit me in anywhere. I really had the lead in *Bernardine* but you couldn't tell from the billing. They'd tested [hundreds of] guys on film for the part so it was quite a coup to get it.

"I thought it would be the start of a brilliant career, but

Alice Ghostley as inept witch and housekeeper Esmerelda

my agent got me minimum, which was two hundred dollars per week in those days, and no billing clause—it should have been 'introducing Dick Sargent' but we didn't get that, so half the kids thought that Dean Jagger was me, but he was one of the stars so he got a lot of my fan mail, I understand.

"But it was heartbreaking because I did get all those notices and there was talk about an Academy Award nomination and everything, but it just didn't happen, so I left there after doing one more picture."

For one season prior to *Bewitched,* Sargent starred in the series *One Happy Family,* and then he became a Universal contract player with roles in *Operation Petticoat, The Great Imposter, That Touch of Mink, For Love or Money,* and *Captain Newman, M.D.*

"A big picture is like a vacation," he says today, reflecting back on his career. "You have the luxury and the time to do it and television is fast and 'get it done.' There are things about both of them and things about the theater I like too."

In October 1991, Sargent shocked the public by announcing his homosexuality to the press.

"[My lover] and I used to play tennis with Liz [Montgomery] and her husband and they would come over for Christmas and we'd go over to their house," Sargent later told Sally Jessy Raphael. "We've remained friends, Liz and myself. In fact we're even closer now. It was a strain on a sponsor level. I don't think [the cast] cared."

"His homosexuality was never an issue," Montgomery was quoted as saying in *People* magazine in November 1991. "That's just the way it was. He's a dear friend."

Sargent was quoted in the *National Enquirer* (October

Samantha (Elizabeth Montgomery) and her mother Endora (Agnes Moorehead) attempt to decipher what dotty Aunt Clara (Marion Lorne) is saying (*photo courtesy Fred Causey*)

1991): "I said I'd been married and divorced. I learned to lie because [coming out] was not an acceptable thing—[at least] not then." At one point Sargent even engaged in a make-believe romance with Connie Francis for the benefit of the fan magazines: "We looked passionately at each other but that was the only time I ever saw her."

"I never really hid it," says Sargent today, hesitating, "I did I guess years ago—I was afraid of the public finding out. The knowledge I was gay could have destroyed my career [but] I'm a gay activist now. I'm out and I'm very proud of it—I think it's time for [gay] role models to step out. I want people to know that we're just people and that we're everywhere. When I first came out in Hollywood we had the rumor that Rock Hudson was gay. If I went to an opening I'd have to take a lady with me. Now I'm not sure who I'm going to take.

"Now, I don't know if I'll ever work again having come out publicly. On a sponsor level, they don't want a known homosexual portraying a loving father or whatever. I'll probably never be allowed to play a father symbol again. I'm afraid for my career. I'm going to probably lose a lot of work but I like myself, probably more than I have most of my life.

"I'm hoping it'll help some people realize that they are not the only ones—that somebody's been accepted in [audience's] living rooms for years who was gay and they didn't know it. There are gay men and lesbian women portraying every type of part right now—they're just not out [of the closet]."

Sargent though will always be remembered as Darrin Stevens. And even he has his own, special episodes: "I loved the one where they made me an old man. It was hard work but it was fun to do. The makeup took two hours every morning. I loved the one, too, with Imogene Coca where she played the tooth fairy. It was a thrill to work with her. *Bewitched* was wish fulfillment."

But at this point all that *Bewitched* remains is a happy memory for Sargent, as financial remuneration stopped long ago: "I'm not rolling in money. I don't get a dime from (*Bewitched*). In those old contracts we got about ten residuals and that was paid off eighteen years ago. My last check was [for] $13.75. I'm okay financially but I do need to work."

And as for Montgomery, as Samantha she was nominated for Emmys five times and always lost. The show ended and so did her marriage, though she was quoted at the time as saying that everything ended openly, honestly, and amicably. Her deal with Screen Gems had snared her a nice stipend plus 20 percent of the *Bewitched* profits. The syndication rights were later sold for $9 million assuring her of at least $1 million.

After the divorce Asher wed Joyce Bulifant (the ex-Mrs. James MacArthur) and Montgomery has since taken up with Robert Foxworth whom she met while filming *Mrs. Sundance* in 1974, one of her many hit TV movies that have also included *A Case of Rape, The Legend of Lizzie Borden, The Awakening Land,* and *Second Sight.*

Today she accepts serious roles, choosing only projects that interest her, and though she shuns publicity, she can often be seen dining quietly in a corner of Le Dome in Los Angeles.

Perhaps Jack O'Brian of the *New York Journal-American* best summed up Montgomery's allure many years ago: "[She] is an uniquely equipped amulet for this feathery hocus-pocus. She has beauty, youth, and splendid subtlety in her reactions, able to register many a mood . . . she manages with the merest moves, eyelash batting and eyefuls of dancing glints in her admirably suppressed 'takes' and just-barely grimaces and amused gloatings."

From Esmeralda's attempting to concoct a Caesar salad and conjuring up Julius himself to the endearing and wacky Aunt Clara with her collection of door knobs, *Bewitched,* which lasted for eight seasons, is a class act that has yet to be matched.

"The shows that have tried to copy *Bewitched* have failed to realize that they need a character like Darrin," says Sargent in conclusion. "The character made the show work with the threat to her using her powers."

Some (such as CBS's short-lived *Tucker's Witch* with Catherine Hicks and ABC's short-lived *Free Spirit* with Corinne Bohrer) have tried and failed. It will take some feat of magic to top the talent and beauty of the fetching Elizabeth Montgomery.

George Tobias, who played Samantha and Darrin's henpecked neighbor, Abner Kravitz (*photo courtesy Fred Causey*)

Lurch joins Morticia and Gomez for an outdoor candid
© *copyright Orion Television Entertainment* (*photo courtesy Orion Television Entertainment*)

SIX

THE ADDAMS FAMILY

(September 18, 1964—September 2, 1966)

There's no place like home! And, that's not Kansas but the musty mansion at 000 Cemetery Lane which, with the 1991 release of Paramount's *Addams Family* motion picture, once again became home to cartoonist Charles Addams's motley clan.

But, other than in *The New Yorker*'s long time series of cartoons, the public's first glimpse of Charles Addams's macabre characters was of a lighter, campier Addams family of the sixties television series. This earlier live-action version, produced by Nat Perrin and starring the late Carolyn Jones as Morticia and John Astin as Gomez, premiered on ABC September 18, 1964—less than a week before the arrival of a rival comic monster family, *The Munsters*, on CBS. *The Addams Family* would finish twenty-third in the ratings at the end of its first season, right behind its aforementioned competition.

Appearing on the tube in a tight, black, fishtail gown, Carolyn Jones made the biggest fashion statement middle America had seen since Marilyn Monroe, in a clinging gown, serenaded JFK at Madison Square Garden on May 19, 1962.

And in the 1991 film version Anjelica Huston, as the new Morticia, submitted to two hours for makeup each morning before donning a telltale gown reminiscent of the one worn by Jones, which was supposed to have been Morticia's wedding dress.

"We lashed Anjelica into a metal corset that created this hips and waste thing," director Barry Sonnenfeld told *Entertainment Weekly* in November 1991. "Morticia has a shape only a cartoonist can draw."

"Morticia was to be beautiful and aristocratic," Addams wrote in his characterizations for the series, "the real head of the family and the critical and moving force behind it. Incisive and subtle, she is given to low-keyed rhapsodies about her garden of deadly nightshade, henbane, and dwarf's hair. She indulges the mischievous activities of the children but feels that Uncle Fester must be held in check."

Composer Vic Mizzy, whose original finger-snapping theme song was also heard in the feature film, says, "I wrote for Carolyn and I told her, 'When you walk, cause you're wearing a long dress, take little short steps so there might be the impression that you might be on roller skates, and I'll write a melody—your theme—to counter what you're doing. And, even when you're standing still you'll have this mysterious charm about you.' [She was] a darling woman, [and she] used to call me 'Vic Misery.' Then I told John Astin, [who was] a very good friend of mine, 'When you walk, try to imitate Groucho Marx.' "

By the time Astin snared the role of Gomez in the original series, he had gone from living in a fifth floor walk-up in New York City to owning his own home in exclusive Westwood, where he lived with his first wife Suzy. In 1973 he and actress Patty Duke were married and had what turned out to be a rocky union which lasted until 1985. He married business executive Verlie Sandobal four years later.

He was born in 1930 the son of Dr. Allen V. Astin, who was on staff at the National Bureau of Standards in Washington, D.C. A bent for mathematics earned young John a tuition grant to Washington and Jefferson College, where he soon learned that he had a penchant for drama, as well as for numbers.

Two years later he drifted on to Johns Hopkins University, paying his way by working as a math tutor. After receiving his degree in 1952, he attended the University of Minnesota to pursue graduate studies in drama, participating in over forty productions at the school.

In New York his first job was Off-Broadway, at $15 per week in *The Three-Penny Opera*. But soon he was making about five times that and dating Suzanne Hahn, a redhead from Louisiana. He made his Broadway debut in *Major Barbara*. Other stage credits include *The Cave Dwellers, Ulysses in Nighttown, Tall Story* (and, in 1993, a version of *H.M.S. Pinafore*). He and Hahn were married in 1956.

To pave their way into a nicer neighborhood, Astin was soon doing voiceovers and character voices. Tony Randall encouraged the struggling actor to go to Hollywood, and during the 1962–63 season he starred as Harry Dickens in *I'm Dickens . . . He's Fenster* with Marty Ingels. Though not a big success, the series landed Astin the role of Gomez on *The Addams Family,* after auditioning for the role of Lurch.

"I had done a movie for Filmways," remembers Astin, "and they had gotten some good preview cards on my performance in the movie. It was a film called *The Wheeler Dealers* [1963], with James Garner and Lee Remick [and Jim Backus and Louis Nye]. They had a few projects they wanted to talk to me about—a couple of movies and a television series. The TV series was an attempt to put the cartoons of Charles Addams on the air and I went into this meeting and was told at the beginning that they were going to build the show around the butler whom I would play and I went away thinking that this was not going to work and I was trying to figure out what kind of makeup and lifts I was going to use to play the butler, and I got a call from the show's creator and executive producer David Levy and over a couple of martinis he told me about his idea for the show.

"I remember him saying, 'This is really *Father Knows Best* and I want you to play the father,' and he showed me a brief character description that had been written by Charles Addams and it didn't have much detail and at that point I began to work on an approach to putting a static cartoon character into a characterization." (Astin was also the voice of Gomez once again in the new animated *Addams Family* series that began in September 1992.)

Astin went on to star with Phyllis Diller during the 1967 season of *The Pruitts of Southampton* and play the commander on *Operation Petticoat* (1977–78), establishing himself not only as a comic actor but also as a top sitcom director.

Astin's leading lady was Carolyn Jones as the lovely Morticia Frump Addams. She had gotten an Oscar nomination for *The Bachelor Party* in 1957 and had costarred with Sinatra in *The Tender Trap* and *A Hole in the Head*, with Kirk Douglas in *Last Train From Gun Hill*, with Elvis in *King Creole* and with Dean Martin in *Career*, among many screen titles that began with *The Turning Point* (1952).

Carolyn Jones was born April 28, 1929 in Amarillo, Texas, the daughter of a branch manager for Allis-Chalmers, the farm machinery company.

"I decided I wanted to be a movie star," recalled Jones in a *TV Guide* article some years before her death, explaining how at the age of eighteen with her nose recently fixed and her teeth newly capped, she had taken off for California and showed up at the Pasadena Playhouse. "I'm a gregarious soul. I like people. I like action. I'm not the girl next door, never was and never will be."

And first husband, Aaron Spelling, an actor at the time, must have known that, indeed, she was not the girl next door when he met her at the Player's Ring Theater in West Hollywood.

"We made a pact," she told *TV Guide*, "We would both make it. I'd help him. He'd help me. We were so well-adjusted in our business life that our marriage—after ten years—went kaput."

(*Facing page*) America's first family—at least at 000 Cemetery Lane: (*clockwise from left*) Jackie Coogan, John Astin, Blossom Rock, Ted Cassidy, Ken Weatherwax, Carolyn Jones, and Lisa Loring © *copyright Orion Television Entertainment* (*photo courtesy Orion Television Entertainment*)

Gomez and Morticia Addams along with hirsute Cousin It © *copyright Orion Television Entertainment* (*photo courtesy Orion Television Entertainment*)

neither Carolyn nor I dated or went out together—we were both with other people. And I think we retained an attraction for one another that we were able to play in the show and I remember years after the show had been off the air I said [to her], 'I miss nibbling your arm.'

"We knew if the script was a little off or something like that. Any tough moment we could just look at one another. The genuine sexual interplay that we had eye to eye was something that would get us in and out of any scene we wanted to play."

On *The Addams Family* set, it was not uncommon for Jones and Jackie Coogan to exchange tongue-in-cheek greetings: "Good morning, you look awful," baited Coogan. "Thank you," quipped Jones.

"She [was] not the kind of star," recalled Coogan years later, "who spends as much time being made up to come to the studio as she spends being made up when she gets [there]. But you [knew] she was a star all the same."

Mizzy recalls Coogan: "I told Jackie Coogan—I'll write something contemporary [for you] because it goes with your character. Then I wrote a theme for Lurch [too] because he always walked slow and lumbering."

Carolyn Jones as Morticia and John Astin as Gomez. © *copyright Orion Television Entertainment* (*photos courtesy Orion Television Entertainment*)

She encouraged Spelling to move away from acting until ultimately he was involved on the production side with Dick Powell, *The Zane Grey Theatre,* and Four Star. It was on Spelling's advice that she play the beatnik in the film of Paddy Chayefsky's *The Bachelor Party* and not the wife. And then the money started to come in. And a year later she and Spelling were divorced.

But Jones always maintained that she still loved Spelling, even crediting him with talking her into doing *The Addams Family.* But she didn't need any heavy arm-twisting at the time. "When I heard it was Charles Addams," she told *TV Guide,* "I flipped. He appeals to my snob instinct. He draws marvelous macabre and wicked cartoons for *The New Yorker,* a snob magazine. . . . He has never appeared on television or in a movie. He does what he wants to do. I like that."

And it was a mutual admiration, for Addams had casting approval for the series and wrote character profiles for all the stars, including Jones: "I think she's terribly attractive," he was quoted as saying at the time. "[She's] exactly right for the part."

John Astin recalls: "I had a great time with Carolyn. During the run of the show we didn't socialize much. We socialized more after the show was canceled. And we remained friends for years, but during the run of the show

Astin and Jones had resumed their passion play in a made-for-television reunion movie, *Halloween With the Addams Family,* in 1977, produced by David Levy (executive producer and creator of the television series) and directed by Dennis Steinmetz. In this Halloween special, written by *Munsters* scriptwriter George Tibbles (who also gave us the music to the campy "A Merry, Shh, Creepy Hallowe'en"), the gang—Cassidy, Coogan, [Lynn] Loring, Weatherwax, and Silla—was brought together once again.

"I scored the [reunion movie] but the whole thing was never any good. [It] was not directed well," Vic Mizzy remembers. "The script wasn't any good, as far as I was concerned. And they wanted to load it with music—it had more music in it than two Disney films put together."

In this disastrous reunion farce, the regular cast was joined by Henry Darrow as Pancho Addams, Gomez's amorous brother; cut-up Jane Rose (*Phyllis*), replacing the solemn Blossom Rock as Grandmama; and zany Elvia Allman (who had played an Addams cousin, Princess Millicent, on the original series) filling in for the incomparable Margaret Hamilton.

As the story unfolded, Halloween Eve drew near, and the Addams clan bustled with unearthly activities in preparation for their annual ghoul bash. Spooks, creeps, hobgoblins, and other oddities—all friends and relatives of the Addamses—arrived for an evening's festivities (not unlike Fester's homecoming gala in the 1991 Addams family feature film).

While being the perfect hosts to this melange of offbeat partygoers, Gomez and Morticia overlooked a trio of bumbling would-be burglars, who were portrayed by Patrick Campbell as Little Bo Peep, Parley Baer (semiregular Mr. Hilliard in the original) as Boss Crook, and Vito Scotti (Sam Picasso and Professor Altshuder in the original) as Mikey.

Despite the return of Mother Frump's handy maid "Ladyfingers" (a female "Thing"), the addition of new offspring Wednesday, Jr. (Jennifer Surprenant) and Pugsley, Jr. (Zen Marquis), and the antics of Gomez and Morticia lookalikes (Dean Sothern and Terry Miller), the reunion movie was no more fun than that other forgettable encore, *The Munsters' Revenge* (1981), which Mizzy also scored.

Even the creative involvement of producer Levy, who also penned the lyrics to George Tibbles's hokey Halloween anthem, failed to make this television movie as entertaining as was the series. Other creative contributions were made by associate producer Paul Pieratt and art director Bill Ross.

As for Gomez, Addams penned a characterization for him, too, in 1965: "Gomez is a crafty schemer but a jolly type in his own way. Sentimental and often puckish, he is full of enthusiasm, and a firm believer in the survival of the fittest."

"I had to write a lot of cues for things," continues Mizzy. "You had to keep the music going with *The Addams Family.* Filmways believed: 'Don't stop the music—just keep it going.'"

But viewers did not hear "Morticia's Theme" or "Gomez's Theme" in the 1991 feature film. And, according to Mizzy, it was only a fluke that his main *Addams Family* theme made it into the Paramount movie. Mizzy had initially contacted the filmmakers in November of 1990 about reviving his theme but without much success. However, after the tremendous response to the Mizzy-scored trailer of *The Addams Family* in theaters the following summer, producer Scott Rudin came around to Mizzy's way of thinking. The end result was the addition of Mizzy's theme (without vocals) and M. C. Hammer's "The Addams Family Groove," which sampled Mizzy's version and played during the ending credits.

"I couldn't get Scott Rudin on the phone. I still have never met him," complains Mizzy. "I was told he had never heard of the [original] *Addams Family* music, he had never heard my music. That shows you what kind of producer he is."

To the contrary, Rudin told *Chicago Tribune* writer Sid Smith at the time of the movie's release that traveling in a van full of coworkers and their children humming Mizzy's *Addams Family* tune provided the genesis of the film. Claiming to have even joined in on the finger-snapping lyrics himself, Rudin added, "I knew we had a movie."

"[But Rudin] didn't want to use my vocals in the picture," persists Mizzy, "he just wanted instrumental. It just goes to show you what [idiots they are]. Everybody knows the vocals—all kids know it, [just like] everybody knows the lyrics to *Green Acres.* Had Rudin picked up the phone and returned my phone call [I could have told him] that *The Addams Family* is a very unique and very special kind of family and I captured it. Without my music it would have been just another sitcom, but my music added that charm. Then they had M. C. Hammer doing this rap thing—'The Addams Family Groove'—but that was so ridiculous. [Today] all producers want is a package—they're not interested in quality.

"[But at least] they're using my main title [in the new Hanna-Barbera animated *Addams Family*]. *The Addams Family* was a cartoon a few years ago but it bombed because they used some canned music from England, you know, they were a cheap outfit then but now they're [using] my music."

In November 1991 Hanna-Barbera released the first two rental titles—"Left in the Lurch" and "Ghost Town"—from the defunct *Addams Family* cartoon series

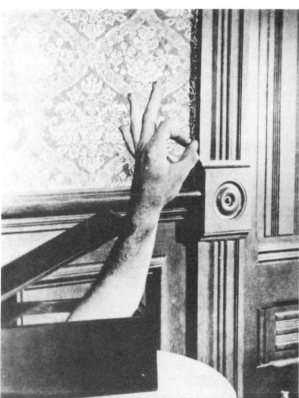

(Clockwise from top left) Jackie Coogan as Uncle Fester, Ted Cassidy as Lurch, Blossom Rock as Grandmama, and the ever helpful Thing © *copyright Orion Television Entertainment* (*photos courtesy Orion Television Entertainment*)

Vic Mizzy, composer of the snappy *Addams Family* theme as well as the one from *Green Acres* (*photo courtesy Vic Mizzy*)

to video stores across the country. In "Left in the Lurch" the Addamses go to Nashville in search of dinosaur bones, but find themselves caught up in a pop festival. Lurch becomes a pop star, in the spirit of Billy Ray Cyrus, and there is trouble ahead when he meets up with a pen pal. (Trivia buffs will recall that Ted Cassidy released a pop single called "The Lurch" in the sixties. The flipside was called "Wesley.")

In the "Ghost Town" video, spooks scare everyone away from the Old Prospector's land until the Addams family arrives on the scene, outspooking the spooks.

The premise of the cartoon series was to chronicle the misadventures of the Addamses as they traveled across the country. In their haunted trailer, complete with a piranha-filled moat, bats in the belfry, family crocodiles, Pugsley's pet octopus, and Morticia's darling man-eating plant, Cleopatra, they went off to see America, from Death Valley to the Great Dismal Swamp.

Character voices included Lennie Weinrib as Gomez, Janet Waldo of *The Jetsons* as both Morticia and Granny, Jackie Coogan as Uncle Fester, Ted Cassidy as Lurch, Jodie Foster as Pugsley, and Cindy Henderson as Wednesday.*

But as far as the original television series went, aside from Mizzy's score, other highlights of *The Addams Family* series included the late Ted Cassidy in a dual role as the seven-foot, harpsichord-playing manservant Lurch (as well as "Thing," the disembodied hand) and the late Jackie Coogan, as the devilishly mischievous and fun-loving Uncle Fester.

"Ted Cassidy, who was seven feet tall, was married to a girl who was a psychologist," explains Mizzy. "She was five feet tall, and she fixed me up [once] before I was married with a very beautiful jazz singer."

"Ted was actually Hamlet in a big body," recalls Astin, "a very serious actor, a very talented actor, and for most of his life, didn't like being known as Lurch. I think that he failed to enjoy the wonderful performance that he gave. It was classic. He got so much into that role—you felt the longsuffering of this man, his dedication to good manners, his intellect and I think you could see a lot of talent in [Ted]. He lived with a certain dissatisfaction in not playing more conventionally honored kinds of roles. You felt the pain inside Lurch [and Ted] as he went through his motions and it was touching and hilarious—all of the characters had that double-edged capacity."

Cassidy is known for his TV work in the films *Genesis II, The Planet Earth,* and *Benny and Barney: Las Vegas*

Undercover, and guested on another popular sixties series—*Lost in Space*—in the "Thief From Outer Space" episode. He died following open-heart surgery in 1979 at age forty-six.

"As for Lurch," wrote Addams, "this towering butler has been a morose presence about the house forever. He is not a very good butler but a faithful one. The children are his favorites and he seems to guard them against good influences at all costs."

"Jackie [Coogan] was very hard of hearing so, as a joke, he'd always call me Tone Deaf," says Mizzy, laughing. "He used to tell me so many stories about Hollywood and vaudeville. He loved talking to me because he could relate to me."

Addams defined Coogan's character for the show: "Uncle Fester is incorrigible and, except for the good nature of the family and the ignorance of the police, might be under lock and key. His complexion, like Morticia's, is dead-white. The eyes are pig-like and deeply embedded and circled unhealthily in black. Without teeth and absolutely hairless, he has a peppery manner and a high-pitched voice."

Born in 1914, Coogan was a top child star in movies and continued in starring and later character roles for more than sixty years.

Coogan was married and divorced several times, first to Betty Grable (1936–39), then to Flower Parry, with whom he had a son before divorcing in 1943. Next came Anne McCormick (1946–50), who bore him a daughter. He married fourth wife Dorothy in 1952 and soon had two more children. Dorothy, also known as "Dodie," went through nine surgeries following a near-fatal car accident in 1967, the same year that son Christopher was born.

Back in 1927, Coogan was number one at the box office, the first major child star. Ten years later he unsuccessfully sued to recover from his mother and stepfather the million dollars he had earned as a child actor. Nonetheless, the suit did result in the Coogan Law, which has protected all child stars since then.

Over the years Coogan managed to recoup his losses, at one time owning homes in Palm Springs and in La Paz, Baja, California. He began his career in *Skinner's Baby* in 1917, and costarred in Charlie Chaplin's first feature-length film, *The Kid,* in 1921. He was Tom Sawyer in the first sound version of the Mark Twain tale (in 1930), but by the mid-thirties he was all but forgotten. He later reemerged as a character actor and worked with Sinatra in *The Joker Is Wild,* Elvis in *Girl Happy* and John Wayne in *Cahill: U.S. Marshal,* among hundreds of others over the years. He was also the voice of Uncle Fester in the animated *Addams Family* series (1973–75).

But it was as Uncle Fester that he became a household name to the TV generation. Coogan died of a heart attack in 1984 at sixty-nine.

---

*Other video releases included "The Addams Family in New York," "Follow That Loaf of Bread," "The Boola-Boola," "The Fastest Creepy Camper in the West," "Mardi Gras," "Aloha Hoolamagoola," "The Reluctant Astronauts," "The Great Balloon Race," "The Circus Story," "The Voodoo Story," "The Roller Derby Story," "Addams Go West," and "Kentucky Derby."

"Coogan was one of the most interesting people I've ever met," says Astin. "It was more fun to spend time with Jack than [with] most people. Often we disagreed [but] Jack's experience, knowledge, flair, lust and gusto for life was so deep. He was a pleasure to be with. I did a lot of publicity gigs with Jack and he was an amazing character."

Not to be missed in *The Addams Family* were tiny Felix Silla as the longhaired Cousin Itt (later he was Twinky on *Buck Rogers*), Blossom Rock as the witchy yet doting Grandmama, Ken Weatherwax as Pugsley, Lisa Loring as the wistful Wednesday Thursday, Hazel Shermet as Cousin Melancholia, Don McArt as Cousin Cackle, Ellen Corby (*The Waltons*) as Mother Lurch, and Margaret Hamilton in guest appearances as Esther Frump, the mother of Morticia and twin sister Ophelia Frump, also played by Carolyn Jones.

"Felix Silla is a nice guy," says Mizzy. "I last saw him at John Astin's wedding. He's an old-timer in the business, a nice guy."

"The show was so much fun," Silla told *People* in November 1991, "At the end of the day you didn't feel tired."

The actual voice of Cousin Itt was that of Carolyn Jones, electronically reproduced.

Later Jones, who was married to actor Peter Bailey-Britton, made a number of television movies, was a regular on the soap *Capitol* and played in the miniseries *Roots*. She succumbed to cancer in 1983 at age fifty-four.

Addams defined Grandmama's character precisely, as he had the others: "[She] is foolishly good-natured, easily led, and some family troubles are due to her weak character."

"Blossom Rock played Grandmama—she was Jeanette MacDonald's sister," Astin remembers, "and there was quite a contrast between the two. She was a lovely woman and she and my mother became friends. They always went out to lunch whenever my mother was in L.A. or Blossom was in Washington, D.C." Blossom died in 1978 at age eighty-two.

Ted Cassidy in earlier times as a college basketball star (*photos courtesy Dr. James C. Bryant*)

"Lisa Loring was the most beautiful nine-year-old I've ever seen," recalls Mizzy. Addams had his own ideas, too, about Loring as Wednesday, as he wrote when he defined her character: "Wednesday, child of woe, is wan and delicate, with her mother's black hair and dead-white complexion. Quiet and sensitive, she loves picnics at the underground caverns." And of course, Wednesday loved to play with her anatomically correct Marie Antoinette doll. In real life no one could have predicted the offbeat turn of events in the life of former child star Lisa Loring. No one would have been more amused than creator Charles Addams himself, a man who married his third wife in a pet cemetery and was fond of visiting mental institutions.

The product of a broken home and only six years old when she was cast in the role of Wednesday, Loring married at fifteen, giving birth to the first of two daughters a year later. By the age of seventeen she was a divorced mother. And as with many other former child stars, Loring had quickly spent her childhood trust fund, so it was soon back to work, this time on the daytime soap *As the World Turns* as Cricket Montgomery from 1981 to 1983.

She married actor Doug Stevenson (*Search for Tomorrow*) in 1983, but soon divorced. Loring then wed Paul

Siederman, also known as porn star Jerry Butler. Loring penned the epilogue to his memoir *Raw Talent*.

"Kenny Weatherwax was such a good kid," continues Mizzy, with Addams offering his own thoughts on the boy's character. "Pugsley is an energetic pop-eyed boy and a dedicated troublemaker." Pugsley's favorite pet was his two-headed turtle and he blew up dynamite caps for kicks. But what could one expect from the son of a man who blew up model trains for fun?

Weatherwax has led a tamer life since exiting *The Addams Family*, working as a key grip on shows such as *The Facts of Life*. His mother Marge told *People* in November 1991: "He builds sets, and he loves the work. He didn't like doing *The Addams Family* but he liked the people."

"I had quite a bit of trouble in junior high and high school," Weatherwax told *The Star* in December 1991. "You want to belong and you want to have friends as a kid and you really can't make friends. I was so recognizable and I was made the center of attention all the time. People around me had trouble accepting me as just another person. I was excluded from sports and any other kind of group activity."

Addams himself once presented Weatherwax with an original drawing, but to young Ken's chagrin he inscribed it "to Pugsley" rather than "to Kenny."

Weatherwax would later join the army where he would experience a degree of anonymity he had not known before. After his discharge and after squandering his *Addams Family* nest egg, ultimately he ended up back at the studios, this time on the other side of the camera. "A couple of friends I grew up with worked as grips; so fifteen years ago I became a grip," he told *The Star*. "After the series was canceled I couldn't get any work because of being Pugsley . . . so that was the end of my career as far as acting goes."

"Margaret Hamilton was a wonderful woman, a very well-educated woman, a darling woman—the opposite of what you would think [from her characters]," says Mizzy. "She was the antithesis of what she looked like [on screen]."

Born in 1902, Hamilton, forever known to moviegoers as the wicked witch in *The Wizard of Oz*, and the definitive spinster lady on the screen in dozens and dozens of films, spent her seventies flying around the country appearing in regional theater productions and on television as Cora, the New England shopkeeper who drank Maxwell House Coffee.

Living Theatre partner Judith Malina, who filled Hamilton's shoes in the big screen saga of the Addamses, says of Granny Frump's creator: "[Charles Addams] was concerned with everything slightly despicable and horrible in human character. He showed a glint of lovingness that made the Addams family embraceable. He looked at wickedness and, instead of regarding it with horror, said 'look how funny it really is.' "

The original TV series also featured character actor Eddie Quillan, who kept turning up in various roles, as he also did on *My Favorite Martian*, and Loyal "Doc" Lucas, who portrayed Andre and also the family witch doctor in "Cat Addams," costarring the infamous Kitty Cat.

One ongoing theme in the series was the chemistry between Gomez and Morticia Addams. There was even a two-parter, "Morticia's Romance" (chronicling the couple's courtship) which was originally broadcast on September 24 and October 1, 1965. Still in love after many years of marriage, Gomez always was turned on whenever Morticia spoke French, never mind that she seldom uttered complete sentences.

A *TV Guide* article at the time of the original run best

summed up the Addamses' relationship: "The exaggerated love scenes that Astin plays with Carolyn Jones are undeniably funny. With old-world dignity, he kisses her hand, and carried away, begins nibbling her arm. And when she whispers something French, he loses his composure altogether and envelopes her with a feverish embrace."

And, the Addamses rarely indulged in petty arguments as did their ghoulish (and low-rent) counterparts, the Munsters. All in all, the black humor of the sixty-four half-hour *Addams Family* episodes is something perhaps better appreciated as an adult than as a child.

Undaunted by the eventual cancellation of *The Addams Family,* Mizzy forged ahead with *Green Acres* and a string of films for Universal: "I scored a lot of movies—a lot of my pictures are classics [now]—I did all of the Don Knotts pictures—*The Ghost and Mr. Chicken* has a big

cult following. I had to play the organ [myself] because the fellow hired to play didn't know how to use the foot pedals. [So] I had to sit down and play the cues and conduct at the same time."

"I did *The Reluctant Astronaut, The Shakiest Gun in the West,* and *How to Frame a Figg.* And I scored the only good picture that Phyllis Diller ever did, called *Did You Hear the One About the Traveling Saleslady?*"

As it turned out, Mizzy's association with Universal and *Green Acres* was so successful, he recently tried to name one of his several race horses (Dizzy Mizzy, ASCAP, and Stradella Road) after the series: "My daughter—she's in charge of them [and] runs the stable—gets a call from the Jockey Club: 'You can't use the name *Green Acres,*' and she said, 'Well, my father wrote it!' [so] we called the horse Dr. Mizzy [instead], but the next time we get another horse, we're going to call it 'Green Acres.'"

Anjelica Huston and Raul Julia as the big screen's Morticia and Gomez, joined by Dana Ivey (left), very tall Carel Struycken as Lurch, very short Judith Malina as Grandmama, Dan Hedaya, and youngsters Christina Ricci and Jimmy Workman (*photo courtesy Paramount Pictures*)

The 1991 Paramount film, produced by Scott Rudin, costarred Anjelica Huston (who got top billing) with Raul Julia, a more charming version of Gomez than Astin.

Though others were considered in the beginning (Mizzy's choices were Cher and Kevin Kline), Rudin says today, "We always wanted Anjelica. She's regal—an original hothouse flower . . . if Anjelica isn't Morticia, then who could be? The Addams family celebrates the freakish and the macabre, yet they're a loving, tightly-knit family. I've always loved the subversive nature of Charles Addams's cartoons."

"She's flirtatious, motherly, suspicious," says Huston of her character, "a romantic soul and quite cool under fire. I see her as a perfect Norman Rockwell mother—just taken to a very dark degree. I wouldn't want to be on the wrong side of Morticia. . . . I'd just come off *The Grifters,* and felt I'd done enough soul-searching. I wanted to play something light and liberating . . . but I consciously avoided doing a Carolyn Jones imitation. She was quite the perfect Morticia [so] I went back to the cartoons. I've known the Charles Addams cartoons since I was a little girl in Ireland. Their life really wasn't unlike ours growing up."

"The Addams family are pranksters," explains Raul Julia. "They're rascals. They are not an evil family and don't really do serious harm to people. They love being a little bad. They laugh at the people who are so preoccupied with being good that they have no fun." Elaborating on his Gomez, he says, "Perhaps childlike in spirit, he's an extrovert who enjoys everything, yet in a matter of seconds he can go from joy to deep anger and depression. But mostly he's just a happy-go-lucky guy who enjoys life and is in love with Morticia and his family."

Costarring was shaven-headed, deeply eye-shadowed Christopher Lloyd as the prodigal Uncle Fester, who has just returned home, having disappeared twenty-five years before following an accident with a tuna net in the Bermuda Triangle. Lloyd told writer Frank Lovece in December 1991: "As long as I can recall picking up a magazine, I was looking for Charles Addams's cartoons—Uncle Fester's always been a favorite of mine, I never imagined I'd be playing him, but I had a feel[ing] about him and I was really excited to [create] that."

Lloyd, born in Stamford, Connecticut, in 1938, grew up in New Canaan, went to high school in Westport, and moved to New York in 1960. He eventually studied acting with Sanford Meisner at the Neighborhood Playhouse and debuted in the 1960 production *They Put Handcuffs on the Flowers.* He finally made it to Broadway in 1969 in *Red, White and Maddox,* and four years later he won the Obie Award and a Drama Desk Award for the title role in *Kaspar.*

Television audiences first got to know the zany actor as Reverend Jim in *Taxi.* Subsequently he played Doc Emmett Brown in the *Back to the Future* trilogy, also made his mark as Judge Doom in *Who Framed Roger Rabbit.* He made his screen debut as one of Nicholson's fellow inmates in *One Flew Over the Cuckoo's Nest.*

Not to be overlooked were Judith Malina as the witchily maddening Granny Frump, and Carel Struycken as Lurch, the guttural, towering butler.

(All five are repeating their roles in *Addams Family Values,* which went into production in late winter 1993, with the addition of Joan Cusack and Carol Kane to the cast.)

Although Cassidy had doubled as Thing on television in the sixties, Struycken did not in this flick. The honor went to Christopher Hart, a twentyish magician.

"Ideally, we were hoping to find a very gnarled hand," casting director David Rubin told *Premiere* magazine prior to the release of the film, "a hand with a great deal of character in keeping with the Addams family style. [Hart] is extremely facile and has really long fingers [and] a pleasant demeanor . . . there are no lines involved. You need somebody with great patience . . ."

"Maybe if this is a hit," joked Hart at the time, "Thing will have his own series." No longer bound by the confines of a box as in the old series, the new Thing perched like a parrot on Gomez's shoulder, ran down a hallway, and turned hitchhiker in an unexpected plot twist. He even leapfrogged across a string of lily pads in what some viewers intrepreted as a flagrant bid for an Oscar nomination.

Director and former cinematographer Barry Sonnenfeld recalled when the first film came out: "We went back to Charles Addams's original drawings, on which the characters were based. It's an incredibly romantic movie. A great love story." One of those classic drawings showed the Addamses preparing to greet Christmas carolers by pouring a giant wassail bowl of boiling oil from the tower. This became the opening scene of the film.

"Their values are different," added Sonnenfeld. "That's what makes them happy. [They] make us laugh and see aspects of ourselves that we try to hide, the darker side of our personalities."

Addams's odd offspring were portrayed this time around by Christina Ricci (Wednesday) and Jimmy Workman (Pugsley). And Ricci was right in step with Charles Addams's vision for her character, perhaps even more so than Loring had been: "It's been a really rough week," she admitted during shooting. "I had to chop off Pugsley's arm, recite Shakespeare, and do this gigantic death scene. It was really exhausting."

Supporting players included Dan Hedaya, Elizabeth Wilson, Dana Ivey, Paul Benedict, and John Franklin as the five-foot tall, hairy-scary Cousin Itt. An additional

Carel Struycken as the 1991 and 1993 Lurch in the feature films
(*photo courtesy Carel Struycken*)

oddity, absent from the television series, was Lumpy, a hunchback with mouth plate and pompadour, played by Ryan Holihan.

The sinister-looking sets were by production designer Richard MacDonald (*The Russia House, The Day of the Locust*) and the outlandish costumes by his wife, Ruth Myers (*Blaze, The Accidental Tourist*). Pungent colors, blood-red wallpaper, a soaring stuffed bear, an elephant's foot filled with popcorn, and the head of a moose were just a few of the decorating tricks used in the original series but MacDonald had bolder ideas—Second Empire grandeur, arched windows, and a brown and gold patina. "The family are aristocrats," he told *House and Garden* magazine prior to the movie's release. "They don't have to keep up with the Joneses—they just carry on in their eccentric manner."

The Addams's picture gallery was hung with copies, albeit in altered states, of paintings by artists ranging from Goya to Grant Wood. MacDonald even turned out some of the forgeries himself. The art nouveau-inspired ballroom was given a pool of gloom feel by the addition of German-romanticized murals, while in the conservatory Huston, as did Carolyn Jones before her, methodically decapitates her roses against the backdrop of a Venetian-style faux floor.

Uncle Fester's big-screen bedroom was haunted by the presence of copies of Gustave Dore's engraved scenes from Dante's *Inferno*. Age-old pots and pans cluttered a gargantuan table in the oppressive kitchen, which was modeled, according to MacDonald, after that of a sixteenth-century Burghley House in Lincolnshire. The exterior of the house was erected in the hills above Burbank, and the interior sets on studio sound stages rose seventy-five feet with an underground river below.

Ironically financially-pressed Orion almost sabotaged the grandiose sets. Three-quarters of the way through filming, the studio, which had gotten the character rights from Addams and distributed the now-syndicated television series, sold the movie to Paramount for $22 million.

"They'd call and say, 'You can't paint the whole set, but you can paint the pillar,' Barry Sonnenfeld told *Entertainment Weekly* a week before the movie was released. I wasn't sure if the movie would ever be finished. It's not a perfect movie. It doesn't really have a good plot. But . . . I really like it. It's incredibly emotional and really funny."

The film's screenplay, written by Larry Wilson and Caroline Thompson (*Edward Scissorhands*), centered around the threat posed to the Addams family when their attorney conspires with a mother-son con team to steal the family fortune. But Sonnenfeld was dissatisfied with the original script so he called in playwright-scriptwriter Paul Rudnick (*Sister Act*) to make much-needed changes.

"The eyelifts got tighter and the temples started to throb," recalled Anjelica Huston in *Entertainment Weekly* in November 1991, making a reference to the arrival of new script pages every hour, on the hour. "It could leave you more wasted than having a very emotional day on the set."

The $30 million film delivered black humor and an ultracreepy ambiance that was truer to the spirit of Charles Addams's thirteen-hundred mordant *New Yorker* cartoons than were the sixty-four half-hour *Addams Family* episodes. The musical score was composed by Marc Shaiman (*City Slickers, Misery*), who collaborated with Betty Comden and Adolph Green on a production number entitled "Mamushka," celebrating Uncle Fester's homecoming.

"I told Marc Shaiman, 'if you're smart, use all those themes that I wrote because people know all those themes,' " says Mizzy today, "[but] Rudin didn't [do his homework], according to Marc. And I told Marc—if you're smart—use all those themes I wrote—people know all those themes. But all they used was the main title." And though Mizzy's popular themes may have been overlooked, Comden, Green, and Shaiman went for broke with their catchy ode to brotherly love which ends with Raul Julia and Christopher Lloyd joyfully shouting "Mamushka!"

Visual effects were under the supervision of Alan Munro (*Beetlejuice*), with special effects coordinated by Chuck Gespar.

And in any case, the more recent Paramount flicks have proven to be a more fitting epitaph for one of America's most beloved, if not most eccentric, families.

Of the same exceptional quality as the feature, and much more amusing than the 1977 reunion, were two half-hour Halloween episodes, "Halloween with the Addams Family" (1964) and "Halloween Addams Style" (1965). The former starred Don Rickles as Claude and was written by Keith Fowler and Phil Leslie, directed by Sidney Lanfield. The latter featured Don McArt as Cousin Cackle, and was written by Hannibal Coon and Harry Winkler and directed by Lanfield.

In 1947 *New Yorker* critic Wolcott Gibbs wrote in the foreword to his book *Addams And Evil:*

The thoughtful reader will wonder about the inhabitants of that crumbling Gothic pile known . . . as "Old Charles Addams Place." What dark and shameful compulsion brought the proprietors together—the haggard ruined beauty and the ignoble half-breed? What unspeakable rites united them, if wed they are at all? We know their little girl has six toes on her left foot, that her little brother likes to mix childish poison brews, and that their only playmates are bats and spiders and probably The Thing that has no face, but wails and drags his chains at night. And we know still less about the shambling giant who ministers their dreadful needs, except that he is apparently dumb and almost certainly a homicidal maniac.

Vic Mizzy recalls, "I met Charles Addams—he visited—he came over and he said, 'I never would have dreamed that anybody could possibly interpret with music what I thought when I created the cartoon characters.' Your music says it all—the finger snapping is so far out, so catchy."

And how did John Astin feel about *The Addams Family* at the time? "It's no great art form," he told *TV Guide,* "but it's no disgrace either. We provide light entertainment for people, and considering the haste with which we work, our quality is nothing to be ashamed of."

But over the years the legacy of Addams's artistic talent and bent humor has transcended the tabloid headlines of Loring's and Astin's sometimes turbulent lives. "Al-though the family was bizarre in its exterior," surmises Astin today, in a somewhat more reflective mood, "what was underneath was healthy. You had a father and a mother who had a very healthy married relationship. There was a supportive attitude in the family. The kids respected the parents. The parents would do anything for the kids. Fundamentally [they] were very sound."

From thirteen hundred darkly humorous cartoons and a classic sixties television series to an animated version (1973–75) and another in the early nineties and a disastrous television reunion movie, the Addams Family endures, the legacy of Charles Addams, an eccentric, almost perverse artist who always kept his public guessing. And in 1991 talents such as Huston, Lloyd, and Struycken breathed life again into character roles vacated by the deaths of Jones, Coogan and Cassidy.

From Addams's fondness for skeletons and tombstones to the embalming table in his living room, was it all for affect or did was he truly a creepy, kooky, mysterious, and spooky eccentric? Buh, duh, duh, dum, snap, snap!

David McCallum as shaggy-haired teen heartthrob Ilya Kuryakin (*photo courtesy Turner Network Television*)

SEVEN

THE MAN FROM U.N.C.L.E.

(September 22, 1964–January 15, 1968)

A light spy spoof of the sixties, *The Man From U.N.C.L.E.* was inspired by the James Bond films. Actually the name Napoleon Solo (Robert Vaughn played the part) was from the Bond feature *Goldfinger,* and was used in *U.N.C.L.E.* with Ian Fleming's consent.

"As an actor I've never liked anything so much," said Vaughn at the time in an interview with *TV Guide.* "It has some parallel with the James Bond role. But I'm playing Solo lighter than Sean Connery plays Bond. I'm surprised at the reaction. I never anticipated anything like this. I'm not yet Robert Vaughn, only Napoleon Solo. You don't get to be known as yourself in TV, only in movies."

"Solo is the name of a minor character in one of [Fleming's] books," says executive producer Norman Felton, who had also produced *The Eleventh Hour* and *Dr. Kildare.* "[Fleming's Solo was] a Sicilian. A very bad man. Not anything like our Solo."

Initially Alden Schwimmer of the Ashley-Steiner Agency had sent Felton the galleys of a novel by Ian Fleming. After early negotiations, Felton received a note from Fleming, dated June 26, 1963, which read:

This will serve as my assignment to you of all my rights and interest in any material written or contributed by me in connection with an original television series featuring a character named Napoleon Solo. I assign to you all rights of every kind to the use of this character and material and I have not used this character or material in any work written or contributed by me nor will I make any use of the same hereafter. The material and the character is original and I am free to grant you the rights assigned in this letter. I hereby acknowledge receipt of the sum of one pound in consideration of this assignment.

98

Unknown to Felton at the time, Fleming had used the character in one of his books and to avoid a lawsuit, Felton finally agreed not to call the series *Solo,* if he was allowed to retain the name for the lead.

And too, as it turned out, the use of U.N.C.L.E. in the title of the series was almost blocked by the United Nations when it was discovered that there was a New York law forbidding the use of the initials U.N. in any commercial venture.

"The initial critical reaction was a mixed bag," said Vaughn in Jon Heitland's *Man From U.N.C.L.E. Book,* "due largely to reviewer's inability to get a fix on the style of escapist fare being served up. Was it action-adventure? Was it spoof? Was it serious? Was it funny? Was it tongue-in-cheek? What was it?"

And what was the purpose of U.N.C.L.E.? Simply to thwart T.H.R.U.S.H., which, according to Vaughn, "was the organization that represented evil incarnate throughout the world. Originally I don't think it did mean anything and people started writing in and saying, 'What does it mean?' So we had to figure out something and then we came up with five words that made some kind of sense."

So T.H.R.U.S.H. came to mean 'the Technological Hierarchy for the Removal of Undesirables and the Subjugation of Humanity.' And Vaughn was not alone in his battle against the evil T.H.R.U.S.H. Little known (in this country) Scottish actor David McCallum costarred as Illya Kuryakin and Leo G. Carroll was Alexander Waverly, head of U.N.C.L.E. (United Command for Law Enforcement).

Ronald Searle said in his *TV Guide* review of the series at the time:

There may be an echo of Bond in the fantasy of the situations, but that by no means diminishes the suspense. With Robert Vaughn, David McCallum, and Leo G. Carroll to give credentials to the incredible nonsense of most of the installments, what might have been merely another juvenile comic strip is jacked up to the level of thoroughly enjoyable rubbish.

And behind the scenes the show utilized the talents of such individuals as producers Sam Rolfe, David Victor, Mort Abrahams, Boris Ingster, Douglas Benton, Irving Pearlberg, Anthony Spinner, and composer Jerry Goldsmith. But the real stars of the show were Vaughn and McCallum.

Born in Glasgow, Scotland, on September 19, 1933, McCallum was the son of classical musicians. David Senior was first violinist of the London Philharmonic;

Dorothy Dorman was a cellist. His parents met while playing in the same orchestra pit in a silent movie theater.

By the beginning of World War II, the family had moved to London, but after the bombings began, David and brother Iain were sent to the country. After briefly attending the Royal Academy of Music, David switched to the Royal Academy of Dramatic Art. He lived for years in cheap London flats and between 1953 and 1956 appeared in more than fifty-two stage productions in stock.

As a child actor he had worked on the BBC: "Perhaps I grew up too fast. When I should have been punching other kids, I was preparing for an artistic career—probably led to my introverted streak." He attended the University College School in Hampstead, London, and after the Royal Academy, he made his film debut in *Prelude to Fame,* followed by two years in the British Army.

Following his discharge in 1956, he came to the attention of the J. Arthur Rank Talent Agency. He and actress Jill Ireland were married seven days after being introduced and in the late fifties they ended up in Hollywood, remaining together until 1967. They had three sons. She then ran off with Charles Bronson, a good friend of the McCallums.

As a mop-haired pseudo-Russian with a vague accent, David McCallum became an idol among teenage girls on the heels of *The Man From U.N.C.L.E.*

McCallum once said in a *TV Guide* interview: "I'm perfectly happy to receive any symbols that indicate success. Part of an actor's metabolism is being insecure. When you get a TV series, you start looking for other places to be insecure. If I am working twelve months a year, I wonder if this is the life I want [but] an actor's sole purpose in life is to entertain. If he doesn't do that, he fails."

McCallum, who had minor roles in such films as *Hell Drivers* (with Jill Ireland and relative newcomer Sean Connery) in 1957, *Billy Budd* in 1962, and *The Great Escape* (with Charles Bronson, among others) in 1963, parlayed his Illya Kuryakin fame into some starring roles for MGM: *Around the World Under the Sea* (1966), *Three Bites of the Apple* (1967), and *Sol Madrid* (1968). After *U.N.C.L.E.*'s demise, McCallum went back to the British stage, but has turned up occasionally on American television—there were his starring role in *The Invisible Man* series in late 1975 and a stint on *As the World Turns* in 1983—and got good reviews for *Mother Love* with Diana Rigg that turned up in 1991 on PBS's *Mystery!*

"David [loved] to do the makeup and wigs and dialects and so on," recalls Vaughn today. "I got to stay clean and be with the girls and he [could] run off to Timbuktu with a fright wig on."

"I was just mad about David," confesses three-time *U.N.C.L.E.* guest star Yvonne (*Batman*) Craig, "I

Robert Vaughn in the title role as Napoleon Solo

thought that he was wonderful and at the time that we did the show, there was [enough] time to sit around and talk. And he had been on a march with Bertrand Russell and I was really impressed because Russell was probably the only person I ever wanted to meet and didn't meet. David and I were talking about the book that he was reading and I was very impressed with his mind. And one day I was in early for a shot and they were still out on the back lot so I was just hanging out by my dressing room—I couldn't get in because the door was locked and nobody seemed to know where the key was and there weren't any people from [the show] there yet. And for some reason David arrived on the set and asked 'Why aren't you in your dressing room?' and I said, 'Oh, I can't get in—it's locked and nobody has a key.' Whereupon he said, 'Piece of cake,' and proceeded to pick the lock. I was immediately in love."

Craig continues, "He was [also] married at that time to Jill Ireland, and he said to me, 'You're a marvelous girl. You should meet this friend of mine,' and I asked, 'Who?' and he said, 'Well, he's very sensitive and he paints and he's a wonderful person.' And I asked [again], 'Who is this?' And he said, 'Charlie Bronson.' I said, 'No, I'm going out with somebody [else] and I really don't want to go out with Charlie Bronson. You may think he's sensitive but I don't.' He said, 'He is helping [Jill] pick out

things for our house.' And it must have been six months later that I saw Charlie and Jill lunching at a restaurant in Beverly Hills and I thought [to myself] that it looked more serious than David led me to believe."

"David was easy to work with," offers another *U.N.C.L.E.* guest star, Diana Millay, the popular sixties ingenue and star of *Dark Shadows*. "He was good, an actor that's decidedly underrated by the American [audience]. He's an excellent actor."

"David clearly became the costar of the show and got comparable fan mail," Vaughn attests. "He was called the blond Beatle by many during that time. The girls who liked him were from a certain age group [eight to thirteen] and the girls who liked me were older."

"The notion of using a Russian agent as a minor character in the pilot came up," explains Felton, "and [we] wondered if, with the Cold War heating up, it would work."

"As for Illya, all I knew was that he was Russian," said producer Sam Rolfe at the time, "but it was a vague, smoky thing, David gave the role life force."

"Illya was a quiet swinger," stresses McCallum. "Nobody [knew] what he did when he went home at night."

"Knowing we were looking for offbeat casting for Kuryakin," Felton continues, "the head of casting at MGM suggested a British actor currently playing Judas in

David McCallum, Leo G. Carroll, and Robert Vaughn (*photo courtesy Turner Network Television*)

Norman Felton, creator of *The Man From U.N.C.L.E.* (*photo courtesy Norman Felton*)

[*The Greatest Story Ever Told*], saying he had a mod look. Before I could check him out an associate came in excitedly to announce, 'I've found a young actor, slim, with long hair, named David McCallum, who is just right!' Paul Kohner, the agent, arranged for us to meet David and we were impressed. An hour later, our director, Don Medford, dropped in to say he had lunch with Charles Bronson, who had brought along an actor now playing Judas and he thought he'd be just right for Kuryakin. I never had any idea he would become the hit he has. His part in the pilot film was only a few lines, and he was just one of many actors we considered. We picked him because he looked different.

"I've worked with David quite a few times," contributes another *U.N.C.L.E.* guest star, Michael Ansara, "We [once] went down to Acapulco and [were] in a movie called *Sol Madrid,* where I played the police captain, and he was a very nice person [to work with]."

"David is one of the very few of my acting contemporaries whom I respect," Vaughn says, though McCallum is more scathing in critiquing his own craft: "We Scots, we tend to be awfully tight inside. We have a tremendous emotion underneath. It has hurt me as an actor to be so—so naturally restricted. I had to learn to expand, to give. Acting is giving."

He was always perplexed by his "sex symbol" image: "With my Calvinist background and my deep Presbyterian blood, with my stiff Scottish spine, to be told you're suddenly a 'sex symbol'—it's just disquieting."

But Yvonne Craig surmises, "David was the one that all the girls were attracted to, if they had any sense at all because he was darling and mischevious and interesting."

Pulling all the strings behind the scenes of the U.N.C.L.E. organization was Waverly, played by veteran actor Leo G. Carroll. Born in Wedon, England, of Irish parents, Carroll begin his professional career in 1911 on the London stage. Broadway followed and by 1934 he was actively involved in the Hollywood scene as well. First known on TV as Cosmo Topper in the *Topper* series, Carroll replaced Will Kuluva, who in the original pilot had played U.N.C.L.E. head Mr. Allison.

And what were the beginnings of the man who created Waverly and his stable of spies? Norman Felton was born in London on April 29, 1913, the son of John Felton and Gertrude Francis. In 1929 he and his family relocated to Cleveland, Ohio. Seven years later, Felton, a high school dropout, joined a theater group headed by a man named Clancy Cooper, functioning as its resident playwright. In 1940 he gained his bachelor's degree at the University of Iowa.

A year later Felton received a master's degree. Then from 1943 to 1948, he was involved in the production of radio shows. By 1952 he was directing in live television on *Robert Montgomery Presents,* which won him an Emmy in 1952 as well as two Sylvania Awards and a Christopher Award.

From 1959 to 1960 he was West Coast producer for CBS's *Playhouse 90.* In 1961 he tackled new challenges as he directed TV films for MGM and received Emmy nominations for *The Eleventh Hour, The Lieutenant* (with Robert Vaughn), and *Dr. Kildare.*

At the time Vaughn first read the script for the *U.N.C.L.E.* pilot he was actually costarring on *The Lieutenant,* with Stefanie Powers's husband Gary Lockwood.

The Girl From U.N.C.L.E. starred Powers as April Dancer and Noel Harrison as Mark Slate. Once again Leo G. Carroll appeared as Mr. Waverly. The original pilot, "The Moonglow Affair," was an *U.N.C.L.E.* episode which guest starred Mary Ann Mobley and Norman Fell.

"Stars begged to play guest roles," says Felton today about *U.N.C.L.E.,* "and when Joan Crawford asked to play a villain, we obliged. When Betty Friedan came to see me in my office, I knew it was time to make *The Girl From U.N.C.L.E.* and we set Dean Hargrove to write the pilot."

One of the reasons that stars were so keen on doing the show was that the dialogue demonstrated a repartee, similar to that of *The Avengers.*

One such episode was "The Jingle Bell Affair," which aired December 23, 1966. It began with an Eastern European head of state in New York to address the U.N., watching a parade with Solo and Kuryakin, who have been given the mission to keep him safe. He is nearly killed when a bomb explodes and later has several more attempts made on his life. As it turns out the would-be assassin is his security chief, who believes that his country is being led down the road to ruination with his talk of peace. J. Pat O'Malley guest starred with Ellen Willard, Akim Tamiroff, Kent Smith, Leon Belasco, Leonid Kinskey, and Joan Tompkins. The episode was written by William Fay and directed by John Brahm.

"The Arabian Affair," which aired October 29, 1965, featured Michael Ansara as Sulador along with Phyllis Newman and Quinn O'Hara. It was written by Peter Fields and directed by E. Darrell Hallenbeck.

"I recall that it was a fun role to do [on *U.N.C.L.E.*] and it turned out very well," says Ansara today of his guest spot. "Before I did *Broken Arrow,* I had done quite a few movies. At the time movie actors didn't like doing television because it [tarnished] their image but slowly the two [mediums] were integrated and some [stars] started doing more and more television. I had done a great diversity of roles—I had played Judas in *The Robe,* I played an army commander in *The Greatest Story Ever Told,* and [aside from these historical roles] I played gangsters and policemen, but when you do a series playing a distinctive role like Cochise, for a while it does

Yvonne Craig, occasional *U.N.C.L.E.* guest star who later became
TV's Batgirl (*photo courtesy Yvonne Craig*)

type you. And after that for a little while I didn't work at all because I refused to do the same kind of [character] but then I did go back and do the second series playing a Harvard-educated Indian who became a United States Marshal [*Law of the Plainsman*]. And after finishing that series, for a while it became difficult to be cast in other roles. They did typecast more in those days than they do today."

"The King of Knaves Affair," aired December 22, 1964, and featured Diana Millay as Ernestine Pepper. It was written by Ellis Marcus and directed by Michael O'Herlihy.

"*The Man From U.N.C.L.E.* was very unusual," says Millay today. "The interesting thing about that was that I had to jump off of a wall and I wanted to jump off myself and that caused quite a [stir] because they would not let me do it and they forced me to wear a dress [style] that the double could also wear—this is the only show I think I've ever been in where I wore one dress for half an hour. The dress was a horror—a great, big, enormous, bouffant, full-skirted monstrosity, because the double had to have that much room in order to jump off the wall. As a result I was stuck in a [prom dress] running through a castle and a dungeon in this absurd outfit. You never [noticed] me—all you saw [was] the dress. We had a great time. It was a silly, silly role and it was very charming."

"I was very, very blessed. I was an ingenue in the truest sense of the word, who actually was lucky enough to play an addict opposite David Janssen. I played a drunk in *The Rifleman* opposite Chuck Connors. That's great for an ingenue to be able to do these things. I ran the spectrum and for that, I am grateful."

Born in Rye, New York, Millay studied acting under Constance Collier, teaming for her professional debut at a charity benefit opposite Garry Moore. At age sixteen she began doing stock in Windham, New Hampshire, and the following fall got her big break in the lead role of *The Seven Year Itch* on tour. She went on to play Dorothy Lamour's daughter on Broadway in *Roger the Sixth*, before moving on to the role of Janet in Moss Hart's *Fair Game*, also on the Great White Way.

"Two of my *U.N.C.L.E.* guest appearances were honest-to-goodness episodes," remembers Yvonne Craig, "and then they added onto [the third] in order to release it as a movie in Europe—I just did add-on [footage]; 'The Brain Killer Affair,' I remember well because I'm tied up in it and it was a horrifying experience. I remember ['The Bridge of Lions Affair']—I was getting ready to go to Europe to do a pilot for a series based on *Three Coins in the Fountain* and they called me back and said, 'We need to do some added takes because we're going to make this into a movie,' and I remember I was very concerned because I had this huge scab on my arm from [just] being

vaccinated and I was supposed to be in a bathing suit and I remember worrying that they were going to see this big scab on my arm and wonder what had happened to me."

Craig surfaced again in a two-parter, "The Alexander the Greater Affair" (September 17 and 24, 1965), playing Mr. Waverly's niece Maude, along with Rip Torn, Dorothy Provine, David Opatoshu, and David Sheiner. It was written by Dean Hargrove and directed by Joseph Sargent. Later it was released theatrically as *One Spy Too Many,* which in March of 1966 set an all-time record in the history of MGM during the London premiere, grossing $282,000 in the first week, says Norman Felton.

Craig was also in "The Bridge of Lions Affair" (February 4 and 11, 1966) as Wanda. Maurice Evans, Vera Miles, and Bernard Fox were among the guest stars. It was written by Henry Stear and Howard Rodman and directed by E. Darrell Hallenback.

"When we did 'The Brain Killer Affair,' " continues Craig, "I was supposed to be tied up to a chair and gagged. And they honest to God tied me to the chair and gagged me and [then] they forgot about me and [I was panicked] anyway because I didn't like being tied up—you're really vulnerable when you're tied up. All stunt people now say, 'You just never do that!' I can't believe I let them do that. So they walked off to lunch and left me until someone remembered."

"The Brain Killer Affair," which aired March 8, 1965, featured Craig with Elsa Lanchester, Cecille Bergstrom, and Abraham Sofaer. Archie L. Tegland wrote the episode and James Goldstone directed it.

Barbara (*Get Smart*) Feldon guest starred in "The Never-Never Affair" on March 22, 1965. In this episode, written by Dean Hargrove and directed by Joseph Sargent, Feldon was joined by Cesar Romero. And *Get Smart* costar Don Adams would show up in "The Minus X Affair" (May 8, 1966).

Other guest stars during the run included Jill Ireland, Anne Francis, James Doohan, Brooke Bundy, Carroll O'Connor, Sharon Farrell, William Shatner, Leonard Nimoy, Kurt Russell, Marta Kristen, Ricardo Montalban, June Lockhart, Madlyn Rhue, Lee Meriwether, Susan Seaforth, Lloyd Bochner, Gavin MacLeod, Eddie Albert, Eleanor Audley, George Sanders, Bonnie Franklin, Sharon Tate, Charlie Ruggles, Vincent Price, Angela Lansbury, Jay North, Diane McBain, James Frawley, Victor Buono, Martin Landau, Eve Arden, Estelle Winwood, Joan Collins, Diana Hyland, Pat Harrington, Jr., Jack Palance, Janet Leigh, Joan Blondell, Nancy Sinatra, Whitney Blake, Victor Borge, Reta Shaw, Sonny Bono, Cher, Telly Savalas, Terry-Thomas, Chad Everett, Carol Lynley, Bradford Dillman, John Carradine, Jack Lord, Michael Rennie, Darren McGavin, and Judy Carne. Even Norman Felton had a cameo as the chess player in "The

Diana Millay, who made several appearances on *The Man From U.N.C.L.E.* (*photo courtesy Diana Millay*)

Giuoco Affair," airing November 10, 1964.

But this illustrious lineup of guest stars aside, what lay behind the success of the show was the special charm of Vaughn, the man who made all of this work. Vaughn, it turns out, had not even been Felton's first choice—other contenders early on included Harry Guardino, Robert Brown, and Robert Culp.

"The network gave a go ahead," explains Felton. "Then followed days of searching for an actor to play Solo, and time running out to film and deliver the pilot on time for the network scheduling of the coming season. Finally I had an idea which led me to call Robert Vaughn who was playing a captain in *The Lieutenant* series, being filmed at a marine base near San Diego. He knew of our project and was delighted when I asked him to pick up a script at the MGM gate when the company returned that evening. Then I called NBC and after haggling, since I assured them Cary Grant and Richard Burton were not available, they gave a reluctant okay to Vaughn."

Vaughn was born in November 1932 in New York City and raised by his mother's folks in Minneapolis. His mother was the Broadway stage star Marcella Gaudell and his father was radio actor Gerald Walter Vaughn. The product of a disturbed childhood, Vaughn has said that he cried all the time. He attended the University of Minnesota's School of Journalism (covering the sports scene for the *Minneapolis Star-Journal*). Later he turned to acting and won best actor award for *Hamlet* at the Los Angeles State College.

In 1951 he was a finalist in the Philip Morris intercollegiate radio-acting contest and went on to study drama at the Los Angeles City College. For two years he was resident leading man at Albuquerque Summer House Theatre. He was discovered by the Hecht-Lancaster people while appearing in *End as a Man*.

Having made his TV debut in *Medic*, he appeared in his first film in 1956, after obtaining a B.A. in drama, and later he pursued graduate studies in political science at Los Angeles City College. In 1958 he starred, as all film cultists know, in Roger Corman's *Teenage Caveman*. In 1959 he was nominated for an Oscar for his supporting role in *The Young Philadelphians,* starring Paul Newman. Dozens of films and TV parts followed, among them *The Magnificent Seven* in 1960, *Julius Caesar* in 1970, *The Towering Inferno* in 1974, and *Superman III* in 1983.

In 1972 he wrote *Only Victims,* an account of the Hollywood purge resulting from the investigations of the House Un-American Activities Committee. Vaughn has portrayed four American presidents—Franklin D. Roosevelt, Harry S. Truman, Woodrow Wilson (*Backstairs at the White House*), and Teddy Roosevelt (*Law of the Plainsman*).

Vaughn starred with E. G. Marshall in a revival of *Inherit the Wind* at the Paper Mill Playhouse in New Jersey in 1985, and in 1990 he appeared with Polly Bergen in *Love Letters*.

"People seem surprised that I'm still alive," says Vaughn today, "When they recover from that shock, they ask, 'Are you still in show business?' or 'Why don't you act anymore?' The truth is, I haven't been out of work ten days since leaving *The Man From U.N.C.L.E.*

"[That show] was an absolute feast of guest stars for me, because I was single at the time [he's been married to Linda Staab since 1974] and we had usually four or five beautiful women on the show every week. We tried, as I recall, to get some ongoing flirtation with one of the U.N.C.L.E. girls in the office. There was a continuing character there who wore the U.N.C.L.E. uniform and the badge. But I don't think that ever came to fruition. I think I tried to use what I knew to be my own working personality with women. Every week there were just lovely, lovely young ladies on the show and it was a pleasure to go to work every morning."

And during hiatus Vaughn, who had once remarked, "Maybe a lot of actors aren't as secure as I am," played *Hamlet* and worked on his Ph.D. in communications at the University of Southern California, while McCallum made movies.

"Bob's a bachelor," McCallum said during the show's original run, "I'm a family man. In Hollywood, as elsewhere, that's two different universes."

"If Napoleon Solo were to place an ad," adds Vaughn, "I guess it would say: urbane, witty, meticulous, energetic, structured gentleman would like to meet all women of all countries in all heights, weights, and colors. Beware, he's also detached, cool. The common operative adjective [would be] 'cool.' He was rarely flustered—coolness under pressure [and a little grace]."

"Bobby had to dance with me [in one episode]," remembers Yvonne Craig, "and I was a trained ballet dancer. We had a scene in which we had to ballroom dance and I was absolutely panicked. I said to him, 'I don't dance,' and he said, 'You're a dancer—I'm sure you can.' I said, 'No, you don't understand. I really don't dance.' Poor thing, he had to shove me around the dance floor and when the scene was over, he said, 'You're right—that's like moving furniture,' [but] I always perceived Bobby as very straight-backed, tight-lipped and uptight."

And Diana Millay, too, remembers Vaughn as something less than a predator: "Bob Vaughn was always fun to work with. I did *Boston Terrier* with him, which was a pilot that didn't go. We worked very hard on it. We liked it—we had a great time and [then] it didn't sell. Bob was the furthest thing from [a big flirt]. He was a very charming, lovely person. We knew each other casually and he was always lovely. He did not come on [to me].

"I found Bob always to be a perfect gentleman. He was

cute and charming and a good [male lead] but offscreen if you had ever given him the incentive he might have [flirted] but I certainly didn't. I was going with my [future] husband so I was never flirting with anybody and that made it very hard for me because at that time, unlike today, there was a casting couch and you were expected to take off your clothes and lie down.

"Right after I got out of school I went out to L.A., although I had been doing television since the age of twelve. I was a real teenager when I was doing the teenage roles. I can remember as a very young girl screaming at Harry Cohn for saying, 'This is it, if you want the part'—he was a horror. I left in tears because I was too young and I came from New York where that really didn't happen and if it did I was too young to know. It shouldn't start when you're [still] a teenager because it's a terrible experience. So many young girls were able to get through it by thinking of the grocery list or the next part [but] I guess I had just been sheltered."

"I didn't believe there was a casting couch," counters Yvonne Craig. "I lucked into the business and I began doing lead roles. Somebody saw me in a restaurant and said, 'How would you like to be in this movie?' I said, 'Oh, no, I don't really think so.' And they said, 'It's opposite John Wayne's son, Pat—we'll pay you a lot of money.' I said, 'Well, maybe.' So I had gone in from the beginning doing lead roles so I didn't ever have to go through any [casting] process. It became established that I was a [leading] actress and they just hired me [based on that]. In the time [period] when I worked they all flirted and played around but we were on such a tight schedule nobody had time [to follow through] so they chose people who were professional [with] work. I was also completely out to lunch. If somebody had not actually thrown me down on a couch I would not have recognized a pass because I wasn't expecting it."

"There was only one man ever in the entire time I was in the business who made a pass at me and it wasn't Bobby Vaughn—it was Desi Arnaz. He was doing a series and he said that he was going to drop the script by my house, which unnerved me because people don't do that. He sat across the room from me and said, 'I would like to keep you.' I said, 'I don't think so.' He said, 'Well, think about it. We Cubans are like this. It has nothing to do with whether you get this part or not. I just want you to know that.' I said, 'Okay.' I called my agent and said, 'I don't want the part but you must not let him know that. Tell him I want the part and we'll see. And so we played it out and

Yvonne Craig and Robert Vaughn in the episode "The Brain Killer Affair" (*photo courtesy Turner Network Television*)

Robert Vaughn seems less than happy over Diana Millay's acceptance of Paul Stevens's attention in the episode "The King of Knaves Affair" (*photo courtesy Diana Millay*)

my playing around with [Desi or not] had nothing to do with it and he offered me the part. I turned it down. I did not play around with him. [But] he was telling me the truth."

Return of the Man From U.N.C.L.E.: The Fifteen Years Later Affair came along in 1983. It was directed by Ray Austin, and Vaughn and McCallum returned as Solo and Kuryakin, along with Patrick Macnee (not as John Steed, but then again, was Sir John Raleigh really his name?). He played the counterpart of the Waverly character created by Leo G. Carroll, who had died in 1972. Other cast members included Tom Mason, Gayle Hunni-

Michael Ansara and Phyllis Newman in the episode "Arabian Affair"
(*photo courtesy Michael Ansara*)

cutt, Geoffrey Lewis, Anthony Zerbe, Keenan Wynn, and George Lazenby in a cameo as "J.B.," driving an Aston Martin DB5 similar to Bond's. Zerbe played T.H.R.U.S.H.'s new mastermind, Justin Sepheran.

In this reunion, written by Michael Sloan, a criminal named Janus engineers the crash of a B-52 equipped with a nuclear bomb and steals the atomic load. Simultaneously former T.H.R.U.S.H. operative Justin Sepheran is being interrogated by U.N.C.L.E. prior to his escape. Raleigh, the new head of U.N.C.L.E., is afraid that there is a plan underway to reactivate T.H.R.U.S.H. And his fears are well founded for that is exactly what Sepheran has planned to do. So Solo and Kuryakin are persuaded to come out of retirement to once again battle the agency's nemesis.

Norman Felton said at the time that the reunion appeared to have been written by a fan who remembered some of the trademarks of the original show and gave them emphasis. Producer Sam Rolfe was less enthusiastic, claiming that the reunion was totally alien to everything that the series represented.

"There's an incredible resurgence of interest in things from the sixties," says Yvonne Craig. "I think that we are in such desperate straits that [the sixties] look like a more appealing time and it's [still] not that far out of touch as say the fifties with Beaver Cleaver's mother in a housedress. Nobody has ever really seen anyone in a housedress. I think [the sixties] are a kinder, gentler place.

"[For instance] I loved doing *Batman*. I've done some comic book conventions since. I've worked with people I would never in my career have worked with had I not done *Batman*. And it did everything I wanted it to for me. Because I came in on the third season it attached a name to my face. It paid me admirably and it's [still] fun now to have people say to me, 'I watched you when I was a kid and now my kids are watching you.'

"[And] I think Bobby and David had a good thing going—they worked well together. *U.N.C.L.E.* was interesting without being supertechnical—it was fun and interesting but it wasn't *Mission: Impossible*."

But aside from the chemistry between Vaughn and McCallum, there were the wonderful props—each gun, created by the MGM special effects department, cost about $5,500. "I wanted one gun capable of shooting single shots or rapid fire automatic shots," producer Sam Rolfe told *TV Guide*, "with sound or silently. I also wanted sleep-inducing darts, explosive bullets, and a gun that could convert to a long-range rifle."

"I think *Man From U.N.C.L.E.* is [still so] popular for entirely different reasons than something like *Dark Shadows*," Diana Millay says. "*U.N.C.L.E.* is popular because it mixed [and I must give credit to Bob] his marvelous sense of humor with terrible plights. People like to see intrigue and [*U.N.C.L.E.*] was larger-than-life intrigue. It was suspense, it was mystery, it was danger, and it had Bob's flair for humor."

But Craig's eulogy for the sixties and Millay's praises of Vaughn and McCallum aside, Felton sums it up more simply: "I think of [*U.N.C.L.E.*] as high entertainment." And he's right.

Fred Gwynne, Yvonne De Carlo, and Al Lewis are joined in *The Munsters' Revenge* by K. C. Martel as Eddie, Jo McDonnell as Marilyn, and Bob Hastings (center) as Lily's cousin, the Phantom of the Opera (*photo courtesy NBC*)

EIGHT

THE MUNSTERS

(September 24, 1964—September 1, 1966)

During the sixties one of television suburbia's strangest and most humorously morbid familes was *The Munsters,* of 1313 Mockingbird Lane. Residing at this address were Frankenstein-like head of the family, Fred Gwynne (late of *Car 54—Where Are You?*) as Herman and onetime film siren Yvonne De Carlo as his oddly lovely better half, Lily. But this romantic coupling was just the beginning. Also in the household were Al Lewis (another *Car 54* veteran) as Grandpa, Butch Patrick as son Eddie, Beverly Owen (and then Pat Priest) as "ugly-duckling" niece Marilyn, and of course, the fire-breathing pet dragon, Spot.

As patriarch of this comically horrifying brood, the tall, gaunt, cadaverish Herman Munster sported a flat square-shaped head, like the Karloffian monster of yore, he had a jagged saber scar on the forehead, darkly-ringed eyes, and bolts screwed into his neck. Though he could at times be dapper, Herman was not a clotheshorse—he was most likely to wear loose, ill-fitting garb.

And how did Gwynne come to look like Herman? Each morning upon arriving at the studio, the top half of a foam latex mask, molded to the shape of his head, was applied to his face with tweezers. Then rubber bolts and washers were attached to his neck. His cheeks, nose, neck, and chin were covered with globs of battleship-gray rubber grease. Next came the powder and black mascara and eyeliner and a nauseating yellowish-green hue, which was applied over the foundation.

A black pencil outlined the ghoulish lips and a black marking pen defined his scars and stitches. The last touches were a human-hair wig and a manicure with black nail polish. Gwynne, at six foot five and 185 pounds,

112

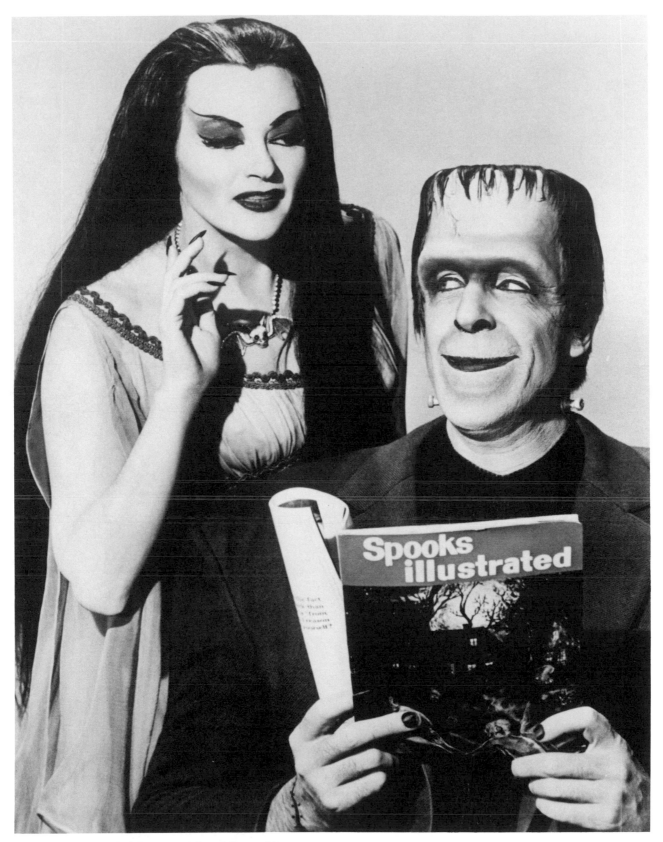

Yvonne De Carlo and Fred Gwynne as Lily and Herman Munster

wore foam-rubber padded trousers, ten-pound elevated shoes, and a shrunken jacket with padded shoulders.

"For the first three weeks," Gwynne confided to *TV Guide* in the mid-sixties, "my back hurt and the high-heeled boots stretched my tendons." Pal Al Lewis consequently suggested that Gwynne hire Julie Andrews's masseuse.

"I felt totally free in my own mind to make my own Herman," says John Schuck, star of the syndicated *Mun-sters Today*, "who was entirely different than Fred [Gwynne's]. He looked different; I wanted a makeup that was much more friendly to me than Fred's was. His main expression primarily came from moving his mouth. And the rest of his face seemed pretty frozen by the makeup. Mine allowed me to move quite well, and when I raised my eyebrows the whole forehead would rise up, and I'm nowhere near Fred's height even in [elevated] shoes that I guess ended up being [only] about six foot seven. I created

In the theatrical feature, *Munster, Go Home*, the family sat for this portrait: (from left), Debbie Watson (standing in for Pat Priest), Al Lewis, Fred Gwynne, Butch Patrick, and Yvonne De Carlo (*photo courtesy Al Lewis*)

a person that was close to me acting like a child. So that was the direction that I went for.

"We only had to wear the makeup twice a week, not every day the way they did, and it took me an hour and a half to put it on and about an hour to remove it. There was one piece which started under the eyebrows and covered the entire head and, of course, the back, and a flap folded down over the ears. The makeup bases have changed an awful lot since the original *Munsters* was done and the

first batch of makeup they gave me irritated me immensely, not so much in the application but in the removal—I couldn't get it off.

"There's been a technological revolution in special effects and plastics and prostheses, makeup bases, emolients, so right now there's a great variety of product out there that's quite comfortable and [we used] one of those space-age technological compounds that somebody mixed together and it worked."

Yet despite Schuck's critique and in spite of his grotesque appearance, Gwynne's Herman had all the charm of a puppy dog and he looked at the world with loving eyes, embracing all with his gentle and innocent warmth. And like a puppy, though he didn't seem to understand everything, and often not much of anything, he exuded loyalty to family. And to provide for those loved ones, he toiled diligently at the local funeral parlor of Gateman, Goodbury and Graves.

By contrast, Lily Munster was hauntingly beautiful and, as some said, as lovely as the day she died. But once you got past first impressions, you realized that she was the same as any other suburban housewife, concerned with homemaking and cooking.

De Carlo arrived at the studio each morning at six to undergo a process similar to Gwynne's. "It's wearisome," she said at the time, "but no worse than being made up as a glamour doll. They used to spend an hour on my hair alone."

And as for her TV rival, Morticia Addams (Carolyn Jones), De Carlo added, "We may become the Casey and Kildare of the witches."

Then there was Grandpa, who at four hundred-plus years of age was a little more than just over the hill. A great practical joker, Grandpa once had formidable powers that over the centuries had dwindled to the simply mischievous, albeit unpredictable.

According to old time vaudevillian and New York City restaurateur Lewis, Grandpa's makeup required "about two hours. I'd get in at six and be ready at eight. About the same time as it probably takes [most women] to put [their] makeup on."

Chalk-face and beady-eyed though he was, Grandpa was idolized by grandson Eddie, who at the tender age of ten was an odd youngster with pointed teeth and ears and a vocabularly consisting primarily of the word "neat."

Not to be overlooked was curvaceous Marilyn with the Pepsodent smile and glossy hair, who was certainly an oddity in her family. Nonetheless, she idolized her surrogate parents and her grandfather, believing, as did they, that she had no beaux because there was something wrong with her appearance. Being the dutiful and loving aunt and uncle that they were, Lily and Herman stood steadfastly by Marilyn, overlooking her "shortcomings."

All in all, the Munsters were a harmless and kind-hearted bunch, and when all had been said and done, were they really any different from the (Ozzie and Harriet) Nelsons or the (Donna Reed) Stones?

So popular was *The Munsters* series, it spawned two feature-length films, *Munster, Go Home* in 1966 and its long-awaited sequel, *The Munsters' Revenge,* a 1981 television movie.

"The first movie wasn't done while we were on the air," says Al Lewis. "*Munster, Go Home* with Terry-Thomas, Hermione Gingold, John Carradine was done after the [series] run. They used a contract player [instead of Pat] for Marilyn."

Today an original *Munsters* cover on *TV Guide* (January 2, 1965) sells for $40 and an original *Munster, Go Home* movie poster sells for $45. And this is just the tip of the merchandising iceberg. There are Herman Munster hand puppets, Herman Munster dashboard dolls, small-scale Munster Koaches, Herman ballpoint pens, and a talking Herman doll which says, "You must come over and meet my mummy."

When these collectibles originally hit the market back in the sixties, they helped to fuel the interest in the first Munsters flick which found the family enroute to England after Herman had been named heir to the title and estate of his distant relative, Lord Munster. Despite the fact that Grandpa changed into a wolf on the high seas and Marilyn had a shipboard romance with a lad whose family was at odds with the Munsters, the clan arrived at Munster Hall on schedule, unaware that their disgruntled and disinherited British relatives had a surprise in store.

Gwynne, De Carlo, Lewis, and Patrick reprised their television roles. Priest, as pointed out by Lewis, was replaced by Debbie Watson. Hermione Gingold appeared as Lady Effgie Munster, Terry-Thomas as Freddie Munster, Robert Pine as Ron Moresby, Bernard (*Bewitched*) Fox as Squire Moresby, John Carradine (Mr. Gateman in the episodes "Herman's Raise" and "The Musician") as Cruickshank, Jeanne Arnold as Grace Munster, Richard Dawson as Joey, Cliff Norton as Herbert, Marie Lennard as Millie, Diane Chesney as Mrs. Moresby, and Jack (*Andy Griffith Show*) Dodson as the shipmate. This flick was written by George Tibbles and Joe Connelly, with Bob Mosher, and directed by Earl Bellamy, who were all involved in the original series.

"The history of *The Munsters* is [that] we did two years [on TV]," Lewis recalls. "We did two films, the second one much later—in 1981. And we did a one-hour show, an Easter special for CBS done on location. I don't where that is—it's kicking around somewhere. That was done during the run."

But Easter wasn't the only holiday that the Munster celebrated. On Thanksgiving Day in 1968 Gwynne and Lewis lounged in the back of the $20,000 Munster Koach

as it rolled through the streets of Manhattan for their fourth the annual Macy's Parade. Gwynne was later quoted in *TV Guide* as saying, "I had to get bombed so I could say hello to little kids for forty blocks. . . . That was my last parade. Four years is too much."

Gwynne, De Carlo, and Lewis, reprised their original roles in *The Munsters' Revenge,* which premiered in late February 1981, in the screenplay written by producers Arthur Alsberg and Don Nelson. Don Weis directed this time around. Edward Montagne was executive producer. Butch Patrick was too old to fill Eddie's shoes, and was replaced by K. C. Martel.

Other cast members included Jo McDonnell as the new Marilyn, and Robert Hastings (who had taken over from Mel Blanc as the voice of The Raven in the series) as Cousin Phantom. Sid Caesar played sinister Dr. Diablo with Howard Morris as his assistant Igor.

This revival was no laughing matter as everyone floundered in a bad script that had Herman and Grandpa being arrested when mistaken for wax-like members of an automated gang. While the rest of the family gathered for Halloween, the two hit the street, a pair of outlaw in-laws on the lam. Gone was the tongue-in-cheek humor that had made the series such a success, and the parody had become caricature.

Though Patrick and Priest were not included in this television movie, they did get the last laugh, along with Lewis in 1985 when the three appeared on the TBS special, *The Best of the Munsters.* Written by executive producer Jeffrey Grimshaw, this reunion was compiled of clips from favorite episodes of the original *Munsters,* as a matronly Marilyn, a grown-up Eddie, and an immortal Grandpa looked back over the years.

"Pat is retired, is a grandmother, and lives in Sun Valley, Idaho," says Lewis of his former costar. "I did a gig in Chicago [recently] and I used [Butch] at a giant disco. We appeared there together. I was doing a weekly show called *Super Scary Saturday* and I used Butch and Pat. I've always had fun working with them. I used them again [when] I did a week with the Shrine Circus in Evansville, Indiana. I did a number of [talk] shows with them—a lot of fun. Two great people."

Yet the special, directed by Rafael Ortiz-Guzman and produced by Toni Pezone, was not the last we'd hear of the Munster clan.

MCA decided to give *The Munsters* a boost again in the late eighties with *The Munsters Today.* Over seventy episodes were filmed during a three-year syndicated run that ended in 1990. None of the original cast members was approached about doing this contemporary takeoff.

"I've never seen [*The Munsters Today*]," says Lewis. "All I can tell you is the reaction I get is they [the old fans] just hate the show. I don't know whether it's because they

Fred Gwynne and Yvonne De Carlo as Herman and Lily fifteen years later in the 1981
TV reunion movie, *The Munsters' Revenge* (*photo courtesy NBC*)

in their minds are comparing it, or on its own they dislike it. They have a terrible aversion to it."

"I'd heard that Al was a little rash in some of the remarks he's made in public," Schuck observes, "but I think he did want to play the part; however, the feeling was if you had one from the old cast, you had to have all of them and that would not have worked. That was the executive decision and I tend to agree with that."

Based on the premise that the family went to sleep for twenty years when one of Grandpa's experiments back-

fired, the revamped *Munsters* show was, at times, overly mock-horror.

"I think [*The Munsters Today*] will be around for a bit. The interesting thing is this show was pretty much presold for that length of time [seventy-plus episodes]," says Schuck. "It's one of the advantages of syndication that stations buy a good number of episodes as opposed to a network situation where they say, 'Well, let's buy six or seven and see how it goes.' So when we signed to do it we knew we had at least one year's worth of shows that we

Pat Priest, Al Lewis, and Butch Patrick got together in the late eighties for "The Best of the Munsters" as a TBS special (*photo by Jeff Slate*)

were going to be doing, and then we knew that if we were picked up it would probably be for the two year period, and it all has to do with merchandising and marketing of products rather than anything regarding whether or not the show's worth being on the air. So it was a little bit of a unique situation in that sense.

"I had seen very few of the [old] shows. I was aware of it. At the time it was on the air, I was strictly a theater actor so I was busy every night. My feeling from the beginning was this—that [the original *Munsters*] was done as well

as it could be. It's a classic, half-hour little comedy show and it was just right for its time, too, because they were still able to make fun of horror movies, and that gave it a satirical edge, and the fact that it was shot on film and in black and white really added to that satirical nature."

Schuck continues: "Lloyd Schwartz was the original [*Munsters Today*] writer and producer for the Arthur Company, and he's a friend and he called up one day and just asked me point-blank if I would consider doing the part [of Herman]."

"On the one hand when Lloyd called, I felt, 'Why are they doing this again? It's been done and it's been done as well as it's going to be.' On the other hand the actor in me said, 'Hey, that's a good a part, Herman's fun. He can be a child one moment and a very deep and philosophical father in another second and that's a very interesting character.'"

"Definitely the story lines [changed] after Lloyd Schwartz left the show at the second half of the first season. I always called us 'Charles in Charge with Green Faces,' but one of the story lines was always some member of the family catching onto the latest craze. We did one whole thing where they moved into an apartment and really went hip with new clothes and all that kind of garbage, only to realize that it didn't make them happy.

"From [our] first script that I read, it was obvious to me that we were going to have the name of *The Munsters* and the character would be the same but there the similarity ended. We were a taped show, we were in color, we were in front of a live audience, and we were an all new cast. Any similarity to the old show was purely coincidental. And there was never any attempt to try to duplicate the old show. We might have done one or two story lines that they had in the first year. We did a show where we ended up becoming fashion models, but that was it.

"I also feel that we did try to imitate almost every family that was on television. It was one of the failings of the show for me because I felt here was a unique family and if they have awaken twenty years later they should retain the same values that they had in the sixties. The uniqueness of who they are as people should affect situations in a very humorous fashion. I think that became [lost] in the approach to the show. I think what you came to see was an attempt to put *The Munsters* very definitely into today's world and in many ways they lost a lot of the innocence that I felt they had."

In addition to Schuck, the new mutant series that ran for three seasons starred Lee (*Barnaby Jones*) Meriwether—hipper than De Carlo—and Howard Morton, who in some ways captures the spirit of Lewis's Grandpa.

"[Lee] is one of the all-time wonderful women of the world, generous of heart and spirit and of great ability," says Schuck. "She's a very serious actress as a matter of fact. She was terrific and again, I felt she and Howard, more than the rest of us, were really able to make their own characters come true. She had a unique way of moving. She would sort of float around the stage and she had a sweetness about her that I really liked. She wasn't quite as cynical or acerbic as Yvonne De Carlo."

"Howard created his own Grandpa, totally different from Al's. Howard is six foot two and very thin and has a tremendous elegance about him. What I just loved so much about Howard's Grandpa was what a wonderful liar he was. He would say one thing and be completely self-righteous and arrogant and extremely selfish. I loved that selfishness about him."

Hilary van Dyke also appeared in the new Munsters show with a bubble-headed interpretation of niece Marilyn, so aptly portrayed in the original series by Monroe look-alike Pat Priest. Jason Marsden was her cousin Eddie.

"It was a producer decision to make Hilary look sexy," explains Schuck, "and it became, as far as I'm concerned, television at its crassest in terms of the clothes she wore. They never really did examine stories that dealt with her character. They concentrated almost entirely on Hilary's looks and that's too bad.

"Jason is really a talented young fellow and again here was a case where I felt we went too far in our stories. Eddie always carried it much too far and he was allowed to talk to his parents in a way that wasn't funny anymore. There's a very fine line and more and more we tended to cross over it. So it's no longer fun but it's almost painful—sometimes Eddie became painful [to watch] in that sense."

John Schuck's TV career goes back to such earlier sitcoms as *Holmes and Yoyo* (he was Yoyo to Richard B. Shull's Holmes) in 1976 and *Turnabout*, a role reversal 1979 comedy with Sharon Gless. And he was Murray the Cop in *The New Odd Couple* (1983). In films, he appeared in *M*A*S*H* and *McCabe and Mrs. Miller*, both for Robert Altman, and on the stage he was Daddy Warbucks in *Annie* on Broadway for over a year and he has appeared on the London stage with Charlton Heston, in *The Caine Mutiny Court-Martial*.

"Sergeant Enright [from *McMillan and Wife*] would probably be the [role] that most people know me by, probably because six years was a pretty good run. We really got on to *Columbo*'s coattails, so to speak, and that was the [show] that really took off and got people to watching the mystery movies. Eventually we developed our own audience."

"The first year [of *The Munsters Today*] we shot in a studio in Hollywood and then the Arthur Company joined forces with Universal and moved its headquarters over [there] so that's where we were shooting, and the first day I went to work on the second season, not only were we shooting on the same stage where I had spent six years with *McMillan* but I had the same dressing room as I had all during that period."

On having worked with Rock Hudson, who lived most of his adult life in the closet, and on the topic of *Bewitched*'s Dick Sargent coming out publicly, Schuck says, "I'm sure [he] still has some residual problems but we've finally come out of the closet [enough] as a society to acknowledge that we do have differences among ourselves. The effects of that admission are far less than they used to be. As long as people are coming out I'd certainly like to see more of it on the executive and producer end. I think that would help the industry perhaps even more than performers. I think overall it's not a bad thing. I think it should one of individual choice—I'm not at all in favor of magazines that choose people that they are going to announce to the world [as] gay. That I think is abhorrent. But if a person wants to I don't think it carries that same stigma, and it certainly doesn't seem to with audiences. And that's where it really counts. Once the industry realizes that someone's sexual preference is not going to affect box office, then you will see the stigma almost completely disappear."

"I've heard nothing about [a *Munsters* revival]," asserts Al Lewis. "My general knowledge of the way Hollywood works [tells me that with the] tremendous success [of *The Addams Family*] Universal might do *The Munsters*."

And Schuck adds, "I don't think it would be a challenge. It would have to have a really unique approach to it that would offer new challenges. I don't begrudge the fact that I did it for a second [but] out of seventy-plus episodes [there are only] five or six episodes that are really good television."

"And even if they did *The Munsters* they wouldn't use any of the original cast," asserts Lewis. "Hollywood thinks that you can be a big star on television, but you're not big enough for the big screen. If they recast *The Munsters* [today] it'd be 'Who's the hot property at the moment?' "

One point to consider about any *Munster* remake is that over the years critics have continually pointed out that Herman and Lily and family were far more mundane though more classic-type horror characters than the upscale Addams Family who played up their uniqueness while the Munsters played at being normal.

Munsters producer Bill Mosher said in the beginning, "We can't worry about the others (*The Addams Family* and *Bewitched*). We are determined to give quality to our show in the hope that the best of the three will survive."

Unless Universal does decide to resurrect *The Munsters*, America's viewing public may have to be content with watching reruns of Lewis and his cohorts as the scheming Grandpa, the bumbling Herman, the nurturing

In *The Munsters Today*, John Schuck and Lee Meriwether as Herman and Lily are joined by Hilary Van Dyke as Marilyn, Jason Marsden as Eddie, and Howard Morton as Grandpa (*photo courtesy John Schuck*)

John Schuck sans Herman Munster guise (*photo courtesy John Schuck*)

Lily, innocent little widow's-peaked Eddie, and dream girl Marilyn.

So what made a show with such an unlikely scenario into a phenomenon that remains popular today? No doubt it was the special talents of an exceptional cast, headed by Fred Gwynne, who in real life was not at all monster-like, but a mild-mannered Shakespearean actor who thrived on such artistic pursuits as painting and sculpting.

"It's twenty-seven years after the fact," Lewis says. "That's the last time we did the weekly show. I think it's endeared itself, running all over the world today in forty-four different countries. It hit a certain part of the pulse of the public and it was, in a true sense, a family show, about a family. It wasn't topical. It didn't date itself. And in spite of the fact that these were people, as we would say, off the wall, they really liked and cared about each another, in spite of their squabbles and whatnot—they really liked each other and the camera picked that up."

And the ever-popular show was frequented by performers who would go on to establish themselves as well-known comedic talents. Among these were Pat Buttram in "All-Star Munster" and Harvey Korman in "Family Portrait," "Prehistoric Munster," and "Yes, Galen, There Is a Herman," which also featured *The Flying Nun*'s Marge Redmond.

Other guest stars included Gavin MacLeod in "The Sleeping Cutie," Don Rickles in "Dance With Me, Herman," and Paul Lynde as Dr. Dudley in "Low-Cal Munster," "Eddie's Nickname," and "Rock-a-Bye Munster." Lynde was later replaced as Dr. Dudley in the second season by Dom DeLuise in "Just Another Pretty Face."

The list goes on: Jane Withers in "Pike's Pique" and "Grandpa's Lost Wife," Alvy Moore in "Bats of a Feather," Bonnie Franklin in "Herman's Sorority Caper," Pat Harrington Jr. in "Mummy Munster," Bill Mumy in "Come Back, Little Googie," Mabel Albertson in "Munster Masquerade," Louis Nye in "Zombo," Charlie Ruggles in "Herman's Driving Test," Emmaline Henry in "Herman, Coach of the Year," Sid Melton in "Rock-a-Bye Munster," Elvia Allman in "The Most Beautiful Ghoul in the World," Dave Ketchum in "Munster the Magnificent," and even Leo Durocher in "Herman the Rookie," and the Standells in "Far Out Monsters."

And the resident cast of *The Munsters* visited the sets of other classic sixties TV programs.

"I did *Lost in Space, Green Acres*—a number of shows," Al Lewis recalls. "I had a lot of fun [on *Lost in Space*). Don Richardson was the director—I had known him from New York. I had a lot of fun working with the cast and [Dr. Smith]." Lewis refers to the "Rocket to Earth" episode of *Lost in Space* (February 15, 1967),

playing Zalto the Magician in a script written by Barry Slater.

Butch Patrick visited *My Favorite Martian* in the "How to Be a Hero Without Really Trying" episode on December 29, 1963, as did Pat Priest in the "My Uncle the Folk Singer" episode on November 8, 1964.

Of his days on the set of *The Munsters,* Lewis recalls, "I never had any problems. Both [Fred and Yvonne] were just super professional people and for me, working with Fred—because I had worked with him on *Car 54*—was an added bonus. Fred Gwynne was hotter than a pistol. The number one voiceover man [for years] and he did movies galore."

"Fred . . . one of our unsung actors," adds Schuck. "One of the best actors we have ever produced. Extraordinary. Anybody who's ever seen him in the theater knows that. A wonderful author [with] his books. They're great. They're quite remarkable. A very brilliant man. I met him only once, years ago at a party down in Greenwich Village."

Gwynne was a Harvard graduate who once made his living as a writer and illustrator of children's books. Though he was born in New York City, as a child Gwynne had traveled extensively in South Carolina, Florida, and Colorado. While attending Groton, Gwynne first attempted to act in the hopes that drama lessons would help curb a speech impediment.

At first he failed but then at the age of thirteen, he was allowed into the thespian society, though he never lost his stammer. After finishing high school in 1944, he enlisted in the navy and served as a radio operator third class on a submarine pursuer in the South Pacific.

Acting was not a priority for six-foot-five Gywnne when he first arrived at Harvard after the war, but it was while there that he began to perform in the nearby Brattle Theater. He soon found himself consumed by the craft, staying on with the Brattle group for two years after his graduation in 1951.

Playing a new role each week, Gwynne was eventually cast in *A Midsummer Night's Dream,* a well-received production which became his ticket to Broadway. It was 1953 and Hasty Pudding Society alumnus Gwynne, whose *Harvard Lampoon* cartoons had been reprinted in *Flair* magazine, soon found himself on the Great White Way performing with Helen Hayes in Mary Chase's *Mrs. McThing.* He also appeared in Brando's *On the Waterfront,* before moving on to countless television appearances.

Though Gwynne had accumulated an impressive list of credits, he decided at this point to supplement his income by returning to writing. Having contributed several stories and cartoons to the *Harvard Advocate,* Gwynne used this experience to land a five-year job with J. Walter Thompson as an ad copywriter, turning out newspaper, magazine, radio, and television advertisements for the Ford Motor Company.

During all this activity, Gwynne, still smitten with the acting bug, also managed to star in *A Winter's Tale* at the Stratford Shakespeare Festival in Connecticut and in *Who Was That Lady I Saw You With?* (opposite Betty White) in Detroit.

The industrious Gwynne juggled vacation time and sick leave to continue with his craft, while branching out as a writer. The end result in the early sixties was several children's books, including *Best in Show, A Chocolate Moose for Dinner,* and *The Battle of Frogs and Mice.*

His canvases were also being heralded at the time at Westchester County art shows, so Gwynne gave up the advertising business. He quickly landed his first major part in a Broadway show, David Merrick's *Irma la Douce.*

In the middle of this successful run on Broadway, Nat Hiken cast Fred as Officer Francis Muldoon in *Car 54, Where Are You?* Hiken was familiar with Gwynne's talents from having used him on *The Phil Silvers Show.*

"There was some sort of fascination when I read the script [of *The Munsters*]," Gwynne told *TV Guide* in July 1965. "I liked the point of view, the satire of old movie monsters. . . . I sensed an aura of what Hollywood used to be. . . . There was an element of parody in the original episodes which ended when the original writers left. . . . But I can't really complain. When you do business you do it for as much money as you can get."

Though still a popular character actor (*My Cousin Vinny*), Gwynne, who with wife Deborah had retired to a farm in Maryland, was diagnosed at age sixty-six with pancreatic cancer. In the spring of 1993 he underwent surgery at Johns Hopkins University Medical Center in Baltimore. He died on July 2, 1993.

While Lily (Mrs. Herman) Munster had a certain style that other female monsters perhaps lacked, she was still a far cry from the seductive Salome, a movie role which had brought acclaim to starlet Yvonne De Carlo.

"Yvonne, as far as I know, is retired and lives in California," says Lewis. "She was here recently and she stopped in to say hello. [But to me] staying in touch is calling each other once a week. I am not great friends with all of them. We had fun working together, but they have their own lives."

De Carlo was born Peggy Yvonne Middleton on September 1, 1922, in Vancouver. Her father was a New Zealander who abandoned her and her mother when young Peggy was three. Mrs. Middleton worked as a waitress in order to pay for her daughter's singing, drama, and dancing lessons at the Vancouver School of Dance. At age seventeen, the young hopeful landed in Holly-

wood, where she enrolled in the famed Fanchon and Marco Dancing School. This training was a prelude to her professional appearances at nineteen in the Florentine Gardens and the Earl Carroll Theatre.

Though she had a number of film roles as a contract starlet beginning in 1942, it would be in *Salome, Where She Danced,* produced by Walter Wanger, that audiences first really became aware of her.

"I'll never forget that audition," De Carlo told *TV Guide* during *The Munsters'* original run. "Mr. Wanger said to me, 'You're good enough so that you'll never have to cozy up to a producer.' " She soon would become Maria Montez's rival as queen of the Universal lot.

Ross Hunter, the fifties and sixties producer (and onetime actor) noted for revamping the sagging careers of

Lana Turner and Jane Wyman, once said that he cut his teeth on "awful ridiculous Audie Murphy westerns or tit-and-sand pictures starring Yvonne De Carlo that I had to make for two-and-a-half dollars."

And along the way De Carlo was pursued in real life by Aly Khan (before Rita Hayworth), Howard Hughes (after Jane Russell), and Lord Lanesborough.

"His Lordship loved my new dress," she once quipped to *TV Guide*. "Little did he know that it was a gift from the Prince of Iran."

Despite her international romances, De Carlo finally settled down with former movie stuntman Bob Morgan, whom she met on the set of *The Ten Commandments*.

George Brown, a British producer, first recognized De Carlo's comic potential when he cast her in the highly popular British film, *Hotel Sahara*. Her appeal as a comedienne resurfaced not long afterward in *The Captain's Paradise*, with Alec Guinness.

Commenting over the years on her role in *The Munsters,* De Carlo often said that she'd never had so much fun as she did on the series. It was, in her estimation, strictly for laughs, and since she'd always wanted to do comedy, it was a wonderful opportunity, as well.

According to her, the cast always kidded one another about the outlandish costumes and makeup. Vanity in no way entered the picture, and certainly had no place in a comedy that was so tongue-in-cheek, she said at the time.

"She has never done anything like this before," producer Bill Mosher told *TV Guide* in the sixties. "But she has picked up the idea wonderfully fast and has given the

Al Lewis hosting the Saturdays-at-noon Superscary Saturday fright fest on TBS in Atlanta (*photo courtesy Superstation TBS*)

character, Lily Munster, warmth and charm."

Tragically, De Carlo's husband Morgan ended up losing a leg in an accident while attempting a stunt in *How the West Was Won* in 1962. To cover rising medical bills, De Carlo—having taken time off to care for her two young sons—went back into acting, accepting anything and everything.

"A lot of [the parts] were no good," she told *TV Guide*. "But I couldn't be fussy."

Though she is more or less retired from show business, one of De Carlo's relatively recent film credits is *The Man With Bogart's Face*, featuring Michelle Phillips, Victor Buono, and Mike Mazurki. And in *Mirror, Mirror*, starring Karen Black, De Carlo turns out to be a real scene stealer despite the allure of brooding beauty Rainbow Harvest as a high schooler who gets even with her uppity classmates with help from an antique mirror inhabited by a demon.

With her comedic timing, De Carlo was the only choice for the daughter of Al Lewis's Grandpa. When Lewis first turned to acting in the twenties he had taken every job that came along. "I've been in the business since 1922," recalls Lewis. "I was [indeed] in the circus. I was about twelve years old. I followed the elephants around. They have no mercy. Then I became a knockabout clown. I also worked the slack wire, rode a unicycle, and played the musical saw. That led to medicine shows; I did vaudeville, I did burlesque."

A native of Brooklyn, Lewis attended Thomas Jefferson High School and then pursued a variety of professions, from salesman, waiter and hot dog vendor to poolroom owner, store detective, and author of children's books and thrillers.

"I did eighteen years of radio [*Mercury Theatre, The Shadow, Jack Armstrong, Little Orphan Annie*]," recalls Lewis. "And the early days of live television. [There was] no transition—not for me. I just did what I had been doing all my life."

In 1949, at the suggestion of a friend, Lewis joined Paul Mann's Actor's Workshop in New York. In the company of fellow students Sidney Poitier, Vic Morrow, and Pat Benoit, Lewis developed his dramatic skills, as well as comic timing. It wasn't long before Lewis was appearing in the *U.S. Steel Hour, Armstrong Circle Theater, Big Story,* and dramas such as *A Tale of Two Cities* and *The Moon and Sixpence*.

"I did about three hundred television shows," remembers Lewis. "Then I found [myself on] Broadway with Phil Silvers, may he rest in peace, and Nancy Walker in *Do Re Mi*. 'Make Someone Happy'. . . great song. I did other Broadway shows, too. Some were flops."

Then *Car 54, Where Are You?* came rolling in in 1961.

"As far as myself personally," Lewis says today, "I had a great deal of fun doing both [*Car 54* and *The Munsters*]. I have never really [made comparisons] because of my background. I just don't engage in that. I would if I were directing the show. [I will say that] *Car 54* had some of the best writing ever done in television. It's difficult to be funny every week, but *Car 54* was beautifully written. The writers were geniuses.

"All I'm concerned about is doing the best I can in the role I am given at that moment. My favorite [role] is the one that I am doing at the moment. I enjoyed playing Grandpa enormously and I had lots of fun playing Leo Schnauser. If I do not have fun doing it, it is a task, a chore, a drudge."

And it must have been fun, for Lewis's enthusiasm for his Schnauser character after a guest spot was contagious; positive response on the part of viewers, no doubt due to his own comedic genius, brought Lewis back on the show as the frustrated doleful Officer Schnauser. *The Munsters* was soon to follow.

Lots of TV guest shots on comedies and drama series came after that. "Then Universal called me to do *The Munsters*. They said they were doing a pilot—would I be interested? I said, 'Send a script.' They sent a script [and] about five days later I went to California."

In the very beginning of his career Lewis couldn't have known that the role for which he'd be best remembered was that of a centuries-old creature in gloves, tux, and swirling cape. Despite the fact that he arrived at the studio at six in the morning to begin his two-hour makeup routine, Lewis says today that he very much enjoyed playing Grandpa.

"I'm always recognized as Grandpa, because you've got to understand that *The Munsters* have been in the United States specifically in syndication for twenty-seven years, never out of syndication. It's so pervasive. If I meet a person who's [thirtyish] or under, they never saw the original, but as *Car 54* is making a comeback on TV, I get those [older fans]. But it'll never catch up to Grandpa."

"[But] I've never seen any of [the episodes]—I've never seen anything I've ever done. I am just not interested. Doing my best is all I care about and that comes from years of training in the circus and vaudeville and burlesque. When I worked vaudeville I didn't go out and wait in the wings for my cue and say, 'Gee whiz, a year and a half ago we had a better singer in Chicago,' It's not my job."

"I went back to live theater [after *The Munsters*]. I worked California, the East Coast, the North, the South, for several years—I did guest appearances, I did personal appearances. I worked carnivals, did movies. I just keep working. I've had the restaurant for five years."

"When I came [back] to New York, I had some ideas, and I met two gentlemen who wanted to open a restaurant with me, so that's what we did. I have a comedy club in New York City. I have a factory in Mt. Vernon that manufactures pasta under the name Grampa's.

"[Not long ago] I did a full-length feature and recreated the role of Leo Schnauser I had [first] done thirty-one years ago in *Car 54*. The only other original cast member was Nipsey Russell. He was Officer Anderson, a switchboard operator. In the movie he plays Captain Anderson. And then I did a wonderful film in New Zealand called *Moonrise*. The last television show that I did, I went down to Orlando and did *Hi, Honey, I'm Dead*. Same old grind—the old mule pulling the wagon.

"I played Mr. Klein, the evil coin collector on *Search for Tomorrow* until they killed me off and then killed the show. Too bad. And a Disney picture, *Save the Dog; Married to the Mob* with that hot director, Jonathan Demme; a video—'The New York City Cabdriver's Joke Book.' "

And that leaves Pat Priest. How did a blond beauty fit into an unlikely familial tableau composed of a serious actor, a sultry film siren, and a former vaudevillian? Replacing Beverly Owen, who left the series after only half a season, Pat Priest was used to being in the spotlight. Her mother was Ivy Baker Priest, the Treasurer of the United States during the Eisenhower administration.

The blue-eyed Priest had tested unsuccessfully for two other series before being cast as Owen's replacement. Born in Salt Lake City, Priest moved with her family at an early age, to a town called Bountiful. During Pat's youth, her mother wrote, produced, and directed road shows for the Mormon Church.

Needing a curtain act to perform during scene changes, her mother taught her to lip synch a comedy record and the act became the hit of the show. Young Pat later performed the routine on KSL-TV in Salt Lake City.

In the meantime, her dad had become more active in politics and soon achieved national prominence. Pat was a junior at Davis High School, when mother Priest was named by Eisenhower to the Washington job, and she took her family with her.

Pat eventually was chosen Queen of the President's Cup Regatta (a major annual Capital social event) and later Queen of the Winchester (Virginia) Apple Blossom Festival and the first Queen of the Azalea Festival in Norfolk, Virginia, a title which both Lynda Byrd Johnson and Peggy Goldwater would later attain.

The five-foot-five Priest had her social coming out at the International Debutantes' Ball in New York and the Thanksgiving Day Cotillion in Washington.

During this time she was elected by a national magazine as one of the Capital's "Ten Most Beautiful Women," making her first professional appearance on her own television show with Art Lamb in Washington, a program she continued for about a year.

Moving to the West Coast, Priest gained dramatic experience in community theater with the Alameda (California) Little Theatre, Oakland's London Circle Players, and Berkeley's Players of the Golden Hind, before heading for Los Altos, where she taught modeling and modeled herself for San Francisco's leading department stores. This ultimately led to television work, including a spot on *Perry Mason,* and films like *Looking for Love* and *Quick Before It Melts,* before being cast in *The Munsters*.

And then there's young Butch Patrick. Long gone were the days of childhood *Munsters* stardom when he found himself settling in Austin, Texas, following a history of substance abuse that began at age sixteen. This downward spiral had culminated in eleven weeks behind bars in 1979. Patrick's mom has been quoted as saying that she regrets ever having let him go into show business. He made the news again during the summer of 1991 when he was sentenced to two years probation, two hundred hours of public service and a $200 fine, as well as $850 in restitution to a limo driver whom he beat up in November 1990.

"I think [Jason Marsden's] parents wouldn't allow [him to follow in Butch's footsteps]," stresses John Schuck, "and I also think he has the ability to make the transition. He's an extremely wonderful cartoonist. He draws very, very well. He does voices, he does a lot of commercials and stuff. He did the *Peter Pan* cartoon. He works a lot. He's very bright, he has a real ability and he works extremely hard. It wouldn't surprise me to see him be a director or something along that line."

As for himself, Schuck says, "I want audiences to remember that whether it was comedy or a serious piece that I always gave them a good time and the thing I would hope my peers would remember is my professionalism. I pride myself on working harder than anybody.

"I'm as amazed as anyone who was involved with [*The Munsters*] that it has run this long," Al Lewis concludes, "and its been nothing but a pleasant experience—wonderful doing the show, and wonderful listening to all the accolades of people all over the world—I travel a great deal—who love the show and who love the character I created and that's why I became a performer sixty-nine years ago. I'd like to be remembered as a great father—a wonderful parent and a performer, who in spite of what you might hear—that he's loud and opinionated and smokes smelly cigars—he always pulled the wagon and got it home in first place. That's all I was ever hired for. That's it. I gave it my best shot. If you can do better, go to it, Jack."

Bob Denver, front and center, with fellow castaways (from left) Russell Johnson, Alan Hale Jr., Dawn Wells, Tina Louise, Jim Backus, and Natalie Schafer (*photo courtesy Sherwood Schwartz*)

NINE

GILLIGAN'S ISLAND

(September 26, 1964–September 4, 1967)

The name Gilligan was actually pulled out of a phone book by creator Sherwood Schwartz. "I wanted the word 'island,' " recalls Schwartz, "and I wanted a name that automatically meant that it was a comedy show."

As it turned out, the viewers may have caught on but the critics did not. At the time of the series' debut it was labeled as inept, moronic, and humorless. In fact, *Gilligan's Island* received the worst collection of overnight reviews since *The Beverly Hillbillies*.

Syndicated columnist Hal Humphrey called it "the kind of thing one might expect to find running for three nights at some neighborhood group playhouse."

"I was not disheartened by the reviews—only a bit angry with the lack of understanding of what was being attempted," complains Schwartz. "Not a single critic reviewed the show from its sociological aspects. But

sometimes the public finds things the critics do not. They tune in to what they want."

Bob Denver, Gilligan himself, said that it didn't take an intelligent person to laugh at a monkey stealing someone's dinner or somebody getting hit on the head with a coconut: "It sounded so silly to me," he recalls, "I could not believe that the network was going to allow us to do something like that! I would finish a script on Friday and say, 'That was the stupidest, silliest one we've done yet,' and a crew member would say, 'Did you read next week's?' And he was right. It was worse [but] it was fun. I don't think the critics were ready for broad, silly, physical comedy."

And Tina Louise, who portrayed Monroe-like starlet Ginger Grant, was even more emphatic, labeling the first show as a cartoon and setting herself up for a misunder-

The Captain and his little buddy, Gilligan (*photo courtesy Sherwood Schwartz*)

standing with the network which continued even after the show ended.

Already having established herself as a sultry fifties socialite, model, and Broadway ingenue, Louise had come to Hollywood expecting *Gilligan's Island* to be her ticket to fame and success. But when she saw the first episode, she claimed to be ashamed of what she had gotten herself into: "I had studied at the Actors Studio and I had started to get some interesting roles and some good reviews. I had heard about what series were like but I really didn't know how it would be. In this medium everyone performs—there's no such thing as a real moment, an honest reaction. You're not acting, not the way I studied it."

Her critique of the series perturbed Schwartz, as he spoke to *TV Guide* at the time about the series: "I dare say Tina may always feel unfulfilled. She's an integral part of a major hit. What else does an actress want? I don't know what would make her happy. It seems to me that she's not a very happy person. I don't thoroughly understand her."

And today he elaborates further: "The fact of the matter is these were not supposed to be real people—they were supposed to be prototypes [and] to help that concept along nobody had a last name—the Professor is the Professor, they never call him anything but that. If I had taken seven offbeat individuals and put them in the jungle, the audience wouldn't understand what I was doing. Each had to represent a different segment of society: the wealthy, the

The castaways after finding a theatrical trunk washed ashore (*photo courtesy Sherwood Schwartz*)

130

Still Gilligan after all these years (*photo courtesy Fred Amsel and Associates*)

Hollywood glamour girl, the country girl, the Professor, the misfit, and the resourceful bull of a man. [They didn't even] wear regular clothes—it was just a very different concept."

"My closet was all red shirts and blue pants," concurs Denver, "and sneakers on the shelf and that was it."

"I'm an enormous believer in uniforms," says Schwartz. "One of the big reasons for the success of many shows is identification—the sheriff with his badge, the doctor with his white jacket. You tuned into *Gilligan's Island* and in one second you knew which show you were looking at. I wanted them to be unique as characters and to be very, very different from each other. I wanted seven prototypes of people in our society. And those were the ones I chose."

But despite the uniqueness and the glamour of her character, Ginger Grant, Tina Louise has still not changed her tune after all these years: "I guess it's a good fantasy show for a lot of people," she concedes, "[but] to think it's being perpetuated—being put out there again!"

From the beginning, the rest of the cast felt alienated from Louise because of her star image. And there may have been some truth to their allegations of her star power, for at one point CBS president James Aubrey relented to Louise's demands and fired a director who had dared to dispute her interpretation of Ginger.

"The only one that had any kind of temperament was Tina," recalls Schwartz today. "I'll tell you what she was promised and this led to strained relations between us. She came out from New York, they paid to get her out of a play. I thought she would be great for the part [though] I did not originally suggest her. She came out and read the first few scripts and clearly saw that the show was mainly the Skipper and Gilligan. She came storming into my office and said, 'I've just read the first [few] scripts and I can't believe what I'm reading. I was told this show was supposed to be about a movie star who gets shipwrecked with six other people on an island and this is not about a movie star. I'm just one of the characters and not even the main character.' I said to her, 'No, you're one of seven very important people and the way the show will be done is to rotate the stories. You have not read a story yet that features the character Ginger. Every fifth week or so you will be the featured player. The Skipper and Gilligan are that main force [though] because it is, after all, not 'Ginger's Island' but 'Gilligan's Island.' You'll have plenty of good roles so take it easy.' I calmed her down. She wanted to go back to New York. She was furious."

But despite the turmoil, Louise managed to keep her cool as she maintained her sexy image through ninety-eight episodes, readily admitting at the time that the character was loosely based on Monroe.

"I was a great fan of hers," she says today, "I knew the quality she had and how to play it so it would work."

She also admits to having admired the strength Monroe showed in manipulating her career toward quality films, a knack which has often escaped Louise despite her own looks and talent.

But Schwartz does give credit where credit is due: "Sometimes you get lucky [if you're aware of people's attributes]," he says. "The character of Ginger Grant as originally written and as presented in the pilot was a Hollywood-type sophisticated kind of lady who said really sharp things and that [wasn't] something Tina could do. Tina could play a languorous, feminine, sexy woman and it was clear as soon as we started rehearsing that the characters needed to be changed. The character was changed to fit [Tina] because she did not fit the character as originally written. You can't force an actress to play against her own abilities. I give [Tina] enormous credit for that characterization because that was never intended. She made it work and I let her."

"I think Tina Louise created a totally original and unique character," agrees Connie Forslund, one of the two actresses who subbed for Louise in the *Gilligan* reunion movies. "I don't think she was imitating Marilyn Monroe—it's just that their two characters were sort of in the same category—beautiful, sexy and kind of [unexpectedly] funny ladies, a kind of innocence mixed with sexuality—they both had that. I loved Tina Louise on *Gilligan's Island.*"

"When I was in Wisconsin, where I grew up," adds Forslund, "everyone watched [the show]—it's a classic. And the funny thing is, when I was a teenager, a couple of friends of mine used to tell me I looked like Tina Louise. I'm not a redhead but I thought that was a tremendous compliment. In a way I wished that I'd let them dye my hair red [for the movie] because I was wearing a wig and wigs are just never quite that flattering."

And it's a fact that Tina Louise, the original redhead, was misled by CBS executives into thinking that the series was to be a star vehicle for herself—a misassumption that caused her to abandon a costarring role on Broadway with Carol Burnett in *Fade Out, Fade In* to report to Hollywood. But even at that, Jayne Mansfield, not Louise, was the network's first choice.

And certainly, there had been a breakdown in communications somewhere along the way, as the pilot had already been filmed without its supposed star, as well as minus Dawn Wells (Mary Ann) and Russell Johnson (the Professor).

"[CBS] had sold her a bill of goods," concedes Schwartz, "telling her that this show was about a movie star—that was ridiculous. Very often, producers are not aware of behind-the-scenes dealings that networks will engage in in order to get a certain performer to do a certain show. You don't know what's going on at the network. [Today] I don't blame her for being angry. She was

Gilligan creator Sherwood Schwartz (*photo courtesy Sherwood Schwartz*)

furious [too] when the show ended and she was typecast. The more successful and the more identifiable the character, the bigger the problem for the actor. The further you can get away from your [recognizable] character the better off you are as a performer.

"To this day Tina Louise believes that the show ruined her life because she started out as a dramatic actress, at least in her own mind. Her intentions were to play [varied] roles but once she got into *Gilligan's Island* and went other places to [read for] a dramatic part, they said, 'What we want is this tall redhead that's funny in a sexy kind of way.' That's why Tina wouldn't do any of the two-hour shows [but] it didn't do her any good because no matter what, when you say her name, everybody says, 'Oh, Ginger on *Gilligan's Island.'*"

"In L.A. they do tend to type," agrees Forslund, "so I think that [generalization connected her to Marilyn]. This was one of the difficulties I had after I played Marilyn Monroe. [My agent would call and say] 'Oh, they want a Marilyn,' and I didn't want to play Marilyn again. For me, I considered it to be a stretch. I didn't want to box myself in and even that was a concern with *Gilligan's Island,* but it was something I couldn't turn down.

"Tina Louise is a very gifted actress," continues Forslund, "and I know from playing Marilyn Monroe [myself] that it gets hard to break away from that image as you get older and want to play [multi]dimensional roles. I don't know why Tina Louise didn't want to do the reunion movies. She may have felt that was then and this is now and [that she wanted to] pursue new things. The one thing that made me reluctant to do it was that [Tina was] so wonderful and, let's face it, when people tune in to watch *Gilligan's Island* they want to see Tina Louise. But I have no regrets about doing it. I had a wonderful time."

The series became so popular in syndication that the cast (minus Louise) was reassembled for three made-for-TV movies: *Rescue From Gilligan's Island* in 1978, *The Castaways From Gilligan's Island* in 1979 and *The Harlem Globetrotters on Gilligan's Island* in 1981.

"The first [reunion] that we did," says Schwartz, "went right through the roof. And that sparked the others."

In it the castaways were rescued, only to be lost at sea again. Luckily that was only a temporary setback, as they were once again saved in the sequel, with the island being converted into a tourist trap to accommodate the likes of guest stars Tom Bosley and Marcia Wallace.

The final installment was a joke. This time around Martin Landau and Barbara Bain came along for the ride as a mad scientist and his assistant who engineer a squad of basketball-playing robots.

The best of the three reunions was *Rescue From Gilligan's Island,* with Judith Baldwin replacing Tina Louise and also featuring Vincent Schiavelli as Dimitri,

Art Lafleur as Ivan, and Norman Bartold as the producer, among others.

Produced by Sherwood Schwartz and Lloyd Schwartz, the teleplay was written by David P. Harmon, Elroy Schwartz, Al Schwartz and Sherwood Schwartz. Music was by Gerald Fried ("Gilligan's Island Theme" by Sherwood Schwartz).

"I don't know how she can think one two-hour movie can tarnish her image when *Gilligan's Island* is showing five times a day everywhere in the country," Bob Denver said of Tina Louise at the time.

But she would not hedge on her earlier assessment of the series: "I don't have anything against it," she insisted, "I'm proud of the success—I think it's charming, amusing—it's [just] something I did so long ago. I had this mass exposure so I thought maybe I could do something I would like to do—if you don't have exposure you don't get to do anything. I didn't take [the series] because I wanted to be in a television series. I didn't feel fulfilled doing [those] shows. Most were not quite inventive."

Costar Dawn Wells, for one, was not surprised: "I don't have any hostile feelings about [Tina's absence]. I do have animosity for those who bad-rap [the shows which brought them recognition]. If you don't want to work on television then don't do it! I haven't seen Tina very much over the years. There were some problems with [her]. We weren't surprised that she didn't do the movies."

"When we were doing *Rescue From Gilligan's Island,* Tina wasn't absolutely sure that she wouldn't do it," Schwartz recalls, "because life had not been too good to her and yet she was torn because she didn't want to do that character again and a lot of money was at stake—we offered her a great deal of money. So she called and said, 'No, I can't do it.' Two days later she said, 'I will do it,' and then she said, 'No' again. She did this for three weeks and finally lost her agent who thought she was crazy. She was great in *Gilligan's Island.* Everybody expected [the reunion] to be a big show and there was a lot of money involved. So [her agent] thought she was being foolish. She left me with exactly five days to find a replacement and that's not easy and Judith Baldwin was the best of the girls that I saw at that time. If I'd had two or three weeks I would have done better."

However, today Louise directly contradicts Schwartz and his offer of big money, claiming that she didn't do the reunion because he didn't offer her enough.

"But, nobody can fill Tina's shoes," insists Schwartz, "because she wears a size eleven—she has very big feet. She really has huge feet. But we needed somebody who could sing [and] Connie Forslund can. That's why we didn't use Judith Baldwin. I didn't think Judith was all that great [as Ginger]. Our problem with [her] wasn't her fault. I'm not saying that Judith was terrible but she

Jim Backus and Natalie Schafer as Thurston and Lovey Howell (*photo courtesy MGM/UA
Television*)

wasn't as good as Connie Forslund."

"I started out in New York and I did theater there," says Forslund, "I did four Broadways plays, the most successful of which was called *Scapino*. I've done a lot of [episodic] television work, like *Thirtysomething, Murder, She Wrote, Magnum, P.I., Making a Living, Love Boat, Taxi,* and *Fantasy Island*.

"Probably the most attention-getting thing I did was a miniseries *Moviola*—I played Marilyn Monroe. That was a year and a half before I did *Gilligan's Island* and I'm sure that's why I was hired. Tina, who didn't want to do it, had [as I've said before] a very Marilyn-like quality. At the time I hadn't even been aware that there had been two *Gilligan's Island* reunions."

Forslund continues: "I remember that [at the audition] all they wanted me to do was to sing and I had been a singer-dancer but I was more of a dancer and not much of a singer, so [Schwartz] said, 'Just sing a song,' and I said, 'I don't really know a song.' He said, 'Sing "Twinkle, Twinkle, Little Star," but sing it really breathy.' So I sang it really breathy and I walked away thinking, 'Well, that was a waste,' but they hired me [and] I was delighted to do it. To spend a month on a sound stage with almost the entire original cast of *Gilligan's Island*, all the Harlem Globetrotters and Barbara Bain and Martin Landau was one of the most fun experiences I've had in my entire career."

But in the end, even if all the allegations of bickering and star tripping were true, who could fault Tina Louise? After all, she was the only cast member with name recognition. When magazines did cover stories on *Gilligan's Island*, it was her picture they wanted, not Denver's or Alan Hale's.

"I thought Bob was terrific," stresses Schwartz, who holds a master's degree in both zoology and psychology. "He's a very, very bright man. You could not have gotten a better Gilligan, although he was not my first choice. My first choice was Jerry Van Dyke. Carroll O'Connor was flown in from New York and was tested along with thirty other guys [for the Skipper] and he was rejected. That was the most difficult character to cast.

"I wrote the [original] presentation which included the philosophy of the show which was basically a social microcosm. If people who, because they are wrecked on an island, have to learn to live with one another, that's really the philosophy—that people, when forced to, find ways to accommodate each other. They may have nothing in common to begin with, but they sure better find ways to deal with each other if they're gonna be stuck someplace, and in this case I chose an island so they couldn't get off.

"So I made this presentation and I went to an agent and [he] directed me to CBS because one of his clients was Phil Silvers who had a deal [there] and with United Artists

and the deal included the fact that Silvers, who at that time was about to start a new show also, and his company could sponsor another show—that CBS would have to give them the money to foot the bill for another series in which Silvers did not appear, and they chose *Gilligan's Island*.

"So I went up to CBS and talked to the head of development on the West Coast. His counterpart in New York was the head of programming, James Aubrey, and they worked like a team, and I had enormous problems with Mr. Aubrey, who felt that it was a show that had nowhere to go because it was a show locked [onto] an island with the same seven people. [Aubrey] said, 'All right, if you guys are in love with a deserted island, we wreck them there the first week. The second week they have a new adventure, they fix the boat and they're off someplace else. I don't like the idea of staying there. I want a charter boat to take people to different places.' So he never understood what I was talking about and kept insisting that the show should be about the Skipper and Gilligan and that the five passengers [were] just for the first week.

"And I said, 'That's not my idea. My idea's the social interactions of seven unrelated people who form a society of sorts on an island—that's the idea.' [Aubrey] said, 'You can't do that idea' and this is the battle that we had—it eventuated in his putting another show on the air called *The Baileys of Balboa*, where he took his version of my idea, and that was a failure [it lasted one season]. And in that series he had Sterling Holloway play the Gilligan part and he had Paul Ford play his [version of] the Skipper. He matched all the characters and did it his way.

"And he felt that the exposition involved in setting up the show each week—if you have to keep giving the background every week—was a major problem—and I used to tell him I would have a song written that would tell all that background in sixty seconds, a tuneful melody with the proper lyrics that would detail the way they got there. At that time the technique was not yet really in use.

"Once the pilot was made [at a cost of $175,000 during a six day stint in a remote section of Kauai] the troubles started. Virtually everybody at CBS liked the premise. Hunt Stromberg, West Coast vice president, was very, very high on it. But Jim Aubrey [still] disliked the show.

"United Artists refused to allow me to do a song at the opening of the show," says a still incredulous Schwartz. "I was told 'No'—no reasons given."

Consequently the pilot was sent to New York sans theme song and rejected outright. At this point Schwartz decided to do it his way: "I was forced to write the song myself to show [Aubrey] what I meant—[that the song] was the only solution to the problem." Next Schwartz reedited the existing footage and sent out the second version of the pilot.

"They tested it with an audience, and it just went right through the roof," recalls Schwartz. "They [even] tested it twice more. Again the audiences indicated that the show would be a hit. This was in the final week of the selling season. They were locking up the 1964–65 schedule. So Aubrey finally gave in.

"But then the badgering started. The network demanded to know who could identify with a Hollywood actress-type. Or a billionaire for that matter. The network brass even labeled the Professor as colorless. On one point the network won out—three of the actors were replaced [by Tina Louise, Dawn Wells, and Russell Johnson], and because recasting characters demanded that new footage be added, Zuma Beach was substituted for Hawaii.

"I wanted the pilot to air first," Schwartz says. "Unfortunately I did not have complete creative control of this show. I was overruled. It was an outlandish beginning. If you're telling a story about people who get shipwrecked, the only honest way is if the first show is about how they got shipwrecked.

"The network did not [air] the pilot episode first. I thought it was ridiculous to start the new series with [the castaways] already on the island. I said, 'I think the first episode has to be how they were wrecked, how they built these crummy huts that they live in, and how they set up housekeeping,' and [CBS] would not permit that, which meant that they wanted to dump the pilot. The pilot is the Christmas episode. The first year I resurrected about 75 percent of the pilot—all of the footage that didn't have the three [players who had been recast]. I shot new footage with Tina, Dawn, and Russell so that viewers saw only about a portion of the original pilot that was shot in Hawaii."

"A lot of the criticism that the show got was that it didn't make any sense starting out on this island with this group of people—how did they get there? Which is a logical question. And I wanted to answer it using the pilot."

In the Christmas episode, called "Birds Gotta Fly, Fish Gotta Talk" (directed by John Rich), Gilligan's Christmas wish is to be rescued.

Gilligan's Island, as the world came to know it, followed seven people stranded on a deserted isle in the Pacific after their pleasure craft ran aground during a tropical storm. Aside from Denver, Hale, Louise, Wells and Johnson, the two other cast members included Jim Backus and Natalie Schafer as the very wealthy Thurston Howell III and his doting wife Lovey.

As for *Gilligan's Island,* Schwartz says, "My personal favorite is one called 'The Little Dictator.' It tells the story of the world. People only know how to behave like they behave. [The dictator] was exiled from his country and having some remorse, the firing squad doesn't shoot him, they just take him to a desert island so he can live out his life and die there. And what does a dictator know how to do? He knows how to dictate so he gradually assumed control of the island. He also had a gun. It's the story of oppression. This particular episode had a lot of philosophy in it. They submitted to a lot of things he made them do because he had the gun. Like any people held under a dictator's thumb, if they want democracy they have to fight for it. So [the castaways] had to scheme on how to get rid of the dictator in order to bring back the democracy they'd enjoyed before he got there. When people are oppressed and they really, absolutely must experience a return of respectability on their own terms, they have to get rid of [oppressors] and that's what [the castaways] did with this guy."

As an interesting footnote, when Ginger finally managed to get the gun away from the dictator, she refused to hand it over to any of the men on the island.

"Eventually there was another revolution in his country and the firing squad came and took him off the island. Because it has very strong political overtones and really tells the history of mankind in its own comical way, that's my favorite episode."

"The Little Dictator" guest-starred Nehemiah Persoff as Rodriguez and was directed by Jack Arnold. The script was by Bob Rodgers and Sid Mandel.

"Every six or seven weeks I would have a [new] character to come aboard to lend a different tone," adds Schwartz, "It was a relief. From time to time we would have a guest [star]. Hans Conreid was on the show twice, and Vito Scotti was on the show [several] times."

Hans Conreid played the title role in "Wrongway Feldman" and "The Return of Wrongway Feldman," both written by Fred Freeman and Larry J. Cohen and directed by Ida Lupino.

Scotti guested in such episodes as "Diogene, Won't You Please Go Home" and "So Sorry, My Island Now" (in both of which he played a Japanese soldier), as well as "Ring Around Gilligan" and "The Friendly Physician" (in both of which he played Dr. Balinkoff).

"It was really fun because each week was so different," Bob Denver told Joan Rivers in November of 1991. "We had good guest stars—we had Don Rickles on and he was good for the first two days and the third day he started [in]."

Rickles appeared as Norbett Wiley in "The Kidnapper," which was written by Ray Singer and directed by Jerry Hopper. Rory Calhoun played Jonathan Kincaid in "The Hunter," written by Ben Gershman and William Freedman and directed by Leslie Goodwins. Sterling (*The Baileys of Balboa*) Holloway played Burt in "The Pigeon," written by Brad Radnitz and directed by Michael J. Kane.

Dawn Wells, who'll always be Mary Ann from *Gilligan's Island* (*photo courtesy Fred Amsel and Associates*)

In reality, he is a thief on the run with over a half million in his possession. This episode was written by Dick Conway and directed by Abner Biberman.

"Most people's favorite [episode]," Schwartz continues, "is 'The Producer'—that was the show with Phil Silvers. [He] lands on the island and we did a very interesting combination of music. We used operatic themes and did a musical version of *Hamlet*."

On a worldwide talent search, Silver, in his arrogance as conniving Harold Hecuba, intimidates the filthy-rich Thurston and Lovey Howell into acting as his butler and maid. The castaways produce the musical *Hamlet* in order to boost Ginger's sinking spirits, as she mourns the fact

Russell Johnson, the Professor, then and now (*photos courtesy Sherwood Schwartz and Fred Amsel and Associates*)

Zsa Zsa Gabor played Erika in "Erika Tiffiany-Smith to the Rescue," which was written by David P. Harmon and directed by Jack Arnold. Erika arrives on the island in her yacht and falls head over heels for the Professor. Henny Backus, Jim's real-life wife, turned up as a native mother in "Gilligan's Mother-In-Law." This episode was written by Budd Grossman and directed by Jack Arnold. Kurt Russell played the jungle boy in "Gilligan Meets the Jungle Boy," written by Howard Merrill and Howard Harris and directed by Larry Dobkin. Gary Nelson directed some episodes, as he had on *The Baileys of Balboa*.

And in "Little Island, Big Gun," Larry (*F Troop*) Storch played mobster Farrell, who lands on the island with his henchman and passes himself off as a missionary.

that she has been away from Hollywood for too long. The episode, written by Gerald Gardner and Dee Caruso, was directed by Ida Lupino, at the time the most prominent (if not the only) female director in television.

"['The Little Dictator'] is a stronger show in terms of [content]" Schwartz admits, "but as pure entertainment 'The Producer' is probably the best show that we did."

Bob Hope was Schwartz's first employer back in radio in 1939. Schwartz began his TV career with *The Joan Davis Show*. His other credits include *The Brady Bunch, The Brady Brides, Harper Valley, P.T.A.* and *The Invisible Woman*, a 1983 television movie with Bob Denver. In 1988 Schwartz did *A Very Brady Christmas*, and a short-lived hour-long series in 1990 called *The Bradys*. Schwartz has even turned down a proposal to do *The Brady Bunch on Gilligan's Island*, claiming "I don't think the public is ready for that."

Most recently Sherwood Schwartz and son Lloyd, along with Sherwood's brother Elroy, have finished the screenplay of *Gilligan's Island: the Movie*. For the stage there is *Gilligan's Island: the Musical* (which has already premiered regionally), written by Sherwood and Lloyd with music by Laurence and Hope Juber.

"I never had [a favorite episode]," confesses Denver. "They were all so silly. The one in which the lion almost attacked me I guess I remember best."

Denver is referring to "Feed the Kitty," written by J. E. Selby and Richard Sanville and directed by Leslie Goodwins, in which a caged lion washes ashore and the castaways form a safari to capture the big cat.

"Bob was married to this wonderful [Southern] lady so it was fun getting to know both of them," recalls Forslund. "In fact we kept in touch for a little while after that. [He] is a really gifted actor and entertainer. In a way, I think *Gilligan's Island* has been a kind of mixed blessing because it's had such tremendous success in syndication—so that he in one way suffers from overexposure. I think he should be doing a lot more [professionally].

"I had a relationship with Barry Bostwick a number of years ago and we had rented a house on Kauai and [there was] a guest book which we signed, and when I met Bob and his wife, Dreama, they said, 'Oh, yeah, we saw your name in the guest book [when we were in Kauai].' I'd love to work with Bob again."

"We filmed next to the Hollywood Freeway out in the San Fernando Valley," recalls Denver. "We usually couldn't shoot until half an hour after rush hour because the traffic noises were too loud. The lagoon was there, too. There were one hundred shows [actually ninety-eight episodes, sixty-two in color and thirty-six in black and white, which Turner eventually colorized] and we kind of stumbled along for the first three or four months and then we got into the top ten and kind of stayed [there] for the three years.

"In 1963 when I signed, no one had any idea things could run for twenty-five years. Plus there were no residuals—you got paid off in two years and that was it. You felt lucky if you got two years reruns.

"I did another series after *Gilligan* called *The Good Guys*, which spiraled right out of sight—in two years it was gone. And then I did another one—a syndicated show called *Dusty's Trail*, a western."

Joyce Van Patten and Herb Edelman were with Denver in *The Good Guys*, and *Dusty's Trail*, a sort of landlocked *Gilligan's Island* out west, was a Schwartz package. Forrest Tucker and Jeannine Riley costarred. Three episodes of *Dusty's Trail* were strung together into a feature film called *The Wackiest Wagon Train in the West*.

"Then I started doing theater—my first love—and so then I did that for about ten years and interspersed [that] with three *Gilligan* movies and whatever Hollywood came up with.

"I'm typecast," Denver admits. "Anybody in a series that's been running that long is just typecast—the viewers love it [so much]—it's from their childhoods. *Gilligan* is going to run forever because viewers love that kind of humor—slapstick."

And Schwartz agrees: "If you look back historically, the characters that were extreme characters [all] had extreme difficulty shedding that image. And this was such a highly unusual show—the characters were not your everyday people. The more different [the characters] the harder it is for those people to work in other circumstances."

Denver says, "I lived in Vegas for five years and [have since] moved to West Virginia. It's just a really pretty area and I like the people. I have a young son, Colin, and he watches *Gilligan*. All my kids grew up with the show. [He also had two children by model Maggie Ryan.] I kind of feel sorry for them being Gilligan's sons—they had to go through the teenage years when they went, 'Oh, boy, thanks Dad!' They wished their father wasn't Gilligan [but] now the older ones are grown and they enjoy [the series]. They got into their twenties and realized it was not that bad. But when they were in grammar school it was kind of hard."

Bob Denver was born in New Rochelle, New York, and at the age of sixteen he moved with his family first to Brownwood, Texas, where they operated a candy manufacturing business, and later to California.

As a law student at Loyola Marymount University in Los Angeles, Denver joined the Del-Ray Players and discovered he had a knack for acting. His college theater work included *High Button Shoes, See How They Run, Joan of Lorraine, The Male Animal*, and *Little Falstaff*.

After he graduated in 1957, he went back for a semester to star in *Harvey* and was spotted by Ben Bard, new director of talent for Twentieth Century-Fox. (Denver's

Connie Forsland, who took over the role of Ginger Grant in *The Harlem Globetrotters on Gilligan's Island*

sister was Bard's secretary and this connection would later lead to *Dobie Gillis*.) Denver would go on to play another nervous young seaman in *The Silent Service*. In the meantime he worked for the post office and as an athletic director and history and mathematics teacher at a children's school in Pacific Palisades.

For his role in *The Many Loves of Dobie Gillis* as teenage Dobie's beatnick buddy, Maynard G. Krebbs (1959–63), Denver is fondly remembered along with Dwayne Hickman (Dobie Gillis), Tuesday Weld (Thalia Menninger, in a recurring role), Warren Beatty (Milton Armitage, for several episodes), Stephen Franken (Chatsworth Osborne), Shelia James (Zelda Gilroy), and Frank Faylen and Florida Friebus (Dobie's parents). There were two pilot revivals: *Whatever Happened to Dobie Gillis?* (1977) and *Bring Me the Head of Dobie Gillis* in 1988, which had Connie Stevens in the role of Thalia.

"Dawn is delightful," expounds Forslund on the perky brunette who was one of the *Gilligan* costars, pert Mary Ann Summers. "She's a lot like her character. She's just warm and bubbly and fun—incredibly youthful with an incredible attitude about life."

"Dawn Wells IS that sweet, little girl next door," agrees Schwartz, "That's her!"

There isn't any cast member more grateful for her role on the series than Wells, a former Miss Nevada and Miss America. The great-great granddaughter of a stagecoach driver, Wells never expected to win the Miss America title in 1960, and though a chemistry major at Stephens College in Missouri, she soon switched to drama, going on to get a B. A. at the University of Washington.

She then gave herself a year to become an actress and having only done summer stock at the Pink Garter Theater in Jackson, Wyoming, she promptly got an agent and landed her first acting job in just six weeks.

She soon found herself portraying poor Mary Ann, who gets marooned on her first trip away from Kansas. This was to be the highlight of her career. Life after *Gilligan's Island* included guest roles in shows ranging from *The Invaders* and *The Wild, Wild West* to *Matlock* and *ALF* (on which she reprised her Mary Ann role, polka dot outfit and all). *Gilligan* also led to two animated spin-offs, *The New Adventures of Gilligan* and *Gilligan's Planet,* with Dawn Wells doing both Mary Ann and Ginger.

Wells, who married agent Larry Rosen and generally avoids the show business spotlight, is grateful that she has been steadily employed throughout the years. She has even taught acting at Stephens College and has also designed a line of clothing. She is not at all bitter about the lack of residuals from *Gilligan's Island*. As it was, getting paid only for the first five reruns, she philosophizes that this alone doubled the salary she was paid at the time.

She even credits her uninterrupted employment to the fact that *Gilligan's Island* is still on the air, and remembers it more fondly than does Tina Louise, labeling it as pure slapstick and simple escapism.

Tina Louise was born Tina Blacker on February 11, 1934, in Brooklyn. After the divorce of her parents (her father was a candy store proprietor), her mother married socialite doctor John Myers, and Tina was enrolled at the exclusive Scarborough High in Westchester. She later studied at Miami University, the Neighborhood Playhouse in New York, and the Actors Studio.

Louise was a surname invented by Tina when she was first bitten by the acting bug. At the Actors Studio she met Joanne Woodward and in 1953 was called New York's number one debutante. By the mid-fifties, having made her professional debut as a chorus girl, she was being spotlighted in such publications as *American Weekly* and was appearing on Broadway in *Two's Company* with Bette Davis and *Almanac* with Orson Bean.

But scandal nipped at her heels when she was battered by a date, leading to newspaper headlines, and though she went on to press charges, the chauvinistic judge was overly lenient with her assailant.

Tina Louise also appeared as Appassionata von Climax in the musical *Li'l Abner,* in the wake of her mother's sensational divorce trial. Both her mother and Dr. Myers charged each other with adultery, with the judge siding with the doctor. Denying her mother's alleged infideli-

Tina Louise as movie star Ginger Grant

ties, Louise went on to Hollywood to receive good notices as sexy Griselda in her first film, *God's Little Acre,* in 1958.

Though much has been said about her rapport (or lack of it) with the rest of the *Gilligan's Island* cast, Louise insists that her character Ginger, next to that of Gilligan, was the most popular: "We were the most outstanding characters that the audience identified with."

On this point Wells is again at odds, insisting that she (as Mary Ann) got the most fan mail, no doubt because of her girl-next-door image.

In the long run, Tina Louise may have made a wise move in not joining the Gilligan reunions. She enjoyed more visibility than Wells in her career in the years immediately following *Gilligan's Island* on stage, screen, and television.

Though she has persevered in her career, her marriage to radio talk show host Les Crane did not last. They separated in 1970, after having a daughter, Caprice.

"Natalie Schafer was marvelously dotty," says Forslund, and Schwartz agrees, "[She] was Mrs. Howell—there's no difference. She was a perfect foil for Jim—like two people living in their own world of high society and yet they were stuck on an island but still tried to live their own lives, which is where much of their humor came from. In real life if you ever had lunch with [Natalie] you'd think you were talking to Mrs. Howell. She'd say the most outrageous things that were so funny. Her attitude about life was funny."

"I'm being recognized but by another kind of people," claimed a surprised Schafer, long a respected veteran actress, during *Gilligan's* original run. "It's supposed to be very good for your ego to have people recognize you in the street. But I look around at the people and I think, 'Oh, dear, if they were just a little more attractive, I'd like it better.' "

And just as Louise had created her own Ginger, Schafer created her own Lovey Howell. She turned her nose up at the tweeds and low-heeled shoes the production team had originally planned for her. "I decided Mrs. Howell should wear mad clothes—and pearls. Always pearls," recalled Schafer. "At first the producers and writers were aghast and they fought the idea but I finally won."

A native New Yorker, born November 5, 1900, Schafer attended the Merrill School and Hamilton Institute (where she studied with Katharine Cornell). Her parents were divorced when she was a child and her mother later remarried. When forced by her mother to turn down a job with the Theatre Guild, Natalie worked as a clerk in a bookstore, eventually walking off the job. Her first stage role was as a stock performer in Atlanta, though she eventually ended up back in New York on Broadway, after appearing opposite Pat O'Brien in a Chicago production of *The Nut Farm.*

She met actor Louis Calhern while performing in *The Rhapsody* on Broadway, and they were married in 1934. Later they appeared together in the New England stock production of *The Guardsman.* Her big break came in 1936 when she joined the cast of *The Show Is On.* Hits like *Lady in the Dark, Susan and God,* and *The Doughgirls* followed. It was the last that attracted the attention of an MGM talent scout.

She made her film debut in the comedy fantasy *The Body Disappears* in 1941, and made about two dozen movies over the years, culminating with *The Day of the Locust* in 1975. (And there were television roles galore, in the live dramas of the fifties as well as on various sitcoms. She even played Lana Turner's mother in the 1969–70 TV series, *The Survivors.* Later she toured for six months as the sadistic lesbian in *The Killing of Sister George.* Her last appearance was in the 1990 cable movie, *I'm Dangerous Tonight,* in which she was wheelchair bound and had no dialogue.

"I had moved to Hollywood, but I left most of my clothes in New York," Schafer once told *TV Guide,* "because I was never very sure about *Gilligan's Island* being a great success. It never entered my head it would go on. Besides, the pilot was being made in Honolulu and I'd never been to Honolulu."

Schafer died of cancer on April 10, 1991, at her Rodeo Drive home in Beverly Hills, leaving a multimillion dollar fortune to her pet poodle, CeCe, a replacement for a former pooch, named "Lovey," after Mrs. Howell on the series.

"Jim [Backus] was a wild comedian whose character was so rich you had to use him sparingly," says Schwartz of the actor who *was* stuffy Thurston Howell. "He was sharpwitted, clever, dedicated to his craft—a terrific actor. He [had] a dramatic role in *Rebel Without a Cause.* He was a great [performer who] started out as a Shakespearean actor and then turned to comedy. He added many ad libs to the script and was very different from Alan [Hale] in that respect. They were very different people, but I loved them both."

"Jim Backus was very ill [during *The Harlem Globetrotters on Gilligan's Island*]," Forslund adds. "They weren't sure he would be able to come in and do the few days [work], but he was able to and everyone was so happy about that. I didn't get to know him."

Backus started out as a radio actor in Cleveland. Born February 25, 1913, the son of industrialist Russell Gould Backus, Jim was educated at the Kentucky Military Institute, the University School in Cleveland, and the American Academy of Dramatic Arts in New York.

In New York, he and his wife Henny (whom he met in 1941) were part of a select group of thespians who seemed to work every show on radio, and he soon created the very rich and very snooty Hubert Updyke III (a forerunner to

Thurston Howell) on Alan Young's radio show.

After World War II he moved to Hollywood and began his movie career, and then played long-suffering Judge Bradley Stevens opposite Joan Davis (as his wacky wife) in the 1952–55 sitcom, *I Married Joan.*

The Backus voice also immortalized the myopic cartoon character, Mister Magoo, both in films and on television. In the syndicated *Jim Backus Show—Hot Off the Wire* (1960), he portrayed PR guy Mike O'Toole. During the 1964 season Backus starred simultaneously in *Gilligan* on CBS and in *Mr. Magoo* on NBC—both programs aired on Saturday nights. Five years later (on February 2, 1969) he appeared in the "Night of the Sabatini Death" episode of *The Wild, Wild West,* along with Alan Hale. (At the end of that episode Hale announced that he was going off to live on a deserted island accompanied by the tune of *Gilligan's Island.*)

"I'd already worked in two weekly shows," said Backus to *TV Guide* about his initial reluctance to do *Gilligan.* "Nobody outside the business knows how physically and emotionally tough it is to do a series. Sometimes in the silence of my lonely room, I would like to do something maybe a little more worthwhile or artistically satisfying. But I enjoy the money and I certainly enjoy the recognition. It [has gotten] very fashionable to rap *Gilligan's Island.* I don't know why we have television critics. To review a television show is a ridiculous thing anyhow. The New York papers have a tendency to hate anything that comes from the Hollywood film factories." Following *Gilligan,* Jim and Henny Backus played J.C. Dithers and his wife, Cora, in the 1969–70 version of *Blondie* and then became regulars on the talk-show circuit.

Backus died of pneumonia on July 3, 1989, at age seventy-six. Though he had suffered from Parkinson's disease for several years and had had a stroke, he had written two books with Henny which humorously addressed his disease: *Backus Strikes Back* and *Forgive Us Our Digressions.*

"Alan Hale was probably the warmest-hearted, most sincere person I have ever met in my life," says Schwartz. "He just radiated [warmth] which is why he got the part. [The Skipper] was very often mean to Gilligan, berating him, hitting him with his hat, telling him he's stupid, and it takes a wonderfully warm person by nature to play that role. Every other actor I tested for that part turned dark and you hated him. I was looking for a Mutt to Denver's Jeff. Bob is so sympathetic that anyone who has to yell at him all the time automatically becomes unsympathetic. I deliberately chose a scene where the Skipper had to blast him. Everybody else that I tested turned out dark and mean but the Alan was lovable.

"I can't tell you how many hours [Alan and I] spent together in going from one room to another in various children's hospitals and orthopedic hospitals, just cheering up the kids. He was terrific at that. I have the finest memories of him.

Hale initially had flown in from film location at St. George, Utah, to test for Schwartz on a Sunday and flew back that same day.

Denver recalls, "Alan Hale and I did all kinds of public appearances after the series was over. We'd go out and get rescued anywhere there was a body of water. And we just had a good time."

An L.A. native, Hale was born in 1918, the son of one of Hollywood's jovial screen stalwarts. Alan Senior was a veteran actor, who began as a leading man at Biograph. He starred in *A Doll's House* with Nazimova and played Little John in *Robin Hood* (the silent in 1922 and the talkie in 1938 and again in 1950).

Alan Junior made his debut while still in his teens and was awarded his first major part while still a student at Los Angeles City College. His film career actually began with *Wild Boys of the Road* (1933) when he was only thirteen, but as with many first-time appearances, Hale was never seen in the final cut except as a photograph.

In 1940 he really launched his career in *I Wanted Wings.* But despite numerous film roles he found himself at one point in the forties selling vacuum cleaners.

After serving in the U.S. Coast Guard, he appeared in a string of movies, looking more and more like his actor dad (who died in 1950). In TV's early days, he starred in the syndicated *Casey Jones* and CBS's *Biff Baker, U.S.A.* (1952–53).

Hale was always curious about the depths of the critics' animosity: "I still think that a couple of the folks who have roasted us have way down deep had a couple of laughs watching [*Gilligan*]."

After the series ended, he continued making appearances on various shows, and did a couple of episodes with his "little buddy," Bob Denver, on Denver's series *The Good Guys.* In later years, he opened a seafood restaurant on the West Coast.

Hale, who'd had four children with first wife, Bettina, before divorcing her and marrying former singer Naomi Ingram, died of cancer on January 7, 1990, at age seventy-one.

Not to be overlooked is Russell Johnson, the remaining *Gilligan's Island* habitué, who played the Professor. Johnson has always been quick to defend his involvement with the series, even during its original run: "In this day and age I'm delighted to have the job, to be working because it's cold out. Boy, it's rough. If you're an actor you should work. You do the best you can with what you've got."

In the fifties, he acted in such films as *For Men Only* (1952), *Loan Shark* (1952), *Johnny Dark* (1954), *Strange Lady in Town* (1957), and the never-to-be-forgotten *Attack of the Crab Monsters* (1957).

In theater his credits include *Delirious, The Management, Romeo and Juliet, The Inspector General, Hamlet, O Dad, Poor Dad, Paradise Lost,* and *Volpone.* (How many actors can list both *Hamlet* and *Attack of the Crab Monsters* among their credits?)

So why did this top-rated series that has so permeated our pop culture end after only three seasons?

"We had unofficially been picked up for a fourth season," recalls Schwartz, who just prior to *Gilligan* had worked for seven years as head writer on Red Skelton's show. "And I learned a bitter lesson at that time. You don't listen to the programming department for renewal—you wait until Business Affairs sends you a letter saying you're officially picked up, and I never got that letter so I learned that when [Bill] Paley found *Gunsmoke* [had been canceled] he removed two shows in order to make room for his and [wife] Babe's favorite show. So they knocked off *Gilligan's Island* and the show to follow both to make room for *Gunsmoke.* [But] it's happened to other [shows]."

"*Gunsmoke* had to go back on," concurs Denver, "and we were picked up unofficially for the fourth season and in the middle of the hiatus we got a call saying we were canceled and Sherwood said, '*Gunsmoke* had to go back on and just bumped us right off [the schedule].' "

But despite the lapse of time, the condemnation of the critics then and now, the sometime ambivalence of Bob Denver and unprocessed hostility of Tina Louise, *Gilligan's Island* endures, coming back again and again.

Denver, Hale, Wells, and Johnson surfaced a while ago (before the Skipper's death) on an episode of *ALF,* and Wells played a Mary Ann lookalike on an episode of *Growing Pains.* In 1988 the entire cast turned up on *The Late Show.* The same year, Schwartz, Schafer, and Wells were heard on "Tom Snyder's Radio Show." Denver and Johnson joined them by phone. Again in 1988 everyone except Backus—but including Tina Louise—showed up at a Los Angeles reunion.

"We were [once] in New York City—the Professor, Mary Ann, and Gilligan," recalls Denver, "[and we were] 'rescued' on a tour boat with over five hundred passengers for whom we signed autographs. We do that two or three times a year so we stay close."

So *Gilligan's Island,* the series about characters who could have stepped from a comic book and named after a guy from the phone book, endures as a testimony to, if not the good taste of, the American viewing public, at least to the savvy and determination of its creator, Sherwood Schwartz.

The cast of castaways
(*photo courtesy Sherwood Schwartz*)

Jonathan Harris as Dr. Zachery Smith joins Guy Williams and June Lockhart as Dr. John and Maureen Robinson

TEN

LOST IN SPACE

(September 15, 1965—March 6, 1968)

In mid-September 1965 one of America's most beloved nuclear families was thrust full-speed ahead into the space age. Television's first intergalactic family Robinson was launched from Earth's Alpha Control aboard the Jupiter 2 in what was intended to be the maiden colonization flight, funded by Uncle Sam at a cost of $40 billion. The year was 1997 and their destination was the Centauri star system.

"The Robinson family was selected from more than two million volunteers for its unique balance of scientific achievement, emotional stability, and pioneer resourcefulness," explained TV commentator Don Forbes on the series.

But the Robinsons were unaware that their spaceship was harboring a spy and the Jupiter 2 was soon thrown off

course by the machinations of saboteur and stowaway Dr. Zachary Smith, who held an honorary degree in intergalactic environmental psychology. And though Smith would eventually manage to endear himself to the passengers of the Jupiter 2, at the time of the eighty-third and last episode ("Junkyard in Space"), almost three years later, the Robinsons were still lost in space.

Lost in Space was created and produced by Irwin Allen. Jerry Briskin functioned as associate producer during the first year, William Faralla, the second and third. The story editor was Anthony Wilson, and L.B. Abbott and Howard Lydecker coordinated the special effects.

The show starred June Lockhart, Guy Williams, Mark Goddard, Marta Kristen, Bill Mumy, Angela Cartwright, and Jonathan Harris in his larger-than-life role as the pathetically and comically ruthless Dr. Smith. *Lost in Space* would become a phenomenon that attracted thirty thousand fans at a cast reunion party in Boston twenty-five years after its premiere.

"You know it was hot—it had romance," recalls June Lockhart today. "It had drama. It had great special effects. It had that fabulous set. The music was wonderful. There was such a potential and it was a wonderful experience for all of us."

"June dubbed me 'Crash West,'" remembers Mark Goddard (the spaceship's pilot Maj. Donald West), who now teaches school in Massachusetts, "because in order for us to have a segment every week on a different planet we had to land somewhere and we had to crash and I was the pilot so I was 'Crash West.'"

"It was the first show of its type," explains Marta (Judy Robinson) Kristen. "It not only combined science fiction but science fantasy, a little bit of tongue-in-cheek, and camp."

"It [was] an arena which no one knew about—SPACE—no one knows what's out there and it's great to fantasize about it," says Billy (Will Robinson) Mumy, the only child of a California cattle-ranching family who fronts three rock bands—Barnes and Barnes, the Jenerators, and the Seduction of the Innocent.

"The effects were great—the music was fantastic. John [then Johnny] Williams did all of our music and you can't get any better than that," Mumy continues. "I'd like to think the acting was decent. To me, at least, a third of [the episodes] are unwatchable—when it came to the episode with the talking carrot, I though it [was] really stupid—I just cringe."

Mumy refers to "The Great Vegetable Rebellion" (February 28, 1968), which was written by Peter Packer and directed by Don Richardson.

"Everyone had to kind of react normally," contributes Goddard, "and play it straight to this guy who [was] a talking carrot."

"My favorite [episode] was something called 'The Great Vegetable Rebellion,'" claims Lockhart, begging to differ with Mumy. "Jonathan [Harris] played a stalk of celery and everytime anybody sat down they took root."

"Dr. Smith—I created him, you know from nothing," explains Harris today. "I created something I'm quite proud of really, especially as [in the beginning] he was none of the things you [eventually] saw. He was meant to be a deep, dark snarling villian and I didn't find that very palatable—I didn't feel Smith had any longevity with no redeeming features. I don't think [that's] a nice thing to watch every week so I began to sneak in little comedic bits—I carefully plotted my character."

"Will [Robinson] really did love Dr. Smith," Mumy adds. "Will was constantly making excuses for him to get him out of the frying pan."

"Actually I patterned him on every child I've ever known," says Harris of Smith. "I did all the things that kids do and never got smacked for it [and] it worked. Of course, my relationship with the robot became very important too—he was my alter ego. I was the very first antihero on TV that became a hero."

Harris elaborates this last point by describing how, in one episode, he devoured a piece of chocolate cake, rearranging the remainder so that it appeared as if a slice had not been taken. When confronted, Smith, right in character, denied that he had been indulging his sweet tooth.

"I had an affection for him," admits Lockhart, regarding Dr. Smith, "even though he did frustrate me a lot."

But all the cast members were not as fond of Smith/Harris, as was Lockhart. According to a 1966 *TV Guide* article, *Lost In Space* was originally supposed to have focused on the exploits of John Robinson, his wife, the children and their copilot. Enter Harris at the last moment as "a lip-curling, no-goodnik who, it was discovered, could be better used for laughs played off Mumy and a sober-sided robot." The rest of the cast, aside from Mumy, were reduced to supporting players.

And though it became Jonathan Harris's show, according to the contracts, he could not rise above seventh place in billing. "This show," Goodard was quoted as saying at the time, "is lousy with ego."

"Will was smart and polite, but he was definitely his own guy. I loved playing the part [and] I always had plenty to do in the first season, as well as in the second and third," explains Mumy. "I had more work [later on] and I suppose everyone else had less but I enjoyed it [in that first season] as an ensemble piece more than as a Smith/Will/Robot piece."

But if creator Irwin Allen was ever pressed about rumors of complaints from his baffled, frustrated, and often unhappy cast, his response was "Complaints? I haven't heard any."

One morning, however, a director positioned the scene-stealing Harris in the foreground of a segment scripted for Guy Williams and his TV wife June Lockhart. Williams walked off of the set and called Irwin Allen.

"He came down and we reached a compromise," Williams told *TV Guide* in 1966.

Williams, who was earning $2,500 a week, reported his displeasure to his agent. Lockhart, at the time, was more philosophical: "We probably wouldn't be here at all without Jonathan."

Guy Williams was born in 1926 in New York. His real name was Armando Catalano and his father was from Palermo, Sicily. Guy became a male model during the forties, studying acting with Sanford Meisner and doing theater and some television.

In 1957, for Walt Disney, he played the swashbuckling

Six-sevenths of the cast of sixties space cadets: Mark Goddard, Marta Kristen, June Lockhart, Guy Williams, and (seated) Billy Mumy and Angela Cartwright

Young Billy Mumy as Will Robinson

Billy Mumy and Jonathan Harris on an excellent adventure

Zorro. The show was short-lived but it earned Williams quite a bit of money. The series ended in 1959, but he was kept on salary for two years while ABC and Disney argued over the network's refusal to allow the producers to switch the show over to NBC. At the time Williams was unaware that his swashbuckling had influenced a young lad who would one day be his TV son.

"I started wanting to be an actor because I broke my leg when I was three and a half and I sat in a cast and stared at Guy Williams as Zorro," recalls Mumy, "and I wanted to do that and I was lucky enough to make that happen. Whatever my destiny was, I jumped on it and I made it happen. By the time the cast came off, I had found my life's destiny and I knew I wanted to be on television. So I whined and bothered my folks enough till they said, 'okay.' "

After *Zorro,* Williams went on to appear in European films like *Damon and Pythias* and *Captain Sinbad* in the sixties. Once back in the States he attempted to fill Pernell Roberts's shoes as a Cartwright cousin on *Bonanza,* but that fell through and *Lost in Space* came along.

"Guy was a joy to be with," Billy Mumy recalls of his TV dad, who died in 1989. " A wonderful, pleasant, happy guy. He was a pleasure to work with. He taught me how to fence and he was always fun. I miss him."

"He was a friend to all of us," remembers Bob May, the man inside Robot. "He was a guy you could always turn to. He was a professional."

And Williams's costar June Lockhart was every bit as professional.

"June is the epitome of rock and roll," Mumy says today. "You know people have an impression of her as being this tame and conservative woman and she's the biggest rock and roller that I know. She used to have the Allman Brothers band play parties at [the studio] and at her home, when we were on *Lost in Space,* and she used to take me and Angela [Cartwright] to concerts at the Hollywood Bowl, and she still goes to concerts every week. She carries a picture of one man in her wallet and that's David Bowie."

And Mumy is right on target in his estimation of the real June Lockhart. So pure was her image on *Lassie* that once when a writer mentioned that she had nursed a Scotch during the interview, she was called up on the carpet and had her wrist slapped by studio executives.

"The series was good for me," recalls Lockhart, "but they couldn't have found an actress more alien, personally, to the part. I've really learned what I know through experience and from my father. Apparently, whatever my image is to the television viewer, I'm a highly salable commodity."

"I've never met a human being, regardless of age, who has a tenth of her energy and it's always positive," Mumy

elaborates. "She is a dynamo. She does episodic work. She's very hooked into the political world, and she's always traveling with journalists or at the White House for something or the other. She's super busy."

There are five stars for the Lockharts on the Hollywood Walk of Fame. Two are for June who, with an Emmy nomination, a Tony Award, and an Associated Press Woman of the Year in Drama citation, has continued the family legacy begun with her famous parents, father Gene and mother Kathleen.

Actually the family performing tradition started with her grandfather, John Coates Lockhart, a respected concert singer. Another famous ancestor, John Gibson Lockhart, was the son-in-law and biographer of Sir Walter Scott.

In his 1984 *Guide to Health and Happiness,* author Kenny Kingston states that the Lockharts (Gene and daughter June) were interested in the spirit world. While living in a house purchased for them by family friend Clifton Webb, Gene wrote the song "The World Is Waiting for the Sunrise," but shied away from publishing other works as, according to Kingston, they were not his own but channeled.

A New Yorker (born June 25, 1925), June was only eight when she made her debut in a stage production at the Metropolitan Opera House. At twelve she appeared as Belinda Cratchit in the 1938 film of *A Christmas Carol,* sharing billing with her famous parents. Before finishing her education at the Westlake School for Girls (also the alma mater of that other queen of sixties TV, Elizabeth Montgomery), Lockhart had appeared in films such as *All This and Heaven Too, Sergeant York,* and *Adam Had Four Sons.*

Following graduation, she was put under contract to MGM and went on to appear in *The White Cliffs of Dover, The Yearling, Meet Me in St. Louis,* and *Son of Lassie.* She also had the title role in *She-Wolf of London* for Universal. In her first Broadway play, she won praise as the ingenue in F. Hugh Herbert's *For Love or Money,* opposite Gig Young.

For this debut performance Lockhart received an Associated Press award. Her Emmy nomination would come later for her role in *Lassie.* Following *Lost In Space,* she spent two years on *Petticoat Junction* as Hooterville's Dr. Janet Craig.

"I just wrote Paul [Henning]," Lockhart told *TV Guide* in 1969, after *Lost in Space* ended, "and said I was looking for a series." Later she also did sixty episodes of the daytime soap, *General Hospital.*

"I never had a frantic ambition to be big as an actress," Lockhart once told *TV Guide* during the original run of *Lost in Space.* "I always regarded the business as a lovely hobby and a way to make money."

"She's a doll," says Bob May on the subject of Lockhart. "She's the one [who] keeps us all together. I still see all [except for Mark who's back East] at Twentieth at yearly anniversary parties."

In the beginning May was on the Fox lot interviewing for a picture when he was called into Irwin Allen's office.

"You always go into a project with high hopes but you never know," says May today. "Basically we gave the public what they wanted and that was a lot of fun between Smith and the Robot and a lot of affection [between] the Robot and Will Robinson. Bill and Angela are [both] just fantastic adults now."

And though May stresses, "Everybody who worked on *Lost in Space* was a tried and true professional," his favorite episode was directed by Albert Salmi (one of two favored directors—the other was Ezra Stone) and called "Junkyard in Space."

This was the last episode to be aired during the original run and was shown on March 6, 1968. In this one the Robot prompts Smith into making an exploratory excursion aboard the space pod to a neighboring planet, but something goes awry. The Robinsons launch the Jupiter 2 in a rescue mission to recover Smith and the Robot and are greeted by the Junk Man. He offers to buy the Jupiter 2 for scrap, but the Robinsons refuse. Consequently their rations start to rust and a famished Smith trades off the Robot's body parts to the Junk Man for food. After using the parts from the dismembered Robot to repair his own android body, the Junk Man announces that he is commandeering the Jupiter 2.

"It was my favorite," says May. "The robot was going to destroy himself to save the family. There was a very touching scene toward the end with the Robot and Will Robinson by the conveyor belt."

But nobody knew at the time that they would not all be returning for a fourth season. "I picked up the *New York Times*," recalls Harris, "and quickly turned to the TV page—'LOST IN SPACE' CANCELED! I was absolutely aghast!"

"It cost too much money," Mumy offers in the way of an explanation. "We were picked up for a fourth season. When we wrapped for the third season, nobody said good-bye to one another. We just went on our little holiday expecting to be back at Twentieth in nine weeks. What I was told was that CBS called Irwin Allen and said, 'We're cutting your budget because it's too expensive a show and the ratings have not been as good,' and he said he would not produce it [for less] and he would take it to one of the other networks and CBS said, 'Go ahead,' and the other two networks said, 'No thanks.' "

"I was very, very disappointed. I was very depressed [after] I heard the news. Show business is an industry you go into knowing it's a temporary reality. You work with these people and some people you carry on a relationship with [but] most people you don't. You finish the script and it's done and you say good-bye.

"If we had known we were going to be canceled, I think we would have resolved the show the same way *The Fugitive* found the one-armed man. We would have returned to Earth. And even if [not], if we'd known we were going to be canceled after the third season, then we could have had a nice little rap party and toasted each other and gone [on] our merry way. But because it was a phone call at home one day from my agent, no one ever really got together and let loose and it was different for me and Angela because we were little kids."

Billy Mumy admits: "I'm much more emotionally connected to that time than Mark or Jonathan because I was ten, eleven, twelve, thirteen. It was such a part of my foundation of life. If weren't for June I might not have started going to rock concerts. If it weren't for Marta [Kristen] I might not have been turned on to the Byrds and Bob Dylan. [These] things became very important in my life. [Today] Marta does a lot of theater work and she travels all over the world. She's very happily married to a real nice guy who's a very successful attorney and she has a beautiful daughter and is still working and she's a real positive force on this planet."

"I read it in *TV Guide*," says May of the unexpected cancellation. "I was shocked because we were all scheduled to come back. We're all still very, very close. Marta is very charming, very talented and very nice. Jonathan is brilliant. Mark is a super nice guy, extremely talented. I would say on *Lost in Space* that he never got the credit as an actor. He'd worked with people like Robert Taylor and he'd worked with many fine, fine actors. He's a pretty good actor and a very nice guy."

"Mark is a wild guy," contributes Mumy, laughing. "I did a convention with him in Atlanta. He's a crazy guy. He's a wonderful guy. I love Mark. When we were doing *Lost in Space* I really looked up to him, and [now] I can't believe that I did that—Mark's a strange man—but I love [him] very much and I wish him the very best. He's teaching high school in Massachusetts and he's a wonderful dad. He's got a handful of kids—some of them are grown up, some of them are babies."

Mumy goes on to describe an adventurous escapade with Goddard back during the show's original run when the two of them would steal the directors' golf carts, drive them around the lot and then abandon them somewhere. One day, according to Mumy, he and Goddard locked May into his Robot costume and left him there while they went off to lunch. When they came back smoke was coming out of the Robot so they ran over and opened May's Robot suit him only to find him inside reading his paper and smoking a cigar.

And what became of the Robot? "[It] ended up at my

friend's house decorated as a Christmas tree," Mumy says.

"Our ratings were great," stresses May today. "[And] still to this day we're number one in Australia. Our show is accepted all over the United States, in Canada and [around the world]. We're all in favor of doing a reunion. A lot of fans would like that. We certainly would like that. We've [even] talked about it."

And May could get his wish now that the estate of Irwin Allen, who died in 1991, has brought the property to Paramount, which distributes the *Addams Family* movies.

May has collected his remembrances of *Lost in Space*, in a video called "Robot Memories." "I've met so many nice people through [the video]—Mike Clark, in particular, [who] coproduced it with me. Mike is a very nice man."

And one interesting tidbit from "Robot Memories" is that May was not the actual voice of the Robot. Mumy explains how the character voice of Dick Tufeld came into the picture.

"I never really knew Dick [Tufeld]," he says. "Bobby did all the acting [as] the Robot and, of course, did all the lines but because he was inside they came out sounding all muffled. Dick was never on the set. He'd come in and loop [the lines] while we were busy shooting on another stage so I was never involved in working with Dick. When I see him there's that warm camaraderie but I never really knew him [that well] in the first place."

After the series ended in 1968, Bill Mumy entered high school and later spent a couple of years at Santa Monica College, where he studied music. Subsequent acting stints included *Sunshine,* a doomed series, and a bit part in *Papillon,* and more recently in a few episodes of *Superboy.* In 1985 he collaborated with Miguel Ferrer on Marvel Comics' *Comet Man* series.

"We had three permanent sets [on *Lost in Space*]," Mumy recalls. "One was interiors, one was exteriors, and the other was an all purpose one. Where Century City is now there used to be the back lot. We had deserts and lush forests, so most of the exteriors were done there. Some were done out at Red Rock Canyon, but a lot was just stock footage.

"Originally [the series] was called *Space Family Robinson*. The original ship was not called the Jupiter 2 [but] the Gemini 12. I wasn't sure if I wanted to be tied to a TV series, 'cause I was working with such great people like Hope, Ball, Benny, and Hitchcock, but the idea of being given a space suit and a laser gun and running around shooting one-eyed monsters was so appealing. So we made the pilot ("No Place to Hide") in 1964. There was no Dr. Smith or Robot in the pilot. Then when the pilot was picked, Jonathan and the Robot were added, and I spent the next three and a half years running around Twentieth."

And Mumy ran head-first into costar Angela Cartwright, who is sixteen months older. After having started out throwing water bags at one another, by the time they were adults they had been engaged. "We were very close. We were as close as you can be," he recalls today. (She broke it off.)

"Today she owns a boutique and she does children's photography," says Mumy. "She's always been a photographer. She's a very good one."

Known for her role in *The Danny Thomas Show* (1957–64), Cartwright returned for *Make Room for Granddaddy* (1970–71).

Her star potential shone through when she auditioned for the Thomas show. They were looking for a seven-year-old blond. She was a four-year-old brunette. The same scenario repeated itself later when she auditioned for the film of *The Sound of Music*.

When Irwin Allen first saw her he said, "Thank God, I expected you to be twenty-one and smoking a cigar."

She was brought to El Segundo, California, by her parents from her native England. Born in Cheshire on September 9, 1952, she and her family moved to Canada a year later and to the United States when she was three. Cartwright had to lose her British accent for the Thomas show.

Many years ago Danny Thomas remarked of Angela, "She's the leading femme fatale in television. Anyone exposed to her for ten minutes belongs to her forever." And ten years later he told *TV Guide:* "She was a most adorable child—a fine child actress who is now a fine young actress."

In 1969, Angela told *TV Guide:* "I may have missed things other kids do, but I've done things they don't. [*Lost in Space*] was a fun show to shoot, I mean we always had a great time."

"I did every kind of episodic TV you could think of, well over one hundred [appearances] in all the sixties shows," recalls Mumy of his own youth. "I had a huge crush on Elizabeth Montgomery, and I got to play her husband and nothing could have made me happier than to kiss her." (And he did, just as he also kissed French bombshell Brigitte Bardot in *Dear Brigitte,* in 1965.)

"I loved *Bewitched* and [Montgomery's] son is a friend of mine who does a lot of guitar work for me, and she was great. It was one of my favorite shows as a kid. *The Munsters* was just a quick three-day [shoot]. I didn't think that was a very great script. I look back on my *Twilight Zones* and 'Hitchcocks' with more pleasure than I do on *The Munsters*."

Billy Mumy goes on: "There are a lot of grown-up child actors who kept on working and kept their wits about them, so to speak. Ronnie Howard, Jodie Foster, Roddy McDowall, Veronica Cartwright, myself, the guys from

My Three Sons, and I think the reason is that all of us were actors and got into television to act. So many child actors who are bitter, cranky old ex-drug addicts were kids who just got lucky enough to play a kid on TV for three or five years, and if you really look at their work they never played characters beyond that.

"They were really never doing other things as actors. They just had the opportunity to kind of play themselves on a TV series for a while and they got a great deal of money and great adulation and that was that and they disappeared and became bitter and cranky. But the ones who were doing it because they wanted to act and play different roles and do different characters and really stick it out for those reasons have mostly turned out to be fine adult actors. I had a concept of work because acting is hard work.

"I've never had to go have a straight nine-to-five job. I've always been able to explore the avenues that I wanted to and that includes music and writing, as well as acting, and I've made a lot of albums and I've toured with a lot of great musicians and I've written a lot of interesting comic books and I've got to explore that realm and if I hadn't had the experiences as a child actor I would have never been that fortunate."

Mumy explains that his grandfather had been an agent and had gotten Boris Karloff the job of the Frankenstein Monster and that his mother had worked at Twentieth as a writers' assistant. His parents, he says, weren't afraid of

June Lockhart, Bill Mumy, and Jonathan Harris, light years beyond *Lost in Space* (*photos courtesy June Lockhart, Bill Mumy, and Atlanta Fantasy Fair*)

show business or threatened by it, so they got him an agent and he started working straight off.

"I got to work with Hitchcock one week and Walt Disney the next and Jimmy Stewart the next," continues Mumy, "and Loretta Young and Raymond Burr and Jack Benny and Lucille Ball and Bob Hope and Dustin Hoffman and Steve McQueen, and I learned from these people. I traveled all over the world working as an actor and I have no regrets. My only regret was that I took a few years off after a film called *Bless the Beasts and the Children*. I wish I hadn't done that."

Regarding his appearance with Shirley Jones in *A Ticklish Affair,* Mumy says, "[She] was a good friend of mine. I had a big crush on her, too. I was in Shaun Cassidy's band when he was a teen idol."

Mumy says of the series that made him famous, "I liked the first season. [It] was the best [with] serious episodes that were more science fiction oriented than science fantasy oriented."

"I prefer the color seasons," counters Jonathan Harris. "They are much prettier. Some of our monsters were fabulous."

"I liked the two-parter we did with Michael Rennie called 'The Keeper' because we really got to stretch a bit further than with the other episodes," adds Mumy. "He had starred in *The Day the Earth Stood Still* and that was one of my all-time favorite films."

"The Keeper—Part One" originally aired on January 12, 1966. Aside from Rennie, Wilbur Evans also appeared as the alien leader. The script was written by Barney Slater and directed by Sobey Martin. In this episode Dr. Smith falls into a trance-like state and is summoned to a nearby cage in an alien's lair. Will Robinson goes for help, returning with his father and Don. The Robot discovers that the cage can produce climatic conditions suitable for varying life forms.

Enter the Keeper, who explains that this spacecraft contains a collection of species gathered from throughout the galaxy and that he wishes to add humans to his collection. As the plot develops in part two (the following week), Smith and the Robot go to the Keeper's ship, where Smith attempts to hijack the spacecraft in a desperate bid to return to Earth.

But Smith's plans are foiled when he inadvertently releases all the creatures. The Keeper confronts the Robinson party at the Jupiter 2, demanding the surrender of Will and Penny as compensation for his loss. This episode, also written by Slater, was directed by Harry Harris.

And there are the inevitable comparisons between *Lost in Space* and that other sixties space adventure—*Star Trek*. "Why compare them?" Mumy asks. "They're both ridiculous—they had their Tribbles and we had our talking carrots. I love both *Star Treks*—I've written three

episodes and three issues of *Star Trek* comic books. I love their characters and I think *Star Trek* was certainly more grounded than *Lost in Space* but trekkies want to rewrite history. You cannot look at *Star Trek* and not consider it to be a silly, campy show. It *was* a silly, campy show.

And Mumy admits that so was *Lost in Space*. "The stupider [the shows] got, the more some people liked [them]. It was a unique era in our society—it was that whole pop art time: Andy Warhol, *Batman, Laugh-In*. The sixties were a unique decade.

"For the most part, it was [all] farce, I think. I look at *Star Trek* more or less as a military show in the space arena and *Lost in Space* was a family show in the space arena. That's really the only difference. Their monsters looked as stupid as our monsters—or as good, depending.

Some of the *Lost in Space* monsters and aliens were played by Dawson Palmer, Ted Lehman, Don Matheson, Albert Salmi, Michael J. Pollard, Kurt Russell, Mercedes McCambridge, Sherry Jackson, Gregory Morton, Sue Englund, Wally Cox, Ted Cassidy, Eddie Quillan, Sheila Mathews, Al Lewis, Alan Hewitt, John Carradine, Lyle Waggoner, and Arte Johnson.

"Their Spock was our Robot. Their Bones was our Smith, only Smith was more of a parody than Bones." And they had their "Menagerie" episode and *Lost in Space* had its "Keeper" episode. "There are certainly similarities there. If we'd had the opportunity to have made five or six multimillion dollar features, then we could compare them. I wish I'd had the opportunity to have made *The Wrath of Khan* as a *Lost in Space* project [but] I'm very glad I got to do something that fit in [with the times] and brought people a lot of pleasure—I had a great time."

And Mumy has his own thoughts on his huge fan following. "When we were in Boston [in 1990], there were thirty thousand people there to get our autographs. It felt great being with the other cast members again, and when [that many] people are out there wanting to shake your hand, it's pretty flattering—it's a nice feeling but it's also like 'don't you guys have something else to do?' "

But these are the same people who spend a fortune each year on such *Lost in Space* (LIS) collectibles as the Jupiter 2 Model Kit, the Jupiter 2 Interior Kit, the Space Pod Kit, the LIS Family and Robot (figurine) set, the LIS Cyclops, the LIS Accessory set (sonic washer, force field projector, hydroponic garden, drill rig, jet pack, water conversion unit/atomic motor), the Invaders from the Fifth Dimension Kit, (comes with ship, base, and two aliens), the Jupiter 2 Diarama (large base with first season crash site scenery), the LIS First Season Laser Gun Kit, the 2nd and 3rd Season Laser Gun and Ship, LIS Basic Kit (comes with Cyclops, Jupiter 2 crew, mountain, and boulder), LIS Gum Card Sets, and the LIS Robot Kit.

Popular publications and books include the *Lost in*

The cast at an early nineties *Space* convention: (from left) Angela Cartwright, Marta Kristen, Mark Goddard, Jonathan Harris, June Lockhart, and Bill Mumy in front (*photo courtesy Innovation*)

Space Scrapbook (volumes one, two, and three); *The Jupiter 2 Operator's Manual; Lost in Space Monthly Yearbook; LIS Handbook: The Story of America's Favorite Space Family* by Paul Monroe; *LIS 25th Anniversary Celebration Book; The Alpha Control Reference Manual; LIS 25th Anniversary Tribute Book; Lost in Space Blueprints* by Shane Johnson; and many more.

And in 1990 to celebrate the twenty-fifth anniversary of *Lost in Space* the series was run daily on the USA Network.

"I don't feel strongly one way or the other about [fans]," says Mumy of the folks who buy all these products. "If I'm out and someone wants to take my picture or wants me to sign something, I'm happy to do it. But for every celebrity of any status there's a psychotic fan. I've learned over the years the hard way that you shouldn't get too close to [fans] because you never know.

"It's too scary a world. I have a son, I have a family. [Now] I don't answer fan letters. I don't feel like I owe anybody anything. I had a job just like anybody [else]. I went to the studio, I hit my mark, I read my lines. I don't owe anybody. It's nice to have people enjoy your work and it's very nice to bring pleasure to people.

"If I write a song and somebody likes that song, then that's great, but I don't write that song for the audience. I write that song for myself—I [don't do it] for adulation. I don't act because I want to be loved by millions of people. I act because I enjoy the process of becoming another character and imagining that I am doing things that I don't normally do.

"After the series was canceled in 1968 I spent several years not wanting anything to do with *Lost in Space*," confesses Mumy. "I wanted to put it behind me and move along with my acting and musical careers.

"But I started to work as a writer, first for television, then for comic books. So I wrote a screenplay for a *Lost in Space* epilogue resolving [the series] and I spoke [of it] in print interviews about ten years ago. I brought the script to the cast, to Twentieth, and to CBS. Everybody thought it was an excellent idea—the studio, the network and the cast wanted to make it [so] I phoned producer and creator Irwin Allen and he said he didn't want to do it. He told me that he wasn't interested in a *Lost in Space* project at that time and, should he decide to do something along those lines in the future, it would be his script and his idea, not mine.

"So I let that go in 1981 when he said 'no,' but people were [still] aware that I had this script. First *D.C. Comics* approached me about turning my script into a limited edition format as a comic book and I said 'great' and so I got my energy back up and they couldn't get the rights to do it. And then an editor at *Marvel Comics* where I had been doing quite a lot of work said, 'Hey, if *D.C.* can't do this *Lost in Space* thing, I'll bet we can do it,' and then they couldn't get the rights to it.

"And then Dave Campiti, from this small company, Innovation, walked up to me and said, 'Hey, I got the rights to *Lost in Space*,' and I said, 'You're crazy, I don't believe you. If *Marvel* and *D.C.* couldn't do it, pal, don't tell me you did it.' He was crushed. He [later] sent me a copy of his contracts and said, 'I want your involvement in this.' "

"By the time I came aboard, he had outlined the way he wanted things to go—it had nothing to do with resolving *Lost in Space* [which is what I had always wanted to do]. Campiti's comics are six years after the Jupiter 2 left Alpha Control. It's just a regular comic book—the continuing episodes of the Robinsons.

"He handed me an outline which explained where he was going with it and I had some difficulties and disputes with him as to where it was going but ultimately, I felt protective of the characters and I pretty much wanted to control where it was going so I reluctantly got into it. The ones I have written I have worked very hard on and I'm happy with my work and I'm happy with the books. It's fine."

"When I realized that Bill Mumy—the writer-actor-musician who has written comics and songs, acted in episodes of *Superboy, The Flash,* the new *Captain America* film and was, of course, *Lost in Space*'s Will Robinson for three years—was wanting to do a *Lost in Space* comic book, I suddenly had the impetus to set things in motion," elaborates Campiti.

"Viacom was dealing with a twenty-six-year-old property, and when they split off from CBS, something fell through the cracks. *Lost in Space* had so many owners, including CBS, Red Skelton, Desilu, and the estate of Groucho Marx."

Fox had only owned the physical property—the $350,000 set, at the time the most expensive ever built for a television series.

"I think the books show how much a labor of love it all was," continues Campiti. "I'm especially thankful that Bill Mumy was so patient with us. Bill was, of course, the first person I called when the clearances finally came through.

"Fortunately, I already knew [Bill], as he played and sang in the rock group Seduction of the Innocent [and] as his almost editor—we nearly worked together on a graphic novel project for an independent publisher in the mid-eighties. When Bill came aboard he accepted the role of looking over my shoulder, reading all the scripts, perusing all the art, and making story or dialogue suggestions.

"Of course, Bill's ear for dialogue for these people is faultless; he lived it, he spoke it, he performed it, and he knew the people who played these parts, making him the ultimate authority. Fortunately Bill also wanted to write some of our *Lost in Space* issues—so to start it off Bill wrote a strong characterization-based story. *Lost in Space* is one of my dream projects and it's been a thrill to work with Will Robinson—Bill Mumy—on [this] project."

"I'm involved in [many] different musical projects," continues Mumy, whose more recent credits include *Matlock* and the film *Double Trouble*. "I've been part of Barnes and Barnes for the last thirteen years. We've brought you 'Fishheads' and 'Party in My Pants.' We've released our eighth album on Rhino Records.

"I have a band with Miguel [*Twin Peaks*] Ferrer called The Jenerators. It's a straight ahead rock and roll band that I'm very much into. Miguel and I are also part of a band [Seduction of the Innocent] that's comprised of people who write comic books, and we have a CD out and that band plays a couple of times a year at comic book conventions only. That came about when we'd go to these conventions and there was always some schlocky band there and we just sort of sat around grumbling, 'We can do better than this.'

"Seduction of the Innocent is a fun little exercise into rock and roll. I've also worked with the band America for most of the last ten years and I've written eleven songs on their last four records [including] *Encore: Greatest Hits, Volume 2*—there're four new songs on that, three of which I cowrote and two of which I produced. I did three episodes of *Superboy* and one episode of *The Flash*—it's all comic book related [but being on *Lost in Space*] was like playing a character from a comic book—it's all fantasy—I can't escape it. It's very strange."

And indeed the saga of the Space Family Robinson is a strange tale. At the time of its original run, creator Allen said, "If the show doesn't stay on the air three years, everyone is bankrupt." And as it turned out, everyone broke even.

Eddie Albert and Eva Gabor as Oliver and Lisa Douglas
© *copyright Orion Television Entertainment (photo courtesy Orion Television)*

ELEVEN

GREEN ACRES

(September 15, 1965–September 7, 1971)

"The kind of people that Lisa and Oliver were are the kind that would be involved in the environment and this has nothing to do with recycling," stresses Eddie Albert (Oliver Wendall Douglas) today. "It has to do with a whole new attitude toward the universe and nature and Oliver was a little sick of the law business and the hysteria of New York and he wanted to see God's good, green earth, and [*Green Acres*] wasn't written for that but it fits perfectly. I played myself—or at least one aspect of myself—and I tried to arouse in the audience things that made them identify with me."

Based on Jay Sommer's radio series *Granby's Green Acres* (which had featured *Petticoat Junction*'s Bea Benaderet), the TV show starred Albert as the Park Avenue lawyer-turned-farmer and Eva Gabor as his wife, Lisa, who reluctantly gives up their Manhattan penthouse to join him in the mythical town of Hooterville.

"CBS bought the show," Albert once recalled to *TV Guide,* "on the basis of [producer] Paul Henning's track record with *The Beverly Hillbillies* and *Petticoat Junction* at a time when the script, let alone a pilot, was just a gleam in Jay Sommer's eye."

And as the scenario unfolded, Oliver, having already climbed the ladder to success, has always dreamt of an idyllic life in the country, a dream which was never crushed, not even when his father nixed his plans to attend Cornell's School of Agriculture, insisting on Harvard Law School instead. Having lost his first job in a law office for growing mushrooms in his desk, following a stint as a pilot in World War II, Oliver returns to New

York to wed Lisa, an internationally celebrated socialite of Hungarian extraction.

Unfortunately, the 160-acre Haney farm in Hooterville turns out to be more than the Douglases bargained for. First of all the bathtub, the kitchen sink, and the stove are all missing. Then there's the matter of no electricity and no telephone.

Junk dealer and horse trader Mr. Haney was portrayed by veteran actor and cowboy sidekick Pat Buttram. Known as the sophisticated rube, Buttram has spent his post-*Green Acres* years as an often-in-demand after-dinner speaker, always adept at glib and witty Will Rogers-style quips.

"Every town has a Mr. Haney," recalled Buttram on a cast reunion called *Green Acres, We Are There,* which aired on Nick at Nite in early 1990. "[He'll] sell you anything. One time I sold [Douglas] a genuine Van Gogh. I said, 'It's very rare—it's one of the few he did in ballpoint.' I sold him so many things. One time a farmer had one cow and I sold him two milking machines and he had no money so I took his cow as a down payment on it.

"Well, I've known people like that. I kind of patterned it after Col. Tom Parker, Elvis's manager. I first met Tom when he was in a sideshow in a fair and he had dancing chickens, Col. Tom Parker's Dancing Chickens. He had a big table and he had sawdust on it and there was about twenty chickens on it and he charged a quarter to get in."

Buttram, who was widowed in 1975, has versatile interests which include owning horses, a radio station in Alabama, and a five-acre ranch in the Northridge section of the San Fernando Valley.

As the *Green Acres* story goes, the doubting Lisa Douglas rallies, despite Haney's obstacles, and with the involvement of handyman Eb (Tommy Lester), store owner Mr. Drucker (Frank Cady), neighbors Fred (Hank Patterson) and Doris Ziffel (Barbara Pepper/Fran Ryan), county agent Mr. Kimball (Alvy Moore), carpenters Alf (Sid Melton) and Ralph (Mary Grace Canfield), and Mother Douglas (Eleanor Audley), a series of mishaps begin to occur.

Moore comments on his introduction to the series, "It was a two-parter and then I was supposed to be gone. And I looked at the series a long time before I realized where they got the idea—the first episode was very straight—was at the end of the second episode. At the very end, Eddie [Albert] turned to me and said, 'Well, what do you think of my farm?' and he looks over this disaster that Haney has sold and the county agent, really seriously didn't know how to answer him and tell him that this thing is a disaster, and so the way I read it—it just happened—I said, 'It's a nice farm; well, it's not a nice farm; well, I guess it could be a nice farm.' And I think that's really where he got the idea but I just happened to read the line that way."

Despite county agent Kimball's astute appraisal of the farm, the Douglases never quite seemed to get around to restoring the property.

Sid Melton, who appeared as Uncle Charley Halper with television-wife Pat Carroll as Bunny in *Make Room for Daddy,* explains why he and carpenter sister Ralph (Canfield) referred to themselves as the Monroe Brothers: "Mom wanted another boy so when the girl came out she called him 'Ralph.' "

Buttram, a collector of books, Civil War relics, and button hooks, offered his own explanation on the 1990 Nick at Nite special: "One of the writers told me, 'They had the sign "Monroe Brothers," ' and it turned out that they didn't want to make a new sign."

Back in Hooterville Lisa quickly assimilates the laid-back culture of the wacky community, incessantly introducing zaftig Arnold the pig as the son of the neighboring Ziffels. Soon Oliver, overwhelmed by a community that is more surreal than silly, is also inadvertently referring to the piglet as the Ziffel's offspring.

And perhaps the highlight of the 170 half-hour episodes was the toast of Hooterville, swine extraordinaire—Arnold Ziffel, who won two Patsy Awards for wallowing in the thespian pigpen.

The prized ham on the hoof was born in Alabama on July 4, 1960, and would spend his Hollywood years battling a weight problem—at one time he shot up to 250 pounds. Arnold, who barks like a dog and watches television addictively, is hidden away by Lisa in one episode to save him from being attached by the Ziffels' creditors.

In other episodes the star porker courts hound dog Cynthia, flies out to Hollywood for a screen test, opens a bank account, and is enrolled in elementary school, where he excels in art class.

"Eddie had the toughest job," recalled Buttram on Nick's *Green Acres, We Are There,* "because he had Eva on one side and me on the other and the pig in the front and he couldn't understand any of the three of us. When I wasn't in the script I used to come to watch [Arnold]. It was fabulous what they had that pig do."

But *Green Acres* was much more than just a pig tale. With Paul Henning as executive producer and Jay Sommers as producer, *Green Acres* was the zaniest of all the southern-fried sitcoms from the sixties with Richard Bare directing and Sommers and Dick Chevillat writing. The series was number six during the 1966–67 season.

Behind the respectable, though gullible Oliver Douglas, was an actor who was equally respected and often even more serious. Albert was an ecologist back when it wasn't always popular. He met with national and local officials over the years in an effort to eliminate pollutants and to encourage that positive preventive measure be taken. In 1969 Albert gave his controversial "End of

The *Green Acres* cast: Pat Buttram (Mr. Haney), Tom Lester (Eb Dawson), Eddie Albert, Eva Gabor, and America's favorite TV porker, Arnold © *copyright Orion Television Entertainment* (*photo courtesy Orion Television*)

Man" speech to a Boeing Aircraft management group in Seattle.

"Ecologist, hell!" he exclaimed at the time. "Too mild a word. We are all part of this giant whirlpool—ecological, if you will. Love thy neighbor [is] no longer a matter of sentiment—it [is] a matter of survival."

Albert, who earlier had starred (with Betty Kean and Ed Begley) in the short-lived sitcom *Leave It to Larry* (1952), takes pride in the role that he has played in raising our environmental consciousness, but even at that, today he says, "We've only scratched the surface. We still have far to go."

Always one to indulge his humorous inclinations as well as his serious causes, Albert is quick to recount one of his favorite stories about his *Green Acres* costar Eva Gabor: "We shot three days a week, so four days a week usually I would travel, talking on the environment at the time. . . . I'd been doing the college circuit, and I'd come back, and [Eva]—I adore her—would say, 'Darling, where was you now?' and I'd say I was traveling in Ann Arbor or Stanford and she'd say, 'Every time you hear about a sick fish you make a speech!' And she'd ask, 'What are you doing?' And I said, 'Well, saving the environment, you know, our resources. For example, this gown you have on with all the feathers—it's beautiful but I'd appreciate it if you wouldn't go in front of the camera.' And she said, 'Why not, darling? It's very chic.' I said, 'That's right—then the ladies will buy that and they'll have to kill a lot of birds for the feathers.' And she said, 'Eddie, feathers don't come from birds!' And I said, 'Where do they come from?' And she said, 'Pillows, darling, pillows!' "

"I love Eva," Albert told *TV Guide* in 1969. "Have ever

since my wife Margo and I first met the Gabor sisters—three frightened little girls from Hungary—at an Ernst Lubitsch party thirty years ago."

But despite the fact that these two performers are as different as were Lisa and Oliver, they have maintained a friendship over the years that was cemented back when Albert was speaking on his off days at campuses ranging from the University of Michigan to George Washington University and Roanoke College, while Gabor was out shopping for maribou kimonos.

What does Gabor have to say today in defense of her chic *Green Acres* wardrobe? "My producers Jay Sommers and Dick Chevillat," Gabor notes, "who were just the geniuses of this business said, 'Eva, have you ever been to a farm?' And I said, 'Yes, I was on a farm,' and they said, 'Well, what did you wear?' I said I just woke up and I was in my nightgown and I went out to see the chickens. And for that I had the most comfortable wardrobe for six years."

"You have to be glamorous on the farm or whatever," she told *TV Guide*. "A woman is a woman and she should never forget it . . . [and] anytime you don't like something, just put ruffles on it. At least you will feel better . . . . All a girl needs at any time in history is just simple velvet and basic diamonds."

For the record, at the Miami Racquet Club robbery in 1964, Gabor was belted by a bandit who made off with her $25,000 diamond ring. Though the robbery received heavy media attention, it was never ascertained as to whether Gabor was wearing simple velvet with her rock.

"You know the crux of the matter," she adds today, "and the basis of *Green Acres* to my mind is—why it was so good was because it was real. Here was a woman who

162

Eddie Albert of the nineties (*photo courtesy Eddie Albert*)

was a New Yorker, who was a chic New York woman, and her husband wanted her to live in the country and she loved him so much that she went with him and tried to do everything that he wanted her to do."

Besides, Lisa Douglas learns that if she and Oliver return to Manhattan, then the cow Eleanor and the chicken Alice will be slaughtered back in Hooterville as there will be no one to take care of them.

Gabor stepped in, after twenty-six other actresses (including Marsha Hunt and Janet Blair) had tested, when Martha Hyer backed out:

"When this series came along," she recalled in a 1967 *TV Guide* interview, "I asked [my husband] what to do and he said to take the test. I would have done whatever he suggested—or maybe I would have taken the test anyway."

But she did have her reservations. "What is a chic Hungarian doing in the barnyard, anyway?" she asked herself at the time. "It's ridiculous, darling!" she exclaimed to a *TV Guide* reporter then. "But deep down inside I knew I had to do it—so many years when I couldn't even get arrested, darling. You can't fight fate."

"They had all the beautiful Hollywood actresses," recalls Gabor today, "and I was doing a play and I flew out to test for it. And I saw these gorgeous girls coming in and out and I said I'd better be different because that's the only way I'm going to get the part. So I dressed like *Green Acres* and I dashed home and I got one of those things when you cook the turkey you use and I got that and I was supposed to do a martini for Eddie and I make that with a baster and I behaved like, I guess, I do and I got the part and it was a joy.

"On *Green Acres* at first they expected me to be difficult or always late. There [was] always the undercurrent—'Here's one of the Gabor girls.' We Gabors were supposed to do nothing but take bubble baths and drip with jewels—I didn't have time to sit in the bubbles. [Over the years] I've worked like a dog. I've lived in bluejeans [at times]. I was hurt because people were surprised I was a good actress. After all these years suddenly I was being discovered."

The youngest of the famed Gabor sisters—daughters of Jolie—Eva was the one who wanted to be taken seriously as an actress. She was born in Budapest on February 11 either in 1921 or 1924 (depending upon whom you ask and what source you consult).

A would-be actress and sometimes café singer and ice skater by the time she reached her teens, in 1939 Gabor met Dr. Eric Drimmer, an American osteopath who was visiting Hungary. After a three-month long distance courtship, she and Drimmer were married in London.

Once back in Hollywood, the doctor realized that his new bride was dismayed to discover that American casting agents weren't falling all over themselves over her

mousey brown hair and voluptuous figure. Undaunted, Gabor toned up and improved her English, soon ending up as a Paramount starlet. She and her doctor husband subsequently split. She was soon to become a legend before her time, as a sometimes film star and fulltime personality.

Sister Sari, a.k.a. Zsa Zsa, soon followed her onto the Hollywood scene. Though Eva was more serious about her craft, who could tell them apart?

"The [Gabor] sisters are highly competitive," Eva's onetime husband Richard Brown told *TV Guide* in 1967. "There is, I would say, a strong sibling rivalry."

Eva concurred at the time: "I've always had to face the fact that my name is Gabor. On every job I've ever had I could feel resentment."

Eva Gabor had gone to New York in 1950, appearing on Broadway in *The Happy Time*, which brought her the first taste of stardom. Later she starred with Noel Coward in *Present Laughter*, before taking over for Vivien Leigh in *Tovarich*.

She went on to do *Blithe Spirit, A Shot in the Dark, Oh Men, Oh Women,* and *Her Cardboard Lover,* and even managed to appear on television with Boris Karloff in *Uncle Vanya*. In 1955 the Gabor sisters, dubbed mythological by that time by Dorothy Parker, appeared together on stage in Vegas.

In Eva's 1954 autobiography *Orchids and Salami,* which Dorothy Kilgallen claimed was based solely on the contents of the icebox, the author revealed the tribulations of her personal life. Having gone through multiple marriages, as had Zsa Zsa, Eva revealed her most passionate (though very discreet) fling had been with Tyrone Power.

Eva's big sister Zsa Zsa was somewhat less discreet when she tangled with international playboy Porfirio Rubirosa, while still married to George Sanders (who, in turn, would later marry third Gabor sister, Magda).

Eddie Albert claims to have learned discipline from Laurence Olivier, with whom he starred in *Carrie* in 1952. He learned other things from his humanitarian mentor Albert Schweitzer. He visited Schweitzer several years back as a representative of the Meals for Millions, a nonprofit organization which provided food supplements to poverty-ridden countries.

"Now that I think of it, Albert Schweitzer taught me about the environment. His credo was reverence for life. He said, 'What is good supports life; what is evil harms it.' I hadn't thought of that in ecological terms. It took me a couple of years to learn what he was talking about. I'm still learning about reverence for life. And the scientific world is beginning to understand. Schweitzer was way ahead."

Eddie Albert had a forty-year marriage to actress, dancer, and singer Margo, and in the 1950s, the two had a sophisticated nightclub act in the posh rooms around the

Eddie Albert and actor son Edward (*photo courtesy The Family Channel*)

country, including at New York's Waldorf Astoria. Margo died in 1985. Pat Buttram was widowed a decade earlier in 1975, when he lost his wife, actress Sheila Ryan, to whom he had been married for twenty-three years. They had met when he was appearing in *Mule Train,* as Gene Autry's screen sidekick. In the 1940s, Ryan had been one of 20th Century Fox's young starlets. She had dropped out of the film business in 1954, following the birth of her and Pat's only child, Kathleen Kerry. At the time of her death, Ryan had suffered from a lung ailment for almost a decade.

As far as Gabor's ever-changing marital status, she was last divorced in 1983, and of late has been a companion of television and casino mogul Merv Griffin.

The turning point in Eva Gabor's life had actually been her role in the film *Youngblood Hawke* in 1964. It led to her being cast as Lisa in *Green Acres,* after Martha Hyer backed out. And what a team Gabor and Albert made! So great was their rapport that they reunited in 1983 on Broadway in *You Can't Take It with You,* when he took over for Jason Robards and she took over for Colleen Dewhurst.

Green Acres fans may have seen that performance as the duo's professional swan song, but that was not to be the case. Having started Gabor International in 1970, Eva was busy running the largest wig company in the world and appearing on such shows as *Hart to Hart* and *The Edge of Night.*

And Albert, too, let no ecologically correct grass grow under his feet. In June of 1972 he was invited to serve as a consultant to Maurice Strong, Secretary General of the U.S. Conference on Environment, which was held in Stockholm.

The field of nutrition, organic farming, and gardening have always been a favorite interest of Albert's and he has lectured frequently throughout the country on these subjects. For many years he grew vegetables organically in the yard of his own home. He's harvested everything from eight-foot-tall corn stalks, tender shoots of radishes, beets, carrots and herbs, and in the indomitable spirit of Oliver Douglas.

And once on *The Ed Sullivan Show* Albert bared his concern for our destructive tendencies by reading Norman Corwin's "Prayer for the '70s" and Bell Records had him record it as a single which sold thousands of copies.

Albert narrated two NBC television specials dealing with ecology: Jules Powers's "The Unseen World" and "Sea of Trouble," which exposed the condition of fish off the California coast. Two days later newspapers heralded reported confiscations of local contaminated fish. In 1971–72 Albert did a very successful series of one-man concerts throughout the United States.

His stance over the years on the environment has led to his being recipient of the Humanitarian Award of the National Conference of Christians and Jews and the Brotherhood Award from B'nai B'rith. "I believe in the principles of Christianity," he told *TV Guide* in 1970, "Philosophy is a crummy word. I'm not a philosopher or anything like that [but] like Gandhi, I say, 'It's a pity it's never been tried.' "

But civic awards and philosophy aside, Albert admits readily that he was much more excited about his two Academy Award nominations (for *Roman Holiday* in 1953 and *The Heartbreak Kid* in 1972) than by any commendation he has received.

Born Eddie Albert Heimberger in Rock Island, Illinois on April 22, 1908, he was one of five children. His father, Frank Daniel Heimberger, was in the realty business and moved the family to Minneapolis when Eddie was a year old. He attended St. Stephen's Parochial School and Central High School.

Albert studied at the University of Minnesota until his junior year, when he grew restless and took a full-time job managing movie theaters, performing magic tricks before each film. Next he went to work in a singing trio which met instant success on the radio, playing stations in Cincinnati, St. Louis, Chicago, and New York.

In the Big Apple, after the trio disbanded in the late thirties, Albert sang in small clubs for three dollars nightly, while he and a friend lived over a speakeasy on West 48th Street in a flat with no electricity. In the evenings they would read the newspapers by the light of a sign on a neighboring eatery that Toots Shor later bought. Often the chef would give them a handout of spaghetti.

Soon Albert teamed up with singer Grace Brandt and went to NBC, which was looking for a musical duo. The couple was on the air for a year as *The Honeymooners— Grace and Eddie.* Playwright Garson Kanin, a guest on the show, was impressed with Albert and cast him in the play *Brother Rat.* Albert had arrived on Broadway, starring in the first of his three consecutive shows for director George Abbott. *Room Service* followed.

Years later Albert would work with son Edward in a revival of *Room Service:* "We did the play that he started his career with," recalled Edward in 1991, "with me playing his part. And at a certain point, the character enters and opens the door, and says, 'Hello, I'm so-and-so—I'm Leo Davis.' And the two of us [are] sitting there and looking at each other, it's a nice way to sort of keep the circle moving."

Eddie Albert recalls, "I opened on Broadway with George Abbott with *Room Service* and then—we were a big hit there. I had just been in *Brother Rat,* and it was also a big hit, and I played this young writer . . . [and] I remember knocking on the door and making my entrance and it was thrilling to me at that time just being out of Minnesota and the wheat fields and so forth, to open on Broadway. So many, many years later I had the privilege

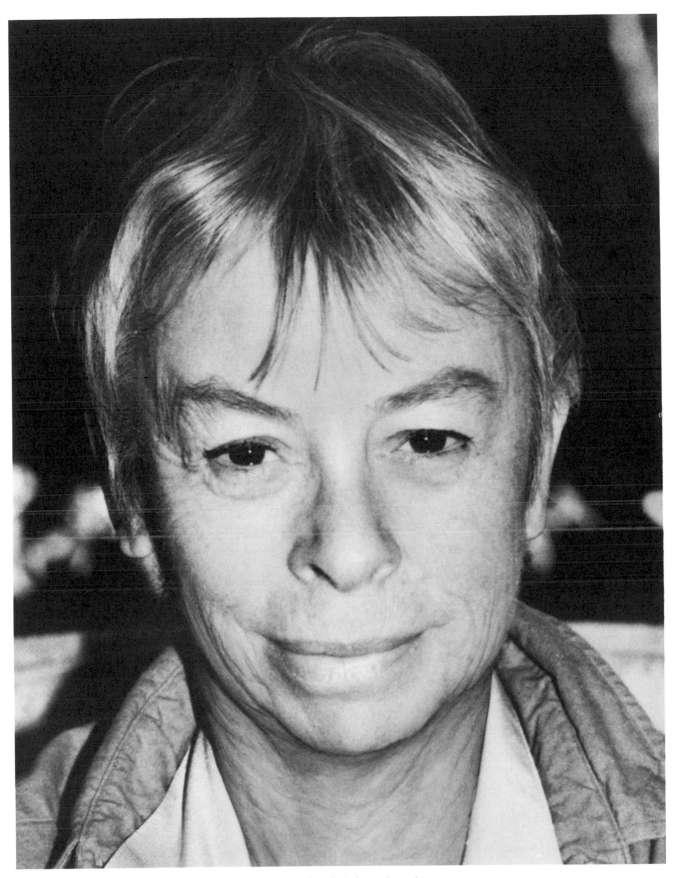

Mary Grace Canfield, who played Ralph Monroe (*photo courtesy Beverly Anderson Agency*)

of being the guy who [Sam Levene did it back then] opened the door, and there's Edward."

Albert also made his film debut in the movie version of *Brother Rat,* along with Ronald Reagan, before returning to Broadway for the Rodgers and Hart musical *The Boys From Syracuse,* again for George Abbott.

One interesting fact that doesn't turn up in Albert's bio is that his role in *The Sun Also Rises* (1957) was not the first occasion he'd had for visiting Mexico. When prompted he admits to having performed in the circus there as a trapeze artist in 1940 with the Flying Escalantes.

"It was just for fun," he says in retrospect, "I traveled with them. You know everybody wants to be in the circus. I had no problems. I wasn't very good on the trapeze—I must tell you that. I just did enough to get by, but I traveled with the people and I loved every bit of it."

Albert served as a navy lieutenant during World War II in the South Pacific and in the Central Pacific at the island of Tarawa. After the war he founded a film company that made two pioneer educational films for schools on sex education: *Human Growth* and *Human Beginnings.*

"At the time there was a great resistance," Albert told *TV Guide* in 1970. "This idiocy arose from the inadequacy of our educational system and ignorance of simple honest facts."

Albert, who has had a long and varied film career, points out that Ray Milland was originally to have played Oliver [Douglas], adding that he himself was cautious about going into a weekly series after Milland bowed out. Albert finally relented and read the script of the *Green Acres* pilot at the urging of his agent.

Eddie Albert's only regular series work since *Green Acres* has been *Switch* (1975–77) with Robert Wagner and Sharon Gless. He has continued guest starring in other shows, like *The Fall Guy, Highway to Heaven,* and *Murder She Wrote,* and for his guest appearance on *Thirtysomething,* in which he played Timothy Busfield's father, he was nominated for an Emmy.

One of Albert's recent projects was the Family Channel's movie *The Girl From Mars,* costarring son Edward, chronicling the adventures of a young girl whose odd behavior convinces one and all that she's from Mars.

"We shot it up in Canada," recalls Albert, "in the rain. But we enjoyed the script and the director was marvelous. They're so used to [rain] there. And they went right out and I remember working at two A.M. and the rain coming down. And I thought, 'These people must be crazy!' But what was really interesting [is] they have such a commitment. They were so excited about the thing. It's not like Metro-Goldwyn-Mayer, you know, twenty or thirty years ago. These people were mostly youngsters, and throwing punches all day long.

"They'd drive you crazy with the costumes and the makeup. They're so eager to be of some service. And so that was fun. That's really like it should be. And we enjoyed all of that. It reminded me, as a matter of fact, a little bit of the fun we had on *Green Acres.* Here again, everybody was committed. And the scripts were marvelous. And the really nice thing to me was to be up there with my son, looking around together. We don't have that privilege very often, and not [while] being paid at the same time, with a per diem.

"The writing, for a change, was very good. I say 'for a change' because a good many of the scripts today are debatable. I don't enjoy them very much."

And one example of this type of writing, unfortunately, was the 1990 reunion movie *Return to Green Acres,* which was panned by critics.

Though semiretired, the eightyish Albert and the late sixtyish Gabor banded together once again, to the delight of *Green Acres* fans, for the two-hour movie reuniting most of the original cast, except for Hank (*Gunsmoke*) Patterson as Mr. Ziffel, who died in 1975. (They also turned up side by side in the 1993 *Beverly Hillbillies* special on CBS.)

Albert says emphatically, "I didn't like it. It wasn't *Green Acres.*" He adds that it could not have been the same without the creative input of Jay Sommers. According to Albert, Sommers was the force that made the original series a quality show.

Composer Vic Mizzy has his own feelings on the reunion: "They took my theme and added to it but they couldn't match the [original] sound." Mizzy had a deal to score *Return to Green Acres,* but got a last-minute call telling him that he had been replaced, although his theme was used. And though not involved with Nick at Nite's *Green Acres, We Are There* special, Mizzy did permit the cable channel to use his original theme song for a rap promo of the series.

As the story of *Return to Green Acres* unraveled, nothing had changed in Hooterville over the past twenty years. Oliver was still unable to grow a crop and Lisa was still assaulting the English language.

A new thespian pig was cast to play the Arnold, now owned by Daisy Ziffel (Mary Tanner), niece of Fred and Doris. Actually, it took three porkers to play the porcine Arnold: a stand-in, a stunt pig, and the big ham himself.

A nasty land developer (Henry Gibson) has stepped in in this reunion movie, buying up the entire town of Hooterville, with the intention of converting it into malls, condos, and fast-food joints. The Douglases had moved back to New York but quickly returned on learning the fate that is planned for Hooterville.

Mizzy offers his own feelings on the continued popularity of *Green Acres:* "I knew it would be a smash. Jay Sommers asked me to do the music and the click tracks,"

The Douglases as American Gothics of the late sixties © *copyright Orion Television Entertainment (photo courtesy Orion Television)*

explaining that this involved editing the opening shots in conjunction with the musical theme.

"Jay and Dick [Chevillat] were top writers," he continues. "Eddie Albert was the most versatile. Eva was a natural. They always went with the first take on Eva. Jay Sommers was the brain—the concept was great!"

"*Green Acres* has never stopped being shown all over the world," stresses Gabor, "and I am brilliant and so is the rest of the cast. We speak fifty-two languages," she adds, laughing. "Eddie held the show together and made it work. I adore *Green Acres*—[it was] a wonderful experience. I'd had successes before but never anything like [that] because nothing is like TV. I just wish I would have more time to watch it."

On the topic of Gabor, Albert exclaims, "She's delightful! She's a wonderful person. Very disciplined. She always knew her lines and she was very generous for working and helping everybody and she considered everybody's welfare and comfort. Yes, she's a splendid person."

But how has Albert reconciled his career with his crusade?

"I bought *Green Acres* on the basis of a remark by my agent," recalls Albert, who apparently was not even second choice for Oliver—Don Ameche was another who turned it down, after Ray Milland. "He said, 'Eddie, I got a series for you.' I said, 'What's it about?' He said, 'City slicker comes to the country.' I said, 'Swell, that's me. Everyone gets tired of the rat race. Everyone would like to chuck it all and grow some carrots. It's basic. Sign me.' I knew it would be a success. Had to be. In a sense Thoreau is the real author of *Green Acres*.

"Different people think differently. The kinds of people that are concerned with the planet, they call me and say, incidentally, '[We] love *Green Acres* very much,' but people who love entertainment [don't] necessarily care too much about the environment. It's two different audiences and they're both marvelous. They're both wonderful. [And] it's very interesting that all [the cast] still love each other. We see each other from time to time and I have dinner with Eva once every couple of months. So we all became good friends, which tells a lot about the show."

TWELVE

THE WILD, WILD WEST

(September 17, 1965—April 4, 1969)

Starring Robert Conrad as James West and Ross Martin as Artemus Gordon, this light-hearted series set in the Old West chronicled the exploits of two resourceful Secret Service agents under the administration of President Grant using prototypes of twentieth century gadgetry to catch their nineteenth century quarry. The megalomaniacal dwarf Dr. Miguelito Loveless, portrayed by the late Michael Dunn, and evil magician Count Manzeppi, played by the late Victor Buono, were just two of their nemeses.

"It was a mix of everything," says occasional guest star Yvonne Craig, "it was a Western but they had futuristic kinds of things, gadgets, and fun things and I think that is always of interest to an audience."

The imaginative show that lasted 104 episodes sported such high-tech toys as plastic explosives, radioactive materials, explosive arrows propelled by telescopic-sighted bows, dragon-headed prototypes of the torpedo, armored robot-knights, computer dating, and even an Amorous Amanda, whose clutching hands would love to strangle West to death. Not bad for the 1870s.

"Go Gothic! Be baroque!" *TV Guide* writer Dick Hobson noted in 1968. "Hang crystal chandeliers in your eerie caves. Put stained-glass portholes in your flying saucers. . . . How would you like to be stuck with U.N.C.L.E.'s tiresome electronics? Gimmick it up with your steam-powered wheelchairs. . . . Your puppet-show marionettes firing guns at Supreme Court justices. . . . Your underwater dragons shooting off torpedoes."

"The beautiful thing about [the show's] formula," adds *Wild West* comic book writer Mark Ellis, "[is that] about any type of story can be told and it doesn't seem out of place."

"It drew on mythology," agrees Rene Auberjonois,

171

another guest star who turned up in both TV movie sequels, and they could just adapt any particular [myth]—they never ran out of stories. They had an unlimited supply of ideas."

"There's a magic that happens every now and then between two performers," Ross Martin observed before his death in 1981. "There was something very special about *The Wild, Wild West*."

"I think that the combination of Bob Conrad and Ross Martin was a good one," assesses Craig. "Ross was a concert violinist and very interested in classical things and [serious] acting and Bobby was very much in the style of John Wayne, and Bobby's tastes certainly didn't run to classical violin. I think he was wonderful in the role."

Craig appeared in the "Night of the Grand Emir" episode (January 28, 1966) as Ecstasy LaJoie with Robert Middleton, Don Francks, and Richard Jaeckel. While protecting a Middle Eastern potentate, Emir El Emid (Middleton), from assassination, dapper James West accompanies him to a cabaret where Ecstasy, a can-can dancer, performs. She makes an attempt on the despot's life, as West disposes of her explosive garter in just the

Ross Martin as Artemis Gordon and Robert Conrad as James T. West, 19th century Secret Service agents using 20th century technology (*photo courtesy Viacom*)

172

knick of time. Ecstasy returns to the lair of her employer Dr. Bey, who has ordered the hit. West follows and falls into a trap.

Craig recalls, "I remember the scene where I was a harem dancer and I was popping grapes into Robert Middleton's mouth, because he was portly and he was dressed up as the Emir. I also remember working with Don Francks [in that episode] from *Finian's Rainbow*. I love him dearly, and I hadn't seen him [in years]. Midway through the filming of that I was looking at him and he had put Bobby Conrad into some sort of horrible contraption

and he was going to kill him, and I wanted to save him and he was a mad scientist or something and he had set in his eyetooth a diamond and I thought he had put [it] in there because the character was foppish and he was going to be foppish and I said, 'Oh, my God, you have a diamond in your tooth!' and then he said 'Yes, only don't say it so loudly.' Anyway he had [indeed] set a diamond in his eyetooth."

Continuing on the subject of her guest appearance, Craig notes, "It's a dancing sequence, ballroom dancing, which I don't do, and [Bobby didn't] ballroom dance either, and I said, 'Oh, thank God, we're in luck because I can lead—I just can't follow.' So he said, 'Okay,' [but] he was going to have a choreographer come in and I said, 'No, no, we can do this, honest to God we can do this on our own,' so we were supposed to do a waltz and waltz is easy and so I led and the director said, 'That's fine [but] could you do it a little faster?' and so we said, 'Sure.' So we did the scene again and we waltzed out of the scene slightly faster and the director said, 'Could you waltz even faster than that?' And we said, 'Okay' and we did it again. I'm still leading, Bobby's still following. Finally the director said, 'Okay, but I'd like that one more time, maybe a little bit faster' and Bobby turned to him and said, 'Listen, you try it in three-inch lifts!' "

"[On *The Man From U.N.C.L.E.*] Bobby Vaughn could lead but I couldn't follow and then I led [on *Wild West*] and I thought Bobby Conrad did just fine."

Craig began her theatrical career at sixteen as one of the youngest members of the Ballet Russe de Monte Carlo. She debuted in films with Patrick Wayne in *The Young Land* and also appeared with Elvis in *It Happened at the World's Fair* and *Kissin' Cousins*. After her stint as Batgirl in twenty-six episodes of the sixties *Batman* series, Craig pursued a real estate career in California, traveling extensively with her husband, while occasionally turning up in series episodes from *Love American Style* and *Star Trek* to *Kojak* and *Six Million Dollar Man*.

"In the early days of pictures, when they worked six days a week, they had to be rugged people, they had to be tough," says Ray Walston, another *Wild, Wild West* guest star. "Conrad had that quality. He was not only really very excellent, he brought a certain aura to it—I don't think it would have been a success without him."

Walston appeared in "The Night of Montezuma's Hordes" (October 27, 1967), playing Dr. Henry Johnson, a would-be archeologist, who, using the name Mallory, meets West at a museum, which was the departure point for an expedition to excavate Montezuma's tomb. Mallory is in the employ of nasty Zack Slade who has ordered a hit on West. West buddies up to Col. Pedro Sanchez, the expedition's military escort, and resourceful Artemus Gordon, master of dialects and disguises, turns up as a

Beverly Garland, frequent *Wild, Wild West* guest, most notably in "The Night of the Bleak Island" (*photo courtesy Beverly Garland*)

Yvonne Craig, who made several appearances on *The Wild, Wild West*
(*photo courtesy Yvonne Craig*)

desert rat and is hired on as a digger. Unfortunately the Indians decide that West and Gordon are the real culprits.

"The director [Irving Moore] threw me quite a curve," recalls Walston today about the Max Ehrlich script. "I had an opening which was two or three pages long and he wanted me to play it fast and furious and loud. And after one or two rehearsals I recall Conrad looking up and saying, 'Wow, wow, wait a minute. Why is Ray so way up?' Conrad's approach to work on the screen was [to be] as realistic, as normal as possible. And Moore said, 'We'll take care of it,' [and] then he got me on the side and said, 'I don't want you to change [anything]—I want you to do it as loud as you can; punch this thing as hard as you can.' And I did it and not until I saw the segment did I realize how bad I had been. I never worked again for any of those producers or any of those casting directors. They wouldn't go near me again ever and it was all because of Moore. He had directed several [episodes] and he was just kind of—as quite often happens in this business—at the point where he was perversely antagonistic toward Conrad."

"The best way I can sum it up is with the picture I did with Billy Wilder [*Kiss Me, Stupid*]. We had a fourteen-week shoot and on the twelfth week [Wilder] looked at me and said, 'The problem is we've just all been together too long and that's the problem.' I think this is what had happened with Moore [and Conrad]."

The behind-the-camera team that made this series such a success included creator Michael Garrison, producer Bruce Lansbury (Angela's brother), associate producers Leonard Katzman and Joe Kirby, story consultant Henry Sharp, and makeup artist Kenneth Chase. Some of these would return to participate in two reunion movies a decade later.

"Burt Kennedy directed the first and the second [reunion]," says Rene Auberjonois, who fared better in his guest appearances than did Walston, "and I had worked for Burt Kennedy before. He asked me if I would do it and I said 'Yeah' and that was the first one and then, of course, the second one brought the character back, a detective from Scotland Yard—a British twit.

"I had worked with Bob Conrad as guest on *Baa Baa Black Sheep* and I remember that he was not very nice to me—he got to be as we worked together, but when we first met he was very standoffish, and sort of distrustful and didn't seem like a very happy camper. When I first worked with him there was a fight sequence between [us] and he was very standoffish about my doing it—he wanted the stunt man to do it, and I said, 'I'm perfectly capable of doing it. I've done a lot of physical work, fencing, and stage fighting, and I know I don't look like that type but I really can handle it,' and he said, 'Well, you could take some hard knocks,' and he punched me in

the stomach and he was trying to catch me off my guard and I anticipated it and tensed up enough so that I could take it. He was at that 'holding-it-together stage' when we did those two reunions.

"I haven't seen [Bob] since that time and in those days he was pretty much what you saw was what you got. And when they broke for lunch he would go out running or riding his horse. And [he] was very proud of himself physically. He had a very macho attitude—that's who he is, a bit of John Wayne, kind of guy. At least that's [how] I knew him to be [and] we finally achieved a level of mutual respect—he was very nice [in the end]."

Conrad is right up there among the TV performers who've starred in the most series over the years. Before doing *The Wild, Wild West*, he starred as Tom Lopaka in *Hawaiian Eye* (1959–63) with Anthony Eisley, Poncie Ponce, and Connie Stevens as Cricket. Troy Donahue came into the cast during the final season.

Following *The Wild, Wild West*, Conrad starred in *The D.A.* (1971–72) after two TV movie pilots to get the show off the ground. In the espionage-spy series *Assignment Vienna* (1972–73), he took the role that Roy Scheider had in the TV movie pilot (then called *Assignment Munich*). Next came *Baa Baa Black Sheep*, in which he portrayed real-life World War II marine flying ace, Maj. Pappy Boyington, in charge of a squadron of misfits. The show limped along under that title during the 1976–77 season and then was revamped and retitled *The Black Sheep Squadron* during 1977–78.

Rugged Bob, who around this time was daring TV viewers in a series of commercials to knock a package of Eveready batteries off his shoulder, continued his tough-guy TV persona into the lead role of *The Duke*, as an ex-prizefighter turned Chicago tavern owner, with buddy Red West. The series expired after just five episodes in 1979. Undaunted, Conrad went into another short-lived 1979 series, *A Man Called Sloane*, which was effectively *The Wild, Wild West* brought into a contemporary era, with an imposing six-foot-five black sidekick (played by Ji-Tu Cumbuka) in place of Artemus Gordon, along with a gaggle of high-tech gadgets.

A decade later, after a slew of TV movies for his own A. Shane Productions, a company named after his young son, Shane, and run by his daughter, Joan, Conrad was back as Jesse Hawkes, a rugged loner running a ranger station high in the sierras with real-life sons Shane and Christian in *High Mountain Rangers* (1988). It too was revamped the following season, with the Conrads being moved to civilization (San Francisco) and the program renamed *Jesse Hawkes*.

Robert Conrad was born Conrad Robert Falk on March 1, 1935, in Chicago and attended Northwestern University. He made his show biz debut as a nightclub singer and ultimately, after taking up-and-coming actor buddy Nick Adams's advice to change his name to Robert Conrad, he was signed to a Warner Brothers contract in the mid fifties. He had roles in several of Warners' popular TV series (*Lawman, Maverick, 77 Sunset Strip*) and finally got the lead in *Hawaiian Eye.*

In films (both TV movies and theatrical ones), Conrad has portrayed such disparate figures as gangster Pretty Boy Floyd in *The Young Dillinger* (with pal Nick Adams), then John Dillinger himself in *The Lady in Red,* infamous jewel thief Murf the Surf in *Live a Little, Steal a Lot,* and infamous White House plumber G. Gordon Liddy in the film version of the noted Watergate figure's autobiography. He also starred as fictional detective Nick Carter in a TV movie pilot.

"I'd like to be remembered as one of the better actors in television," says Conrad today. "I [had] hoped that the public might see *Centennial* and say that I've learned a little bit about acting [but] of all the things I've ever done in my life I couldn't wait to get off of *Centennial.* [He was Pasquinal, the French-Canadian trapper.] It was the greatest role of my career [up to that time] and it was written by James Michener and in the first five hours I had the principal role. I [worked] with one of America's greatest actors—Richard Chamberlain. He went to England after he had the tremendous success in *Dr. Kildare* to study as a Shakespearean actor, and working with him was a tremendous experience."

But Conrad will always be first and foremost a tough guy, according to Ray Walston: "He was absolutely wonderful in *The Wild, Wild West.* He spent every moment off screen and his lunch hour practicing, training to be a fighter. He was quite serious about it. Along with three or four other guys that were with him all the time [like stuntman and actor Red West], I used to call them Conrad's Raiders. One of them was [ex-boxer] Roland LaStarza. He was teaching Conrad and Conrad was quite serious and as a horseman he was superb and he was well liked by all the actual cowboys, wranglers, and so forth—he was tough."

And Ross Martin once illustrated Walston's point: "[Once] Bob had to throw Red [West] in one of the scenes—there was a big fight, a tremendous fight sequence, and Red was playing the heavy, doubling [for] somebody and doing the stunt. Bob grabbed him and threw him down a bar into a piano, and there was something that wasn't supposed to be there and Red hit it and went right into the piano and opened [up his] head. We thought in Technicolor it would be unusable—it would look like the whole head was bloody [but] you couldn't see anything."

"Bobby nearly killed himself [in 'Night of the Grand Emir']," reports Yvonne Craig, "There's a scene in which a stuntman was supposed to have swung off a chandelier, and Bobby insisted upon doing it himself. Because he's not a stuntman he didn't understand the mechanics of it, and when he took off and jumped onto the chandelier it snapped his neck. Bobby nearly broke his neck—we were really worried about him. It looked scary and he was injured. And then he couldn't act like he was injured even though he was because he wanted to continue with [the scene]."

Back in the sixties, around the time of things like *Palm Springs Weekend* as a young Warners contract player, there was another side to Conrad, usually reserved especially for the female of the species: "When I met Bobby Conrad it was interesting," tells Craig, "because I was immediately taken with the fact that he had probably the bluest eyes I had ever seen on anybody except maybe Paul Newman. I mean, really riveting blue eyes, and he stuck out his hand and said, 'Hi, I'm Bobby Conrad, the short James Dean.' I would never even have remembered that he was short but now all these years later that's all that I remember because he said that. I think it was a bad move on his part—I wouldn't even have paid attention [otherwise] but anyway he had a great sense of humor about it."

Diane McBain, another member of Conrad's "class" at Warners (she went on to star in *Surfside Six*), found him in another light—at least in *Movieline* magazine in June 1992; "Arrogant and elevator shoes" was how she summed him up.

"Keep Jim West simple and uncomplicated," said a *TV Guide* article on January 6, 1968, "his face a mask. It takes a great many muscles to make a smile—make sure Conrad doesn't use more than two or three. . . . West is never to fall in love or even to show compassion. . . . Bobby looks great with his shirt off. Strip him to the waist at least once per episode."

"I didn't see him as being macho," continues Craig, "[but] I think any actor who wants to do his own stunts—and I preface that by saying I did my own stunts in *Batman,* but the difference was that nobody was taking punches at me—has a macho outlook. Apparently America thinks that being an actor is a less than manly occupation so they have to do something else like do their own stunts so people will not think they are effete, but off camera Bobby had his family around him so he was very much a loving father. He wasn't macho other than [in] doing his own stunts."

And Craig was certainly not the only female guest star to take note of Conrad over the years. Beverly Garland appeared in two episodes, the first of which was "The Night of the Cutthroats" (November 17, 1967), written by Edward H. Lakso and directed by Alan Crosland Jr.

West journeys on a stagecoach with an ex-con (Bradford Dillman) who's quite the dandy. Arriving in New

Athens, the two traveling companions find the populace fleeing. The sniveling sheriff (Jackie Coogan) explains that the town is surrounded by a band of cutthroats. Gordon is at the local saloon owned by Sally Yarnell (Garland) investigating the disappearance of agent Mason. The fiesty mayor (Walter Burke) finally reveals that West's dapper stagecoach friend is actually the leader of the cutthroats come to wreak vengeance, rob the local bank, and sack the town for his wrongful imprisonment.

Garland had designs on a priceless gem left by an eccentric millionaire in "The Night of the Bleak Island" when she made another appearance on the series on March 14, 1969. The script was written by Robert E. Kent and directed by Marvin Chomsky.

West sets sail to remote Bleak Island to claim the Moon Diamond which has been willed to the National Museum by the late Joe Bleak. Bleak's housekeeper Celia Rydell (Garland) confesses that she was also his mistress and now fears for her life. Enter respected British detective Sir Nigel Scott (John Williams). The will is read, strange things begin happening, and the diamond mysteriously disappears.

Garland, the veteran actress who played Fred MacMurray's wife on *My Three Sons* later in that series and Kate Jackson's mother more recently in *Scarecrow and Mrs. King,* debuted in the 1949 flick, *D.O.A.,* and became one of the prolific dramatic TV performers. For *Medic,* the early doctor series, she was nominated for an Emmy.

Today, aside from occasional acting, she operates two hotels, the Beverly Garland Hotel in North Hollywood and the Beverly Garland Hotel in Sacramento. Her daughter Carrington appears on *Santa Barbara.*

Another notable actress guest starring on *The Wild, Wild West* was Agnes Moorehead, who won an Emmy for her role as Emma Valentine in "Night of the Vicious Valentine" (February 10, 1967). This episode was written by Leigh Chapman and directed by Irving Moore.

A visit to a print shop leads West and Gordon to Emma Valentine, a society hostess, who arranges the marriages of men of substance to lovely young ladies of the night. She, of course, controls each and every new bride by blackmail. Her ultimate goal, by controlling the nation's wealth, is to turn this country into a monarchy with herself as Queen Emma.

Ross Martin was himself nominated for his Artemus Gordon role on *The Wild, Wild West.* But as for the show, it has been immortalized by such keepsakes as collectible plates at $29.50 each from the Hamilton Collection as a part of its Classic TV Westerns series, and through a new series of comic books.

Florida-based Mark Ellis, who has written for *Innovation* comics, and his partner Paul Davis, who has written for the business section of the *Providence Journal* in Rhode Island, have collaborated on a four-issue full-color

Wild West comic book series. The two formed a new comic company called Millenium Publishing.

Ellis, who has also written such comics as *The Justice Machine, Star Rangers, Ninja Elite, Warriors,* and *Death Hawk,* says, "I thought [*The Wild, Wild West*] would be great for a comic book adaptation, because it had all the elements: the crazy villains, the gadgets, the plots that always had some kind of apocalyptic thing happening."

178

Ross Martin and Robert Conrad brought Artemis Gordon and James T. West out of retirement in *The Wild, Wild West Revisited* in 1979 (*photo courtesy Viacom*)

Dave Campiti of *Innovation* was not initially interested in the idea when Ellis approached him, so after he and Davis decided to go into business together, they asked illustrator David Banks, who had done *Cyberpunk, Hero Alliance,* and *The Justice Machine,* to do the graphics.

The end result was "The Night of the Iron Tyrants," which is based upon historical fact, with embellishment, such as the Knights of the Golden Circle, a subversive group which West believes orchestrated the assassination of Abraham Lincoln. So West and Gordon go in search of the eighteen pages missing from assassin John Wilkes Booth's diary.

According to Ellis, the Knights enlist the aid of evil Dr. Loveless in an attempt to come up with advanced airships. He would also like to bring back in other issues the mysterious culprit, Count Manzeppi.

Victor Buono, who created the role of Manzeppi in "The Night of the Eccentrics" (September 16, 1966), had Richard Pryor as his ventriloquist in that episode, written by Charles Bennett and directed by Robert Sparr.

A government agent is murdered in a Mexican border town by a group of assassins called the Eccentrics. In the course of the investigation James West arrives at a deserted carnival where he discovers Count Manzeppi and his associates including hulking strong man Titan (Mike Masters) and Deadeye (Anthony Eisley). Manzeppi is planning to bump off Mexican President Benito Juarez and to frame West for the killing. But West hooks up with Miranda (LeGrand Mellon), one of Manzeppi's Eccentrics, who agrees to help him escape.

Buono, incidentally, made his initial *Wild, Wild West* appearance the previous year in the series' premiere episode "The Night of the Inferno" as an immense Chinese merchant named Wing Fat. Buono's Manzeppi came back in "The Night of the Feathered Fury" (January 13, 1967), written by Henry Sharp and directed by Robert Sparr.

West and Gordon again tangle with Manzeppi who, it turns out, is on the trail of a certain toy chicken and eventually snares West in a bird's cage. The prize in this one is the mythical Philosopher's Stone, which, on a full moon, will turn the object nearest to it into gold.

Over the years other colorful villains were played by John (*Addams Family*) Astin, Jackie (*Addams Family*) Coogan, Bernard (*Bewitched*) Fox, and Jim (*Gilligan's Island*) Backus.

Astin appeared in "The Night of the Tartar," which aired February 3, 1967. This episode was written by Robert C. Dennis and Earl Barret and directed by Charles Rondeau. West and Gordon are given orders by the president to deliver a prisoner named Feodor Rimsky to Siberia in exchange for an American diplomat but Rimsky is killed in an attempted escape and Gordon assumes his identity and sets off with West for Vladivostock. When the two refuse to sail on the same Russian ship with their contact, they are taken prisoner. Ending up in a cell with the diplomat, West is accosted by saber-wielding Cossacks under the orders of the evil Count Sazanov (John Astin), who wants the $5 million that Rimsky had accumulated operating an immigrant extortion ring.

In "The Night of the Winged Terror," a two-parter (January 17 and 24, 1969), Jackie Coogan guest starred along with Bernard Fox, William Schallert, and Michele Carey. The script was written by Ken Pettus and the episode was directed by Marvin Chomsky.

The U.S. and Mexico have joined forces to investigate a series of mishaps in which men in high public office have psychotic breaks, becoming criminally insane. Mayor Pudney (Coogan) blows up the train in his tranquil hamlet after being given a new pair of glasses by a sinister optometrist, Dr. Occularis (Bernard Fox). With Artemus off on special assignment West and his cohort Frank Harper (Schallert) are soon on the trail of the mastermind, the real Occularis, who has been sending a stooge out to do his evil bidding. The stooge is done away with and Harper is brainwashed by the doctor to kill West. Occularis is a part of the corrupt Raven organization which has planned to murder the Mexican Ambassador to the U.S.

"The Night of the Sabatini Death" (February 2, 1969) guest starred *Gilligan's Island* cohorts Alan Hale Jr. and Jim Backus together with Ted De Corsia, Jill Townsend, Bethel Leslie, Donald "Red" Barry, Eddie Quillan, and Red West.

In this episode, written by Shirl Hendrix and directed by Charles Rondeau, dying gangleader Johnny Sabatini (De Corsia) asks West to deliver a key to mortician Fabian Swanson (Backus) in Missouri. In turn a gift from Swanson will be entrusted to the care of a young blind girl named Sylvia (Townsend). Ned Brown (Hale), West's assistant, precedes him to town and discovers that a huge army payroll was stolen there years ago by a man named Nolan. West gives the key to Swanson but before the latter can complete the transaction, he is murdered. Sylvia directs West to outlaw Harry Borman (Barry), who may be in possession of the gift, which is actually the $500,000 payroll. Borman, along with Nolan's sister (Leslie), are determined that none shall have the money except themselves.

Additional name guest stars during the series' four-year run included Suzanne Pleshette, Leslie Parrish, Robert Loggia, Ruta Lee, Jeff Corey, Nick Adams, Leslie Nielsen, Martin Landau, Diane McBain, Burgess Meredith, Sue Ane Langdon, Lloyd Bochner, Don Rickles, Keenan Wynn, Boris Karloff, Sammy Davis Jr., Peter Lawford, Patsy Kelly, William Windom, Carroll O'Connor, Ricardo Montalban, Harold Gould, Madlyn Rhue, Lana Wood, John Drew Barrymore, Edward Asner, Harvey Korman, Michael York, Jeannine Riley, Norman Fell, Sherry Jackson, Lynn Loring, Pat Paulsen, Leslie Charleson, and Susan Seaforth.

"In the first [reunion] the villain was Paul Williams, a sweet man, very nice," remembers Rene Auberjonois, who today portrays galactic Constable Odo on *Star Trek: Deep Space Nine*. "Wilford Brimley, who does the Quaker Oats commercials, played Grover Cleveland in it. He was there just as a day player basically and he was in a prison cell—he had a couple of lines. They were setting up the cameras and I went in and sat and talked to him and we got along very nicely. He was very nice, he was an actor but he wasn't hungry for a career and he would do whatever came along.

"[Then] a few months later that film with Jack Lemmon

Rene Auberjonois played stuffy Britisher, Captain Sir David Edney, in the two *Wild, Wild West* reunion movies (*photo courtesy Rene Auberjonois*)

[*The China Syndrome*] came out and that's what made Brimley. From then on he never really stopped working. Now, of course, he does very well."

In *The Wild, Wild West Revisited* (May 9, 1979), Paul Williams plays Miguelito Loveless Jr.; Jo Ann Harris, Carmelita Loveless; and Auberjonois, Captain Sir David Edney. Harry Morgan was brought in as West and Gordon's boss, Robert T. "Skinny" Malone, with Burt Kennedy directing the script by William Bowers.

The year is 1885 and West and Gordon are called out of retirement to hunt down the infamous and equally diminutive Dr. Miguelito Loveless Jr. who is carrying on in the sinister tradition of his late father. He has kidnapped and cloned the heads of state of the United States, Great Britain, Spain, and Russia, replacing them with doubles.

"I think that whatever kind of magic we had," said Ross Martin at the time, "we hope to catch echoes of [in the reunion], particularly since we're not trying to catch exactly the same circumstances. It's these two guys ten years later. They move slower. And you hit a guy and he doesn't go down and you make a pass at a girl and she giggles in your nose."

"Emma Samms was in the second [movie]," Rene Auberjonois recalls, "along with Jonathan Winters, who was fabulous—a wonderful person to be around. For me the high point of doing the second one was to get a chance to spend some time watching Jonathan because he's such an amazing creature. I know Harry Morgan, also a wonderful man, but we didn't [have any scenes] together. I had worked with Victor Buono in *The Man From Atlantis*, and Victor and I had a lot in common and had worked with the same people and had done a lot of Shakespeare. My scenes were basically with Ross [Martin] and Emma. That was her first job in Hollywood."

In *More Wild, Wild West* (October 7 and 8, 1980), Jonathan Winters stars as invisible man Albert Paradine and assorted Paradine relatives, with Harry Morgan, Victor Buono, Randi and Candi Brough, Liz Torres, Dave Madden, Avery Schreiber, Gino Conforti, Jack LaLanne, and Emma Samms as Merriwell Merriwether. Auberjonois returns as Edney.

In this spoof West and Gordon are recalled to service once more by Skinny Malone (Morgan) to pursue evil genius Paradine.

Auberjonois, who has had an extensive career in the theatre (a Tony award for *Coco* and nominations for *Big River* and *City of Angels*), television (Emmy nominations for the TV movie *The Legend of Sleepy Hollow* and for his costarring role in *Benson* as Clayton Endicott III, the governor's officious aide), and in films, has his best memories of *Wild, Wild West* costar, Ross Martin.

Over the years as Artemus Gordon, Ross Martin disguised himself as a Viennese geologist, a desert-rat prospector, a hammy Shakespearean actor, a derelict Civil War veteran, an old Swedish railroad worker, a Chinese coolie, a Parisian art collector, and even President U.S. Grant.

"Ross thought of himself as a very versatile character," says Auberjonois," He prided himself on that and I guess that's what the show really gave him a chance to do. "I had worked with him before [*Wild, Wild West Revisited*] on *Night Gallery*—we worked together in a two-character piece. Ross and I had a little more in common [than Conrad and me] because I'm primarily a theater actor and he had come out of the theater. That was not anything that Bob had ever done—he was a different sort of animal. Ross and I sort of had more to talk about."

Ross Martin was born Martin Rosenblatt, in Grodek, Poland on March 22, 1920. Young Rosenblatt, the son of a sheet metal worker, was brought to the U.S. at the age of six months by his parents.

Martin grew up on Manhattan's Lower East Side, speaking four different languages (though not English until he was four). At the age of ten he tied with another youngster—Red Buttons—in an amateur contest. At that time Martin was lying about his age and playing violin in the symphony orchestra at Teachers College of Columbia University.

Encouraged by his mother, Sadie Rosenblatt, who insisted that he study business administration, education and law, Martin graduated from City College of New York in 1940. Taking the name Mickey Ross, he toured vaudeville circuits with partner Bernie West, before enrolling at the National School of Law in Washington, D.C. He held an M.A. and law degree from Washington University. In 1941 he met and married Hunter College art student Muriel Weiss. He and his wife, and later their infant daughter, lived in Maryland while Martin etched a living in the nation's capital.

Martin worked as a department-store buyer, a government economist, and a PR man before moving into network radio. Eventually he was hired as an actor and announcer by the CBS affiliate WTOP in D.C. Next came New York and the theater with parts in *Hazel Flagg* and *Shinbone Alley*, as well as the road company of *Guys and Dolls*. After a bout of marital woes, the first Mrs. Martin would die of cancer.

A late fifties TV episode of *Peter Gunn*, directed by Blake Edwards, was Martin's big break in Tinsel Town. Six months later Edwards offered him the role of Andamo, star John Vivyan's partner, in *Mr. Lucky*. Not long afterward, Edwards gave him an important role in *The Great Race* (1965).

Perhaps Martin's most noteworthy film role was as the deadly asthmatic stalker in *Experiment in Terror* (1962). Martin was nominated for a Golden Globe Award. "That was a scary picture," he once said, "one of the best directorial jobs that Blake Edwards ever did."

"Ross I had known from New York," recalls Ray Walston, "He was in the theater [there] and so was I. And so it was an opportunity to work with him [in *Wild, Wild West*] which I had never done before. I had always liked him very much and always thought he was a very good actor with a wonderful voice and a very, very charming personality."

Among Martin's theater credits were *Mother Courage, The Chinese Wall, Becket, The Firebrand, I Do! I Do!* and *Deathtrap*. Martin died in 1981 of a heart attack at the age of sixty-one while playing tennis. He had suffered a previous attack in 1969.

"As I recall," Walston says, "he was complaining bitterly about the hours they were working from very early in the morning until eight or nine every night, and that's, in a sense, unusual even for television, particularly in those days in the sixties, and when I did the show it was the third year and I was surprised that the front office was [allowing them] those kind of hours, and I said to Ross, 'Why don't you and Conrad go to the front office and tell them, "Look, we've got a hit, now let's don't run it into the ground," ' and he said, 'I can't do that and Conrad would not do it,' and I said, 'Why?' and he said, 'Because he loves to come to the studio—he lives for this. This is his life. He loves to come here in the morning and he loves to stay as late as he can.' The cost was a heavy one because later [Martin] had a very serious heart attack."

"I can't say I'm happy being second banana," Martin once said of his playing second lead to Conrad's James T. West (just as David McCallum would do to Robert Vaughn in *The Man From U.N.C.L.E.*). But in any case he certainly had come a long way from the little Polish-speaking boy in the Bronx to supremely confident Bob Conrad's sidekick Artemus Gordon in *The Wild, Wild West*.

Ray Walston and friends, guest starring in the episode "The Night of Montezuma's Hordes" (*photo courtesy Ray Walston*)

The once and always Jeannie made a second return to TV in 1991 in *I Still Dream of Jeannie* (*photo courtesy Barbara Eden Fan Club*)

THIRTEEN

I DREAM OF JEANNIE

(September 18, 1965–September 1, 1970)

One of the most irresistible sitcoms of the sixties revolved around an Air Force astronaut who uncorked a bottle after crashing on a deserted island, releasing a sexy two-thousand-year-old genie, named Jeannie. Barbara Eden portrayed the genie, Larry Hagman was flyer Tony Nelson, and Bill Daily was his girl-crazy fellow astronaut, Roger Healey, and Hayden Rorke was their commanding officer, Col. Alfred Bellows.

"Hayden Rorke—I liked him very much," recalls Michael Ansara, Eden's one-time husband and occasional director and guest star of *I Dream of Jeannie*. "I liked him because he liked me and he liked my directing. He thought I was talented. He thought I should go on as a director. He was such an old pro—he was beautiful to work with."

"I always kept in touch with Hayden Rorke," says Eden, "because he made sure that we did. He always kept us together."

In the original NBC series, General Stone was played by Philip Ober, General Peterson by Barton MacLane, General Schaeffer by Vinton Haworth, and Bellows's wife Amanda by Emmaline Henry. The creator of *I Dream of Jeannie* was Sidney Sheldon in the years before he became a mega-selling novelist.

In the fall of 1968 in an episode called "The Wedding," written by James Henerson and directed by Claudio Guzman, Tony and Jeannie were married. Jeannie's wedding gown like all of Jeannie's clothes was created by Joie Hutchinson; however, having the nuptials was perhaps an unwise move since Hagman has avoided any association with the series ever since.

184

(*Bewitched*) Asher, with Hugh Benson producing. The teleplay was written by Irma Kalish, the story was by Dinah and Julie Kirgo and Irma Kalish. It was the eleventh highest rated TV film for the 1985–86 season.

And once again Eden reprised her role as a contemporary genie in October 1991 in *I Still Dream of Jeannie*.

"A lot of high concept shows have been done lately," said Eden at the time, "but this is high camp—a Jeannie is a genie and she's made to serve. Jeannie wasn't a wimp or a robot. She really had a mind of her own. Jeannie was certainly an independent woman. She was never a doormat. [And] naturally when you do something like *I Still Dream of Jeannie,* something that's going to be compared with something that's still on all over the world, you start looking in the mirror.

"To reprise something you did like twenty-five years ago is pretty scary," she told *TV Guide*. "I'm human and of course I thought about it more than twice. If I were playing any other part, I think I would have to grapple with its appropriateness, but Jeannie is different. She's a classical character. What really concerned me about my age is that I didn't want to disappoint the audience who is

The Jeannie television viewers have been dreaming about since the mid-sixties—and with her master, astronaut Tony Nelson (Barbara Eden and Larry Hagman)

"The wedding episode was my favorite," says Eden today. "Her love for her husband and master is very honest and very real and certainly direct and I wouldn't call that sexist. Actually I did not see all of the episodes [but] when I did *Dallas,* Larry said that he knew people who had all of the episodes on tape and asked me if I would like to buy them. We both bought copies, so now I have all five years."

In fact, the series remained so popular—even after the end of its five-year run—that Eden and Daily reteamed in 1985 for *I Dream of Jeannie: 15 Years Later,* with Wayne Rogers in place of Larry Hagman, who had gone on to more lucrative work as TV's J.R. Ewing. Hayden Rorke also returned as Colonel Bellows.

When first approached about *I Dream of Jeannie: 15 Years Later,* a reluctant Eden reconsidered when Daily and Rorke said they would come back. The Nelsons' son was played by MacKenzie Astin (son of Patty Duke and John Astin) and the production was directed by William

Larry Hagman as Capt. Tony Nelson and Barbara Eden as his "girl Friday," Jeannie

used to seeing me as Jeannie looked twenty-five years ago. But I just decided to go ahead and do it.

"I [still] hear from Bill [Daily]. We just make a career out of doing reunions—we had a good time up in Vancouver [where *I Still Dream of Jeannie* was shot]. Boy, did we have a good time. We always have a nice time together."

"Bill Daily is fun," concurs Ansara. "He was a lot of fun to work with. He's funny onscreen. He's funny offscreen. He's easy and fun to work with. They wanted me to do [*I Still Dream of Jeannie*] but things got a little crossed and I didn't do it."

Born in Des Moines, Daily got his start in show business after his stint in the military, entering Chicago's Goodman Theatre upon his discharge. Later Daily landed a job at NBC and soon he was submitting comedy material for Dennis James's program *Club 60*, upon which he eventually was asked to perform. Around this time he also began doing stand-up comedy in various clubs around Chicago.

All of these experiences snagged him a writing job on

The Mike Douglas Show, where he soon began to perform himself, drawing the attention of Steve Allen. Once in L.A., Daily guested on *Bewitched* and *The Farmer's Daughter,* while performing solo at Ye Little Club in Beverly Hills.

He was always a versatile performer—even during *I Dream of Jeannie,* he was producing, directing, and starring in *Bill Daily's Hocus Pocus Gang,* a syndicated children's variety show.

Daily has also appeared in the role of annoyingly pushy airline pilot Howard Borden on *The Bob Newhart Show* for nearly seven years. He has acted in numerous theatrical productions, has worked on the Toronto TV production of *The Comedy Factory,* and has written a play *Lover's Leap.* He also has turned up as guest on Bob Newhart's subsequent series, *Newhart* and *Bob.*

Today Daily is a resident of Albuquerque and has his own commercial TV company. He has dabbled in other series—*The Comedy Shop, The Lou Kelly Show, Small and Fry,* and *Starting From Scratch*—but none have equaled the popularity of either *Jeannie* or *Bob Newhart.*

"We were never really a big hit," says Daily today of the original *Jeannie* series. "Like every thirteen weeks Sidney Sheldon would come up and say, 'We're picked up another thirteen weeks,' but it was never like, 'Wow! We're gonna be a hit for five years!' "

"The worst place Jeannie ever blinked us—we were out on the water and the water's about twenty feet high and they were supposed to spray warm water and they sprayed ice-cold water on us and we were screaming. They thought it was good acting."

"I like the way Larry Hagman works better [than Bob Newhart]," continues Daily, "because he's an actor and he likes to rehearse, and [Bob] doesn't, but he's probably the nicest, sweetest man I've ever met—the nicest of the two was [definitely] Bob Newhart."

"Larry was more like J.R. because he was from Dallas—he lived like that when we did *Jeannie*. He was an incredible human being—like he would have parties after the show and he was J.R., a classy guy—a bigger-than-life guy. I loved working with Larry. Larry's great."

Noticeably absent from *I Still Dream of Jeannie* was Hagman, as he was six years before in *I Dream of Jeannie: 15 Years Later* when Wayne Rogers subbed.

In this latest, Eden is faced with raising her teenage son (Chris Bolton) while husband Tony Nelson is away on a prolonged secret mission in space. But enter evil twin, genie number two—also played by Eden—who reminds Jeannie that she has been "single" for so long that she must find a new master before the next new moon or return to Baghdad forever.

Consequently Jeannie explores the nineties singles scene as her wicked sibling sabotages her every step of the way. Jeannie is given two weeks to find a new master, during which she ends up in single bars as her fingers do the walking through the classified personals.

Meanwhile when her diabolical sister kidnaps Tony Junior, Jeannie joins forces with his high school teacher (played by Ken Kercheval) to find the missing lad.

After Junior is recovered, Jeannie realizes that she could have asked bachelor Simpson to be her new master. He has already gone but returns to the house to retrieve his car keys just moments before Jeannie's curfew is up. Desperately Jeannie ensnares him and he agrees to be her new master.

It's ironic that Hagman's nemesis from *Dallas* plays Eden's leading man in the *Jeannie* movie presentation. As for Hagman's absence this time around, she said at the time, "We asked him—we wanted him but he'd finished thirteen years of *Dallas* and he was tired and what he told me was that he [was going] to Europe for a vacation."

Kercheval, a thirteen-year veteran of *Dallas,* was born in Wolcottville, Indiana, and grew up in Clinton. He attended the University of Indiana and the University of the Pacific in Stockton, California, majoring in music and drama before moving on to the Neighborhood Playhouse School of Theatre in New York City.

Trained as a singer, Kercheval appeared on the Broadway musical stage and later moved on to dramatic roles, including *Happily Ever After, Who's Afraid of Virginia Woolf? Fiddler on the Roof, Cabaret, Here's Where I Belong,* and others.

Christopher Bolton was born in Toronto, and lives and works in Vancouver, British Columbia. He played Kirk Stevens on *My Secret Identity*.

On *Jeannie,* he says, "I remember sitting in front of the TV with a bowl of cereal, watching *I Dream of Jeannie,* when I was young. I was always a big fan. Who would have ever dreamed I would become Jeannie's son? It's not something I would have ever imagined."

Other members of the reunion movie cast included Al Waxman as Wescott, Peter Breck as Sahm-Ir (the role that

Jeannie's abode in *I Dream of Jeannie*

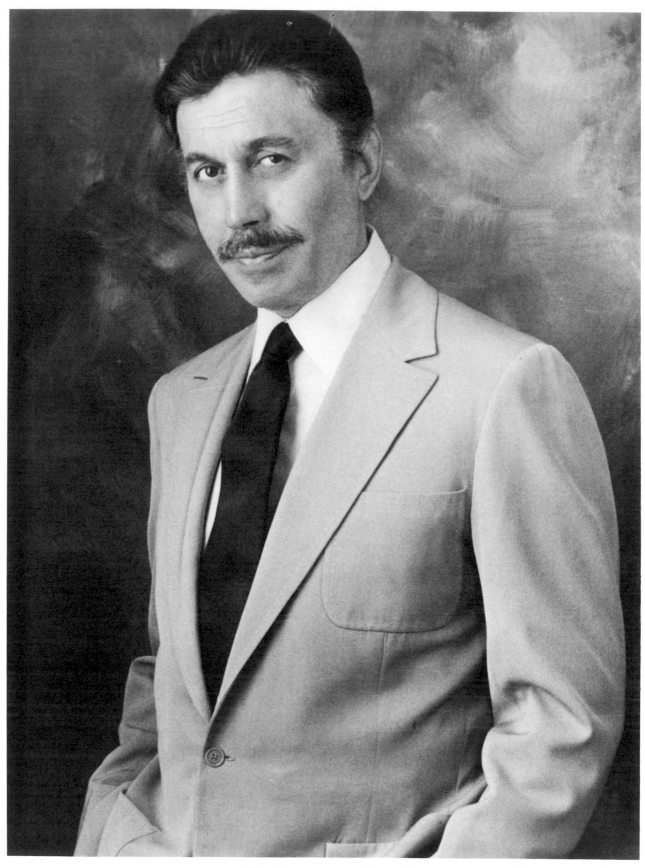

Michael Ansara, occasional *Jeannie* director and guest star and former husband of Barbara Eden (*photo courtesy Michael Ansara*)

Ansara was to have played), Brent Stait as Eddie, Jason Scott as Guzer, and Gary Chalk as Carlyle.

During the movie's filming in Vancouver, Eden, who at fifty-plus is still, as Wayne and Garth might put it, a babe, was treated to a surprise birthday party. The cake was shaped like a genie bottle and a large floating card was suspended by balloons and she was presented with a sweatshirt inscribed "We will always dream of Jeannie."

Joe Scanlon was the director of the latest movie, which was written by April Kelly. Carla Singer was executive producer, and Joan Carson producer for Jeannie Entertainment, Inc., in association with Columbia Pictures Television and Eden's own Bar-Gene Productions.

Though not reunited in either of the *Jeannie* movies, Eden and Hagman were back together again (actually this time at each other's throats) in several episodes of *Dallas* during its final season.

"I loved working on *Dallas*," say Eden today of her guest appearance on the former nighttime soap. "I think it [was] the most fun I have had in ages. Working with Larry, it felt as though we had never stopped—he was wonderful [but] we are both working people, and we go in different directions."

Hagman, who was nearly bounced from the original *Jeannie* series for making too many demands, has less fond memories of the series than does Eden.

"When Larry Hagman was critical over some aspects of the series in the early days and nearly lost his job as a result," director-producer Claudio Guzman told *TV Guide,* "guess who consoled him and insisted that he was the right man? Barbara puts up with people as a sister, mother, best friend. Even women like her."

But just as Jeannie led Tony around, Eden led Hagman around with her easygoing nature. She even defended him at the time: "He was so sweet. I think Jeannie kind of led him around, really [but] whenever Larry feels strongly about something, it's for the good of the show. He's never out to hurt anyone."

And Hagman admitted to *TV Guide* in 1966 that life on the *Jeannie* set was less than rosy at times depending upon his temperament: "I'm kind of a troublemaker on the set."

And indeed, some crew members threatened to quit over disagreements with him. However, Hagman has fared well since though he has his quirks. He charges fans for autographs in the way of a poem, a prayer, or a song. Born on September 21, 1931, and having been known to dabble in numerology, Hagman is defined by that school as artistic, friendly, sociable, and as having learned how to cooperate with others without losing his individuality. Apparently he's risen above his sometimes troubled days on the *Jeannie* set.

Today, living a spontaneous life in Malibu, Hagman (who has been on sixteen *TV Guide* covers over the years)

sometimes indulges in a self-imposed vow of silence for twenty-four hours at a time.

Hagman's motto is "Life is a celebration." He adds, "[J.R. is] such a miserable crud. I love him. I really do." And as for himself, he continues, "I don't gamble. I am not a womanizer. I have two great kids and am [still] married to the same wife." Living well is, indeed, the best revenge, as Hagman tells it.

"Well, as an actor [Larry's] fine," comments Ansara, "a good actor, very responsive. As a director in the beginning, I don't think he accepted me because he knew me so well as an actor and his leading lady's husband. I don't think he particularly liked me directing the show, but as we worked he softened up and seemed to accept it. Everything was okay and I liked working with him because he's very talented. We're [still] very, very friendly when we run across one another."

Hagman's mother, Mary Martin, was only sixteen when he was born in Weatherford, Texas, and while she was courting fame on stage, Larry was raised by his grandmother. A rambunctious youth, he burned down a two hundred-year-old dormitory at his prep school and passed out after drinking a whole bottle of gin in his mother's hotel suite while she was performing at a matinee.

After one of his periodic spats with his famous mother, Larry, while staying with his father in Weatherford, flirted with the idea of becoming a cowboy but that was soon nixed.

"There's just so much of baling hay," he told *TV Guide* in 1966. "No matter how proficient you become, there's just so far you can go."

His mother presented him with a trip to Europe as a graduation gift after he finished high school in 1948. Afterward he found himself in New York. By then the acting bug had bitten. Low marks at Bard College at Annandale-on-Hudson, New York, had given way to acting lessons with Margo Jones in Dallas.

Additional drama studies included a season with Eva Le Gallienne and Margaret Webster at Woodstock, New York. Hagman's first real job though was as an assistant stage manager with St. John Terrell's Music Circus in Florida. Through his Florida connections Hagman ended up in Lambertville, New Jersey, where he worked as prop-man/stage manager and actor/singer/dancer. It was at this place in time that his mother finally caught up with him again, popping the big question: would he like to go to London and be in *South Pacific* with her?

Hagman would spend the next five years in England, doing a bit part in his mom's show and starring in a late-night act at another theater, where he sang and did a little comedy routine. Following this were four years in the Air Force, producing shows in Europe and keeping company with an attractive Swedish dress designer named Maj Axelsson. They married in 1954.

Back in New York, Hagman found work readily on and off Broadway, and in almost six hundred television shows in New York, ranging from *Hallmark Hall of Fame* to *Play of the Week, Studio One* and the soap *Edge of Night.*

For nine years the money rolled in and then for nine months there was nothing. Hagman went from raking in $2,000 a week to taking home zip. So what else was there to do except move to Hollywood?

Five TV pilots presented themselves and *Jeannie* turned out to be Hagman's ticket to the big time. In 1966 Hagman would receive recognition for his first significant film appearance in Sidney's Lumet's *The Group.* His performance was lauded as "first-rate" by *Saturday Review.*

Other film credits include *Fail-Safe*, another Sidney Lumet venture, *Ensign Pulver*, with Joshua Logan directing, and Otto Preminger's *In Harm's Way.*

Barbara Eden will always be remembered as the girl called Jeannie. "I enjoyed it—I enjoyed it a lot," she says today. "I guess it's a character that I can pull all the stops out with. And then I play my naughty sister, too, so you see I can have a good time. The first year I was pregnant [and viewers] never saw but, boy, was I pregnant! They used a lot of close-ups."

"We had a big full grown male lion and this was when I was pregnant and I had done a couple of features with lions so I'd had a little bit of experience," she recounts, "and I knew you were supposed to go over, like with any animal, and let it become familiar with you, and I was over there feeding him raw meat and I went over to Larry and I said, 'Larry, you have to go over and make friends with the lion.' He said, 'I don't want to meet a lion. I'm not going to go over and meet the lion.' Larry, in the context of the scene, thought I was popping in a little puppy. So they put a bowl of raw meat by my side and I blinked and they brought the lion in and he put his big paws over the sofa and he ate the meat. They brought Larry in. He sat there. They said 'Action!' and the lion turned around, looked at Larry and went 'Braghhhh!' Well, there was not a man on that stage. Everyone ran. The camera was on its side. And I had this six hundred pound lion [purring] in my pregnant lap!"

Barbara Jean Moorehead was born on August 23, 1934 in Tucson. At three young Barbara Jean was taken to San Francisco by her mother, who had divorced her father and married Harrison Huffman, a Pacific Telephone Company lineman. Years later, after changing her name to Eden, she tried nightclub singing and studied at City College in San Francisco for a year and studied acting with Elizabeth Holloway before moving to Hollywood. She also studied music at San Francisco Conservatory and sang with bands in the Bay Area on weekends.

A producer from 20th Century-Fox spotted her in *The Voice of the Turtle* at the Laguna Playhouse. She soon found herself in the syndicated *How to Marry a Millionaire*, which ran for two seasons (1958–60). It was a TV spinoff of the Marilyn Monroe–Betty Grable–Lauren Bacall movie. Next she was a semiregular on *The Johnny Carson Show*, which was a primetime series in 1956.

Then she married Michael Ansara of *Broken Arrow* in January of 1958. Next came films such as *Voyage to the Bottom of the Sea* with husband Michael Ansara; *The Wonderful World of the Brothers Grimm, Five Weeks in a Balloon*, and *The Seven Faces of Dr. Lao.*

Says Eden of her early film career: "I was kissed, rescued, and sung to by Pat Boone, Fabian, Frankie Avalon, Gary Crosby. Elvis—twice. I didn't get to cry too often. It was very frustrating."

Life after *I Dream of Jeannie* included not only a continuing string of TV movies, both comedies like *Your Mother Wears Combat Boots* and dramas such as *A Howling in The Woods* (with Hagman), but also a busted 1974 pilot called *The Barbara Eden Show*, the semi-hit series *Harper Valley P.T.A.* (1981–82) and the unsuccessful *Brand New Life* (1989), as well as seventeen Bob Hope specials.

And she even found the time back in the 1960s to do an album on Dot Records called *Miss Barbara Eden*. During *Jeannie* hiatuses she toured in such musicals as *Pajama Game, South Pacific, The Unsinkable Molly Brown, The Sound of Music, Annie Get Your Gun*, and *The Best Little Whorehouse in Texas.*

In the seventies Eden became known for her L'Eggs pantyhose commercials and went on to play Vegas and the dinner theater circuit.

Eden never demanded a fancy dressing room as did Elizabeth Montgomery and she never drove a $16,000 Ferrari as did Sally Field. "She can have anything," director Claudio Guzman said at the time, "[and] she asks for nothing. She dresses in an old trailer and thinks she's lucky to have that."

Kasey Rogers of *Bewitched* recalls that time: "*Jeannie* started after [our show]. We were shooting side by side on that lot for a number of years. Barbara and I would see each other in makeup. And everyone thought *Jeannie* was an imitation [of *Bewitched*], though it was different and it turned out to be very popular."

Preston Beckman, vice-president of programming and scheduling at NBC, makes an interesting point: "Barbara has a following. She has had enormous success in made-for-TV movies. We're dealing with an extremely popular star and an extremely popular vehicle at a time when these nostalgia things seem to be working."

And indeed nostalgia is all the craze today. How many people will remember that the first *Jeannie* episode in which Michael Ansara appeared was "Happy Anniversa-

Wayne Rogers, the "new" Tony Nelson in *I Dream of Jeannie: 15 Years Later*

The "revamped" Jeannie—navel and all—in the eighties (*photo courtesy Barbara Eden Fan Club*)

ry," featuring Arthur C. Romans and Donald Mitchell? As the Blue Djinn, Ansara attempts to wreak havoc on Jeannie and Captain Nelson's plans to celebrate their first anniversary. The episode was written by Sidney Sheldon and directed by Claudio Guzman.

"Yes, I did appear maybe three [times]," recalls Ansara today. "I don't think a lot of people are aware of that. A lot of people know that I was married to Barbara—we worked together and we traveled together and we did some movies together, but I don't think it's a prominent thing that I did the Blue Djinn. I directed one episode toward the end there. I've directed plays but that's the only television that I've ever done. I wanted to get into it, but it's like getting started all over again, it's very difficult for them to see you as a director when they know you as an actor.

"I wanted to do more. As a matter of fact, if it was going to be picked up for another year, they told me I could direct half the shows after that, which would have opened up a new career in directing, but as it turned out, that was the last year of the show."

The episode which Ansara directed was called "One Jeannie Beats Four of a Kind," and it featured Herbert Rudley as Martino, Vinton Haworth as General Schaeffer, William Wintersole as Provost Marshal Rose, Tony Giorgio as Torpedo, and Walter Burke as The Boss. The episode was written by Perry Grant and Dick Bensfield.

Ansara's next guest appearance was in "The Battle of Waikiki," in which he portrayed King Kamehameha. Featured players included Theodore Nobriga, Marc Towers, and Pat Meikle. The episode was written by Marty Roth and directed by Hal Cooper.

His last was "My Sister the Homewrecker," featuring Farrah Fawcett as Cindy. Ansara played Biff Jellico. Eden doubled as Jeannie and her sister in this episode, written by James Henerson and directed by Claudio Guzman.

At the time that Ansara and Eden were married, at least fifty of his paintings hung throughout their house.

But interests as well as spouses sometimes change: "I haven't painted in a long time. I did for a while—I was painting every single day, but I haven't done it in a long

Barbara Eden post *Jeannie* (*photo courtesy Barbara Eden Fan Club*)

time. I've gotten away from it. I keep thinking I'll go back to it but I haven't yet. I love it but I really don't have room [for it]. I've taken up golf. I have a group of guys I play with and one of my golf friends is Tom Bosley. I really enjoy it—I guess that's why I haven't been painting at all. I get invited to these celebrity golf matches—like the Crosby golf match—around the country and I love doing it. That's why I've gotten away from painting."

"*Broken Arrow* is the most prominent series that I did," Ansara points out. "I, of course, have free-lanced a lot. Another TV series of my own was *Law of the Plainsman*. That was in the early sixties. I still get letters from foreign countries [particularly] Germany and France."

"Yes, I do wish I had a series," said Ansara during the *Jeannie* run. "It's steady, it's secure. People don't know you unless you're a superstar, and I am not the all-American-looking boy."

Today Ansara asserts, "I said that a long time ago. I'm more or less semiretired now and I suppose I felt that way for a time and that's true, especially in those days when doing a series was like thirty-nine episodes per season compared to twenty or twenty-two episodes and the networks dominated television at that time so if you had a series on a network and it ran two to four years, it made you a very, very prominent personality and it still does but not to the degree that it did in the past because of cable and all that [taking] away from the networks.

"[Barbara] has a following. She's very popular—people like her and as the years go on and we get older, we [both] still have a following—like I still get fan letters for Cochise, and she has a very strong following and they keep calling for her to come back and do that kind of role. That was her most prominent thing, and she did many things before that [but] they keep asking for *Jeannie*. People have seen me in many things but they keep referring to me as Cochise.

"I think most actors feel that [a series] is only a step in the direction for an ultimate goal of being bigger and better and more diversified in the things you do, more versatile. A lot of actors after awhile resent playing a particular role and they leave a show to go on to bigger and better things and that doesn't very often happen. Once you leave a show sometimes you die for a while and don't get work, so I don't think anybody feels this is the position that [they] want to be in for the rest of [their] life while doing a series. It's wonderful doing it—the money is good, the security is good, but they feel it's only a step to bigger and better things.

"If a role has really made your career and helped you move forward even though you haven't achieved what you want to achieve, [though] you don't want to feel that you're only known for one role, you've [still] got to be grateful. I mean I'm grateful for having done Cochise because it made me prominent and before that I did many things and they said, 'Oh, I know that face, but I don't know his name,' but after Cochise they knew who I was. You have to be grateful for the role that makes you famous.

"I don't watch episodic television. I made my living at it, television and motion pictures, but really I don't like episodic television. I like to work at it, but I don't like to watch it. So I didn't see (*I Still Dream of Jeannie*)."

Ansara once said in *TV Guide*, "Barbara is intelligent, but not mixed-up intelligent. She gets mad like anyone else—when she's dieting she's mean as a tiger—but her anger doesn't linger and corrode. She's stable—but even the most stable people, especially actresses, need attention, applause, and appreciation. After eight years and one child, we're no longer just two people—we're a couple."

He stresses today when reminded of his words, "Remember [then] I was married to her, and being married to someone and close to someone, your opinions are very, very colored, and you pull together and you work for each other, and they are not always objective. Not that what I said was wrong at the time, maybe what I said was right at the time, but now . . . I would say I wouldn't [be a fan of hers]. And this has nothing to do with her talent or ability or what she does on the screen. [Jeannie's] just not the type of character I would follow.

"[Today] I would not be a fan of Barbara the actress. She's not the type of screen personality that appeals to me [to the extent] that I would go out of my way to watch her on television and that's not to degrade her talent or her ability, it's just personal likes and dislikes. No, I would not follow her. I don't think I would be a fan of hers.

"To a degree [we are still friendly]. We have a son [Mathew] and we've had some problems and we disagree on certain things concerning our son, so we have been friendly and we would be again but we don't communicate very often anymore. We did for a while, but we don't anymore. I have my own life—she has her own life."

"I never look back at past relationships or compare them with my present one. That's not fair," counters Eden today. "What I like about my [present] marriage is that we share the same interests and we like to do the same things. Sharing everything in all respects, that makes me feel good and wonderful as a person. I never thought I'd like sharing things as much as I do with Jon [Eicholtz]. We have great respect for each other and we don't compete with each other and that's why it works. It's a waste of time not to be happy. I'm always saying that worrying is a waste of time. I like to work—I love it. I'm lucky. I'm very, very lucky."

Eden and Ansara divorced in 1972. She later married Chicago newspaperman Charles Fegert, whom she divorced in 1982. She dated plastic surgeon Dr. Stanley Frileck for awhile before marrying husband number three, architect-engineer Jon Eicholtz, following a seven-year courtship.

Over the years, many big stars and later names guested on *I Dream of Jeannie:*

Dabney Coleman appeared in "Anybody Here Seen Jeannie," written by Arnold Horwitt and directed by Gene Nelson. Bill Mumy was in "Whatever Happened to Baby Custer," written by Austin and Irma Kalish and directed by Nelson. Lurene Tuttle turned up in "What House Across the Street," written by Arthur Alsberg and Bob Fischer and directed by Theodore J. Flicker.

Butch (*The Munsters*) Patrick appeared in "My Master, the Author," written by Sidney Sheldon and directed by Dick Goode. Paul Lynde was in both "Everybody's a Movie Star," written by Mark Rowane and directed by Claudio Guzman, and "Please Don't Feed the Astronaut," written by Ron Friedman and directed by Hal Cooper.

On the eve of her early nineties tour of *Last of the Red Hot Lovers* (*photo courtesy Barbara Eden Fan Club*)

Bob Denver guest starred in "My Son, the Genie," written by Bill Richards and directed by Guzman. Ted Cassidy appeared in "Genie, Genie, Who's Got the Jeannie," written by James Herndon and directed by Hal Cooper, and in "Please Don't Feed the Astronaut."

Sammy Davis Jr. played himself in "The Greatest Entertainer in the World," written by Sidney Sheldon and directed by Claudio Guzman. Jamie (*M*A*S*H*) Farr appeared in "Get Me to Mecca on Time," written by James Allardice and Tom Adair and directed by E.W. Swackhamer. And in "Biggest Star in Hollywood," *Laugh-In*'s Judy Carne, Arte Johnson, Gary Owens, and George H. Schlatter all played themselves in a script written by James Henerson and directed by Guzman.

Milton Berle appeared as Charles in "The Greatest Con Artist in the World," written by Allan Devon and directed by Guzman. David Soul and Don Rickles were in "My Master, the Weakling," written by Ron Friedman and directed by Guzman. And Jim Backus appeared as General Fitzhugh in "Help, Help a Shark!" written by Henerson and directed by Guzman.

Dick (*Bewitched*) Sargent and J. Pat O'Malley teamed together in "Jeannie for the Defense," written by Bruce Howard and directed by Hal Cooper. Fran (*Green Acres*) Ryan appeared in "One of Our Hotels Is Growing," written by Robert Rodgers and directed by Jerry Bernstein. Jackie Coogan guest starred in "Guess Who's Going to Be a Bride?" (parts one and two), written by James Henerson and directed by Cooper. Farrah Fawcett and Howard Morton appeared in "See You in C-U-B-A," written by John McGreevey and directed by Cooper.

When people talk about early Farrah Fawcett, they think of Jill on *Charlie's Angels,* but actually Farrah started out as Cindy on *I Dream of Jeannie.* Later she played the girl next door to David Janssen in *Harry-O.*

In 1973, there was a revival of America's favorite genie in a Hanna-Barbera cartoon series called, simply, *Jeannie.* In this version the animated Jeannie is ruled by adolescent master Corry. The two hang out with Corry's friend, Henry, and Jeannie's brother, Babu, traveling cross country on Corry's motorbike. The kids' dog Surfer even tags along. Julie McWhirter provided the voice of Jeannie; Marc Hamill, Corry; Bob Hastings, Henry; and Joe Besser, Babu.

Today having sold her *Jeannie* residual rights, Eden gets no money from the series, but she's not bitter. "It was a very stylish piece, not characteristic of its time. Our show hasn't dated—its subject matter is sort of ageless."

Eden, unlike *Bewitched*'s Elizabeth Montgomery, has not shunned her sixties sitcom persona. And why should she? It has given her worldwide recognition as one of the most popular characters in the history of television, it has given her a movies-for-television deal with NBC; it has

Barbara Eden (*photo Charles W. Bush. Courtesy Barbara Eden*)

given her two top-rated reunions movies; and it has given her a star on the Hollywood Walk of Fame. It has even given her an honorary doctor of law degree from the University of West Los Angeles School of Law.

"[Jeannie's] easy to be with," says the actress who starred in 139 half-hour episodes of *I Dream of Jeannie*. "She's fun to portray. This is a fantasy, a modern-day fairy tale that has nothing to do with women's liberation. It's not making a political statement, it's entertaining people."

"Listen, she's a beautiful, sexy lady," says Wayne Rogers, Eden's costar in *I Dream of Jeannie: 15 Years Later,* "and that's the way she's portrayed on TV, and every man wants to lust after her and I'm no different—I don't think—than any other man, and if that's sexist, I'm a sexist."

And indeed, Jeannie was an object of desire, wearing a minimum-cleavage bolero jacket of rosewood velvet, harem pantaloons lined with silk to make them opaque and an eight-inch girdle, also of rose-colored velvet. (The standard joke in those years was that she had no navel, thanks to the NBC censors who wouldn't allow it to be shown.)

Sidney Sheldon said at the time, "What makes Jeannie sexy is that she doesn't play sex."

But Tony Randall, who starred with Eden in *The Brass Bottle,* also dealing with a genie, and *The Seven Faces of Dr. Lao,* countered, "Barbara has a wonderful bawdy sense of humor that not everyone gets to know."

In the long run though, life hasn't always been easy for the comely blond named Jeannie. According to Sherry Hansen-Steiger and Brad Steiger, authors of *Hollywood and the Supernatural,* Barbara Eden has visited Angela Louise Gallo (who has forty years of experience as one of Hollywood's most esteemed astrologers). At first, according to the Steigers, Eden visited anonymously under the name Huffman (her stepfather's name). She had actually had a chart done about twenty years earlier, say the Steigers, that had said she would experience the highs and lows of a roller coaster career, making a lot of money and losing it by listening to the wrong people.

But Eden has landed on her feet and Hagman has gone on to make a fortune of his own. Series creator-turned-novelist Sidney Sheldon had this to say of Hagman at the time: "He can be difficult, but it stems from being such a strong perfectionist. He wants to own the world and own it this afternoon."

And later as J.R. Ewing, Hagman did, at least for an afternoon.

Edward Platt, as harried as ever as Chief (*photo courtesy Leonard B. Stern*)

FOURTEEN

GET SMART

(September 8, 1965–September 11, 1970)

"I am probably the most exposed comedian on TV," Don Adams once boasted in *TV Guide,* "I was a regular on *The Perry Como Show* for a year and a half, a regular guest on the [Jack] Paar and [Ed] Sullivan shows, and worked a year on *The Bill Dana Show.* The result is that everybody knows my routines—but no one knows my name. If they do call [to] me, [it's] 'Hey there, Glick!' "

The Glick character that Adams was referring to was the bumbling hotel detective he portrayed on *The Bill Dana Show,* a forerunner of Agent 86, a.k.a. Maxwell Smart, of NBC's *Get Smart.* Byron Glick was a cartoon-like character—Smart was more or less real, more dedicated, more intense, and more concerned with his job. And despite the popularity of Glick, the Dana show was canceled in 1965. But the genesis of the character went back further than that.

"In 1954 I wrote a routine for myself," Adams told *TV Guide* in the late sixties, "about a pompous detective who gathers all the suspects in a room and proceeds to sum up one of those unsolved murder cases. He gets so confused that nobody knows what he's talking about. I took that voice from the way William Powell talked in the old *Thin Man* movies. He sounded clever and sophisticated but I exaggerated it a little and it came out funny."

"I used to love Don's act—Don was a stand-up comic," comments Dick Gautier, who was Hymie the Robot on *Get Smart,* "and Bill Dana was a writer and he used to write Don's nightclub material. Don did a very, very funny act. Don's character on [Dana's show] sort of took off, so when they created *Get Smart,* Don was the logical choice. There was something very brittle, kind of high-pitched and a little bit whiny about [Maxwell Smart]. Don

Don Adams and Barbara Feldon as Maxwell Smart and 99 (*photo courtesy Leonard B. Stern*)

loved to do impressions and when he did William Powell, it sort of [saturated] his character."

In *Get Smart* Adams's inept Powell-esque detective was joined by sensible sleuthing cohort Agent 99, played by Barbara Feldon, working for CONTROL. The Washington-based counterintelligence operation usually thwarted the machinations of the evil KAOS organization despite the ineptitude of Smart and 99 (no known name), who were married in November of 1968.

Executive producer Leonard Stern headed a winning creative team, including producers Arne Sultan, Burt Nodella, and Jess Oppenheimer, associate producer Harry R. Sherman, and creators Mel Brooks and Buck Henry, and composer Irving Szathmary, who happened to be Bill Dana's brother and wrote the show's theme.

"It's funny," says Stern today of *Get Smart.* "Much of current comedy is not funny and it's truly unfortunate. People laugh at *Smart,* and that's refreshing for them. Throughout, the history of television has been dotted with shows that are truly funny and they seem to endure—*Lucy* is funny, the *Honeymooners* are funny, *Barney Miller* is funny. Generally, they had high standards. In early television demands were made by the comedians who all wanted to be funny and had their own particular view of what was funny."

Five-time Emmy nominee Stern was also involved with *I'm Dickens . . . He's Fenster; He and She; Run, Buddy, Run; Holmes and Yoyo;* and *McMillan and Wife,* among other TV series.

"Originally *Get Smart* was developed for ABC," explains Stern, "and they didn't like the first script and we did a second script and they asked for their $7,500 [back] so we were stuck with a script and no outlets because in those days all pilots were generally commissioned before the first of the year and generally were delivered in late February and the programming was made up in March, so we had nowhere to go. But NBC had Don Adams under contract and they were looking for a vehicle for him and [network president] Grant Tinker felt that this was perfect and so it was adapted to Don's personality but it had existed before he was even a thought in any of our minds."

Smart and colleagues had to drop through the fake floor of a phone booth in order to get to CONTROL's offices. Smart literally walked on his phone—it was in the heel of his shoe.

"We had a fortunate motto to parody," Stern says, "and that was James Bond, and interestingly enough, initially *Get Smart* wasn't successful in England because they thought Bond was a satire and a spoof and we were compounding a perspective."

On *Get Smart,* Edward Platt portrayed the exasperated CONTROL boss, The Chief. Gautier was the robot Hymie, and Dave Ketchum was Agent 13. Bernie Kopell

was KAOS mastermind Conrad Siegfried; William Schallert was Admiral H. Harmon Hargrade; Jane Dulo, 99's mother; King Moody (Ronald McDonald in later years), Starker, Siegfried's assistant; Stacy Keach Sr., Professor Carlson; Robert Karvelas, Larabee, the chief's bumbling assistant.

"I loved Ed," Gautier recalls. "He was the sweetest, nicest man. He was an opera singer—he had a wonderful voice. He was the sweetest guy in the world, sort of like an island of sanity with all of us crazy people running around. Bernie was nuts and Don was and I was and we were all kind of goofy on the set and had a good time and got crazy."

Platt is best known for such films as *Rebel Without a Cause, Written on the Wind,* and *They Came to Cordura.* He died of a heart attack in 1974 at age fifty-eight.

"I had seen [Edward] in *Rebel Without a Cause,* recalls Stern, "and I was very impressed with the performance and he had a deep sonorous voice but I wasn't sure about his comedy credentials—I wanted somebody who would give authority and when he came in I liked him tremendously personally and then he told me he had been a band singer and immediately burst into 'Old Man River'—I knew that I had the right person. [He had] a remarkable singing voice and that deep baritone gave him authority."

"Dave Ketchum was Agent 13 but before Ketchum was Victor French," explains Gautier. "He was the first one. French [who played Agent 44 for awhile] formed an alliance, a friendship with Michael Landon and worked with him for many years. When he left *Get Smart,* he was replaced by Dave."

"I saw Dave doing a Jack Benny radio warm-up," Stern remembers, "and I thought that he was highly inventive and imaginative and then over the years he was on *I'm Dickens. . .He's Fenster,* my first show that I did on my own. And he became like Bernie Kopell—family members, so whenever I had the opportunity to work with him I would always do so because [they both] were always innovative."

"We all had good senses of humor," continues Gautier, "because we all had nightclub backgrounds and when you're a nightclub comic that's the way you think—you think funny. We liked to kid around and have fun on the set. Barbara just sort of took it all with great aplomb.

"Barbara was very nice, very professional, a terrific lady. She came on the set, did her job and then she left. [She] is extremely intelligent and I have a lot of respect for her."

Feldon, a onetime model known for her pre-*Get Smart* TV commercials, also appeared occasionally in films like *Fitzwilly* (1967) and *Smile* (1975). Most recently, she portrayed "Spy Girl" in an episode of NBC's *Mad About You.*

Dick Gautier, who played Hymie the Robot (*photo courtesy Dick Gautier*)

Leonard B. Stern, *Get Smart*'s producer (*photo courtesy Leonard B. Stern*)

"Barbara was doing commercials when we first saw her," says Stern, "and we put her under contract and then we had her in various of our projects until *Get Smart* was ready because we thought that she would be the perfect 99. Barbara is a person who reads voraciously and her interests were not in acting as much as in philosophy and thought and for a while she did an interview program and now she earns money as a voice-over—[one of] the most in demand in New York and so she's very content."

"There just aren't any good roles for mature, attractive women," says Feldon today. "The women who are scoring in TV today, for the most part, are all in comedy."

Feldon has also hosted not only *A.M. America* and a half-hour magazine show called *Special Edition* (1978), for which she was praised by *Variety,* but also *The '80s Woman* for the Daytime Cable Network. She does voice-overs, and in 1986, appeared at a press conference with other female Screen Actors Guild (SAG) members, protesting male dominance in voice-overs.

A native New Yorker (born March 12, 1939) with a Pittsburgh society background, Feldon (born Barbara Hall) started out in the early 1960s doing hair tonic commercials. She graduated from Carnegie Institute of Technology as a drama major, and married Lucien Verdoux Feldon, a Belgian-born photographer whom she met at Carnegie Hall in 1958.

In 1957 on *The $64,000 Question* she copped the top prize. She and Lucien opened an art gallery with the winnings. Later that would seem appropriate, as Feldon would come to describe her 1960s TV persona as "Pop Art on camera."

At this time she was also modeling for Pauline Trigere quite a bit, having lost forty pounds, and it was these television commericals that finally caught the attention of the columnists. Riding high on her newfound celebrity, Feldon headed for the West Coast and began getting TV work.

Feldon wasn't doing too badly for someone who had been described as having a droopy eye, skinny legs, and buck teeth. "I'm the girl with the drooping eyelids," she would say in *TV Guide* after making it in Hollywood, primarily in Revlon "tiger" commercials. "Men are always accusing me of leading them on with my so-called 'bedroom eyes.'"

Soon she caught the attention of Buck Henry and Mel Brooks, who were developing *Get Smart*. They cast her in the black and white pilot of the comic spy series. (The following 137 episodes would be in color.)

"As a performer, Barbara's camp," continued Stern, "as a human being, this is a girl totally without guile."

Feldon has often defined comedy as having a pace and style all of its own, and her appreciation of that vitality and energy is what no doubt led her to accept a role that took her miles away from her husband for long periods of time.

Maxwell Smart was a square prig and in no way exploited the new generation of the sixties though Feldon's Agent 99 was among the first women in TV sitcoms who was not subservient.

Feldon was reluctant at first, not relishing the idea of being separated from Lucien. Agent 99 was an intriguing character she could not resist portraying, however. Still cautious though, she initially agreed to do only three more episodes after the pilot if, indeed, it was sold. And wisely she chose not to sever her ties with Revlon.

"Agent 99," Feldon told *TV Guide* after the show premiered, "is an ingredient in the overall soup. She isn't the meat; she is the spice. She is a character, not a person."

And Stern expressed his own ideas about Barbara, the woman, in *TV Guide:* "A man's wife can be seated next to him while he's being enchanted with Barbara yet the wife feels no resentment.

"Barbara [in her TV commercial debut] stepped out of the shower," Lucien has said in the way of an explanation for her unexpected sex appeal, "with a towel wrapped around her, not seeming in the least surprised to find you in the bathroom."

"The show is Don Adams," she told *TV Guide*. "Without him, nothing. My softness, sincerity, gullibility, and loving despair are simply a foil for his brittle vitality."

But if anything, 99 was intellectually superior to her male colleague, which Feldon proved so effortlessly in episodes such as the spoof of *The Avengers* with villains Snead and Mrs. Neal, "Satan Place," in which Smart posed as a German surgeon and Feldon as his nurse, and "Tequila Mockingbird," with Smart and 99 posing as cabaret singers in Mexico in search of a missing jewel.

"We did many take-offs," says Stern. "Unfortunately our titles were never printed [onscreen] and some of them were quite hilarious. 'Tequila Mockingbird' [January 18, 1969] was one."

"Satan Place" (November 13, 1965) starts off with the kidnapping of The Chief and a demand for a $200,000 ransom. Maxwell Smart goes to the rescue. Joseph Sirola played KAOS agent Dr. Satan, who had meanwhile frozen The Chief. Smart and 99 pass themselves off as a doctor and nurse, rescuing their boss and freezing the villains. Luck was on their side as they had only been able to raise $600 in ransom money.

"Run, Robot, Run" (March 16, 1968) was a parody of *The Avengers* with Gautier as Hymie, John Orchard as Snead, and Lynn Peters as Mrs. Neal. The Chief assigns Smart to work under Hymie on a case. Snead and Neal of the CAD division of KAOS have sabotaged the world's great track stars, which means Hymie must compete—

and he wins!

In the end *Get Smart* took its toll on Feldon's marriage. She was divorced in 1967, a year after the series had hit number twelve in the ratings. "[Women should] not blame men all the time," Feldon once said. "I have always found men to be willing helpers and not envious of women's success."

But this had not been the case with her personal life, though professionally she was on a roll with two Emmy nominations. She later moved in with *Get Smart* producer Burt Nodella.

By the late 1960s, it was felt that the show was becoming dated, and to fix the sagging ratings NBC decided to marry off 99 to Max. The wedding occurred on November 16, 1968, with Adams's real-life second wife Dorothy, a June Taylor dancer, playing the part of a bridesmaid. The episode, "With Love and Twitches," found Smart and 99 tying the knot at last despite an attempt to sabotage the wedding by injecting Max with an allergy-causing serum. Alan Oppenheimer, Jay Lawrence, Larry Vincent, and Sharon Cintron guest starred. In the end the only disturbance of the nuptials is a fistfight in the aisles with KAOS agents.

"They changed the format," says Gautier, "and Smart got married and had twins. I had just kept doing Hymie except for the last year. [Then] all of the regulars ceased to do the show."

NBC dropped *Get Smart* at the end of the 1968–69 season and CBS picked it up, continuing the new format domesticating the spy couple.

In "And Baby Makes Four—Part One" (November 7, 1969) Max gets off to a rocky start as a father when he mistakes a KAOS map for the map to the hospital and delivers 99 into the enemy's lair as she prepares to give birth. Jack Gilford, Dana Elcar, and Jane Dulo (as 99's mother) guest starred.

In Part Two (November 14, 1969) Max and 99 escape from the KAOS facility and head straight for the legitimate hospital where 99's mother saves the day when she slugs KAOS agent Simon (Gilford).

But this marital espionage didn't work; as a matter of fact, it only backfired. The introduction of twin offspring may have strengthened the Smart marriage, but it wasn't a smart move creatively and hastened the end of the series.

"[That last season] they just didn't ask us to come back," elaborates Gautier, "and they wanted to go in a different direction. I think they felt at that time they had kind of tapped the resources comedically of what they could do with the show and so they wanted to try something else and I think that's why they did the more domestic stuff, just as a change of scenery, some fresh air. It's very hard to come up with new funny ideas [for] each show but I still think *Get Smart* is the only successful satire that's ever really been on the air."

And how did Feldon and Adams remain icons of American Pop culture, despite the show's sagging ratings?

Feldon was always appetizing, wearing Gernreich suits, Galanos evening gowns, and pearls from Van Cleef and Arpels, and carrying Chanel handbags. This bit of haute couture, mixed with the aplomb of which Gautier speaks, was an intoxicating mix.

"I can't stand the way I look," confessed Adams to *TV Guide*, during the show's original run. "I never went to school—I went to movies. Three times a week, maybe four. I loved all those little guys—Cagney, Garfield, Widmark. You just have to accept the fact that you're not Cary Grant and then you're all right."

"Don's a little too slight and he has that curious look around his eyes," quipped Stern. "He's just a little short—only about an inch from being a leading man."

"Those little guys were tough," said Adams in his own defense. "They were cool, and they were only five-feet-eight. Alan Ladd was five-feet-six." Adams was five-feet-nine and weighed in at 150 pounds. Yet he had a certain debonair—though offbeat—quality, that was endearing. His hair stylist Joe Torrenneva worked around Adams's ill-matched ears and triangular head and fashion designer Ron Postal concealed his slight frame with appropriate suits and clothing.

New Yorker Don Adams (né Donald James Yarmy) was born in 1927. His father was a Hungarian Jew, his mother Irish Catholic. According to Adams, when they married both families disowned them. Childhood playmates were Larry and Jay Storch. Another buddy was future writer/actor/director James Komack, who wrote and directed *My Favorite Martian* and created and produced *Chico and the Man* and *Welcome Back Kotter*. He also acted in *Get Smart* and *The Courtship of Eddie's Father*.

Storch, who kicked around show business as a nightclub comic and appeared often in films with navy buddy Tony Curtis, made it big as crafty Corporal Agarn on *F Troop* (1965–67). He would later appear in "The Groovy Guru" episode of *Get Smart* on January 13, 1968.

In this episode Storch launches a huge drugs-sex-and-rock 'n' roll marathon in Washington, but Maxwell Smart and 99 nip this KAOS-inspired insurrection in the bud.

Adams took a stab at high school but became a dropout, going into the construction business and trying out as a steel worker. Then he and his twin cousins William and Robert Karvelas decided to join the Marine Corps, the three of them ending up in boot camp together. He saw active duty at Guadalcanal, was shot, came down with blackwater fever, and yet survived to return stateside and work as a drill instructor after receiving his honorable discharge. "I got blackwater fever on Guadalcanal," he told *TV Guide* during *Get Smart*'s heyday. "Almost

Dave Ketchum, Control's pliant Agent 13 (*photo courtesy Dave Ketchum*)

everyone dies of blackwater fever. I blew up like a balloon. They put a death watch on me but I told the guy he was wasting his time because I wasn't going to die. I did a lot of praying then. In about three days the swelling went down and I was all right."

Following his discharge from the service, he enrolled at the Terry Art Institute, hoping for a career as a commercial artist. This turned out to be a transitional period in his life. "I was never very happy [working] at that, and am not very good at it. I was married awfully young and I felt trapped. I wanted to be a comedian and I felt my life was being wasted." He had four children with his first wife, Dell.

But soon he was was doing impersonations with Jay Lawrence at a club on the beach in Miami.

"We had about fifteen really good impressions," recalls Adams, "but we overwhelmed the audience with fifty or sixty."

While in New York for his mother's funeral in 1954 he auditioned for *Arthur Godfrey's Talent Scouts*. This was the beginning of the big time. He would go on to work with Perry Como, Jack Paar, Ed Sullivan, and Garry Moore. And into his nightclub routine he incorporated a sleuthing detective along the lines of William Powell's *Thin Man* character.

Bill Dana, who had just ended a partnership with Gene Wood, caught Adams's act and liked what he saw. Soon *The Bill Dana Show* had spun off from *The Danny Thomas Show* (as had *The Andy Griffith Show*). In the beginning Dana teamed with Gary Crosby but the mix wasn't right and Bill was then joined by Adams, who at the time (1963) was doing the voice for the animated *Tennessee Tuxedo and His Tales*. Then came *Get Smart*.

"Don is not just an actor who is facile with comedy lines," producer Jay Sandrich told *TV Guide*, "not just a film comic. He has learned through the years what an audience reacts to and he brings [that] to the show."

"I am a quick study," boasts Adams, "I can memorize a script in an hour." But on the set of *Get Smart*, the scripts were always changing, right up to the last minute. In these cases, Adams would simply memorize five or six lines and then wing it.

"They encouraged our personal creativity to change things," Dick Gautier recalls, "to make them work better for us because we all had a sense of comedy and they were trading upon that—that's why we were there. And that was encouraged by the directors we worked with—they were very helpful.

"On the very first show [I did] there was a scene where Don and I were in a closet together because I had been drinking—he didn't know I was a robot at this point; he just thinks I'm a new agent and I'm actually working for KAOS—and the champagne didn't mix well with [my body chemistry], so Don takes me into the closet and says, 'Hymie, spying and alcohol do not mix,' and I look at him and I reach over and kiss him on the cheek and he says, 'A simple nod will do,' and it was a very funny moment [for us]."

But despite the humor behind the scenes, at times the pressures of TV took a toll on the cast.

"Put me in front of an audience and I'm secure," said Adams at the time of the show's original run. "[TV] is a little different—a different craft. I try hard to keep the spontaneity and it's hard because we shoot and reshoot the scenes. I think it takes a little off the performance."

And what did Feldon think of her *Get Smart* costar? "As for our relationship offscreen, I adore him, but I don't know him. We are of another world."

And Gautier agreed that professional relationships are, even at their best, tenuous: "I don't always socialize with the people I work with. A lot of people through the years have magnified [my participation] in the show. When I came out to L.A. I started doing television, and [on] *Get Smart* I was really a recurring character—I don't think I did more than seven or eight shows. They just happen to have some sort of impact. It was the least of my accomplishments—it's just the one that seems to be living on in reruns. [Though] I did very few shows, people seem to remember because we are forever haunted by reruns.

"Hymie never helped my career in any way because there are not anymore robot roles. There are definite parameters in [such] a role that don't give you a lot of leeway—you really don't get to act. It didn't help my career [and] I've never really felt a part of that series if you will."

But others who had recurring *Get Smart* roles were Angelique Pettyjohn as Charlie Watkins, Joey Forman as Harry Hoo, Robert Cornthwaite as Professor Windish, Ellen Weston as Dr. Steele, George Ives as Dr. Bascombe, Byron Foulger as Professor Bush, Frank DeVol as Professor Carlton, Martin Kosleck as Dr. Drago, Del Close as Dr. Minelli, Milton Selzer as Professor Parker, Ann Elder as Dr. Simon, and Roger Price as Dr. Arrick.

"Roger was probably the most inventive and creative man I ever knew," insists Leonard Stern, "and I think our basis of friendship was my great admiration for him. He was the most unique comedy thinker [to come along] in several decades."

"It was a year [or so] before I came on," says Gautier of *Get Smart*. "It was just a guest spot. I had just come from Broadway where I had created the role of Conrad Birdie in *Bye, Bye Birdie*. C. F. L'Amoreaux—he used to be a cowboy actor named Gary Clarke—wrote a 'Hymie' segment and they asked me to come in and see them about it."

"When a writer by the name of Amoreaux had this idea

for the robot," Stern recalls, "I knew that Dick could do this stony-faced individual—he did it at parties, where he would not laugh or would not respond and when he came in he read it and he was right on."

"I did the first [guest spot] and it just took off," Gautier says. "It had enormous popularity and then I came back and did another one [and then again], and before you know it I'm appearing in all these magazines as a part of the show. I was a nightclub comic originally. I did stand-up all over the country in New York and San Francisco. I got my break on Broadway when I went in and sang and read against seven hundred fifty guys and got the role of Conrad and was nominated for a Tony Award so that really started my career—that was a smash hit.

"I've also done both Mel Brooks television projects. He's only done two—*Get Smart* and *When Things Were Rotten* [in which] I played Robin Hood. I didn't work with Buck Henry [on *Smart*] but I've worked with him since, we've done plays together and that sort of thing—Buck and Mel created [*Get Smart*] and then Mel disappeared at that point and went on to other projects and Buck kind of stayed as story editor for a while but I never saw Buck [on the set] or Mel."

In spite of his ambivalence about Hymie, Gautier remains philosophical about his career: "[Remember me] as a creative, eclectic individual. I'm working on my sixth book [and] I used to be a commercial artist and a portrait painter and a cartoonist and I wrote a book for Putnam called *The Art of Caricature*. I'm now doing *The Career Cartoonist* for them. I've written *Actors As Artists* and then I'm doing a sequel to that and I've written movies. I work for Hanna-Barbera a lot doing a lot of character voices."

Dave Ketchum, a fellow *Get Smart* alumnus, also has picked up a pen. "My writing is the biggest thing [that's happened to me since the show]. It was fun [later] being on the staff of *Happy Days* and *Laverne and Shirley* because Garry Marshall is an unusual guy to work for. You know he used to play the drums when I did my nightclub act—I used to do stand-up. And he used to play the drums for me so we got to be good friends. I really enjoy it. I'm doing a book for Leonard Stern [who has gone into publishing]. It's called *The Adult Scratch and Sniff Book*.

Ketchum, who has also written for *The Love Boat*, sums up his career in one statement: "Remember me as a nice guy who figured you'll never get out of life alive."

Many 1960s celebrities were eager to play KAOS rogues and rascals, equipped with invisible rays, retrogressor guns, laughing gas, and high-calorie heat waves. And each was well suited to combat Smart, whose boy scout qualities made him sincere, trustworthy, intrepid, brave, cheerful and, quite often, an inept opponent.

Michael Dunn, the dwarf actor, and character actor Vito Scotti appeared in "Mr. Big" on September 18, 1965. Barbara Bain starred in "KAOS in Control" on October 30, 1965. Conrad Janis showed up on December 4, 1965, in "My Nephew the Spy."

Johnny Carson was the conductor in "Aboard the Orient Express" on December 11, 1965. Leonard Nimoy popped up in "The Dead Spy Scrolls" on January 22, 1966. Janet ("Judy Jetson") Waldo joined semiregular King Moody in "All in the Mind" on February 5, 1966. Ellen Corby was in "Dear Diary" on February 12, 1966.

Alice (*Bewitched*) Ghostley guest starred in "The Last One in Is a Rotten Spy" on April 30, 1966. Harold Gould joined Stacy Keach Sr., as Professor Carlson in "Island of the Darned" on November 26, 1966.

Ted Knight played opposite Angelique Pettyjohn in "Pussycats Galore" on April 1, 1967. Farley Granger played a villain in "Supersonic Boom" on October 28, 1967, with an appearance by Adams's pal Bill Dana. Carol Burnett popped up in "One of Our Olives Is Missing" on November 14, 1967.

Wally Cox was the special guest in "Dr. Yes" on November 25, 1967, and it was Steve Allen in "The Mild Ones" on December 9, 1967. Johnny Carson came back for a repeat performance in "The King Lives" on January 6, 1968, and Arlene Golonka played opposite Don Rickles and Ernest Borgnine in "The Little Black Book" (parts one and two) on January 27 and February 3, 1968.

Milton Berle was highlighted in "Don't Look Back" on February 10, 1968, and Bob Hope followed in on February 17, 1968, in "99 Loses Control."

Robert Culp was a no goodnik in "Die Spy" on March 30, 1968, and Cesar Romero and Anne Baxter camped it up in "The Reluctant Redhead" on April 6, 1968.

Jamie Farr was in "The Impossible Mission" on September 21, 1968, and Alice Ghostley came back, with Tom (*Happy Days*) Bosley, in "The Frakas Fracas" on December 7, 1968. Don Rickles made a return appearance in parts one and two of "To Sire, With Love" on February 15 and 22, 1969. Tom Poston came along on March 1, 1969 in "Shock It to Me."

Vincent Price was the comically sinister guest on December 12, 1969, in "Is This Trip Necessary?" and Bill Dana returned on December 19, 1969, in "Ice Station Siegfried." Victor (*Wild, Wild West*) Buono showed up in "Moonlight Becomes You" on February 1, 1970, and Gale Sondergaard appeared in "Rebecca of Funny Folk Farm" on January 23, 1970.

William Schallert was in "Witness for the Execution" on February 7, 1970, and *Lost in Space*'s Jonathan Harris guested in "How Green Was My Valet" on February 13, 1970. And, Vito Scotti turned up again in "Hello Colum-

Kenneth Mars as Commander Drury, who took control of Control in the 1989 reunion movie, *Get Smart, Again!* (*photo courtesy Kenneth Mars*)

Roger T. Price, who was Control lab technician Dr. Arrick (*photo courtesy Leonard B. Stern*)

bus, Goodbye America" on March 1, 1970.

After *Get Smart* left for that great syndication room in the sky, Don Adams (who won three consecutive Emmys as Outstanding Lead Actor in a Comedy Series) went on to star in the short-lived one-season series, *Partners* (1971–72) with Rupert Crosse. The two played a pair of slightly daffy police detectives. In 1975, *Don Adams' Screen Test* had Adams hosting an entertaining "game" show, although there really was no game involved.

Later, 1983, he began voicing the animated series *Inspector Gadget*, and two years later he began starring in the Canadian-made syndicated series, *Check It Out*, as the harassed manager of a supermarket who sounded suspiciously like Maxwell Smart.

So popular was *Get Smart* in syndication that in 1980 there was the big-screen feature *The Nude Bomb*, a.k.a. *The Return of Maxwell Smart*, directed by Clive Donner, in which Adams starred with Andrea Howard, Vittorio Gassman, Dana Elcar, Pamela Hensley, Sylvia Kristel, Robert Karvelas, Norman Lloyd, Rhonda Fleming, and Joey Forman. The script was by Arne Sultan, Leonard Stern, and Bill Dana.

This was not the first attempt at a Smart movie. Actually, the three-parter "A Man Called Smart" (April 1967) had originally been planned as a feature length film. But in the farce *Nude Bomb*, Agent 86 becomes involved with a madman whose bomb will destroy the world's clothing. Scriptwriter Bill Dana played a fashion designer named Jonathan Levinson Siegel.

But Dana's cameo was not the only surprise. CONTROL had been changed to PITS or Provisional Intelligence Tactical Service. But unfortunately, Feldon was not around to add her special luster. And also missing was the much-needed input of creators Buck Henry and Mel Brooks.

As for Brooks, he and wife Anne Bancroft had a son in 1972 whom they called Max, which may or may not have been coincidental. And not only did he cast Gautier in his next series following *Get Smart*, but he also chose Bernie Kopell as Alan-a-Dale.

Henry went on to write the screenplay to *The Graduate* and *Catch-22* (and acted in both) and has become known for his characterization of Uncle Roy in frequent guest spots on *Saturday Night Live* over the years.

1989 brought us *Get Smart, Again!* a TV movie directed by Gary Nelson that reunited Adams with Barbara Feldon, Dick Gautier, Dave Ketchum, and Bernie Kopell, as well as Robert Karvelas, King Moody, Harold Gould, Kenneth Mars, Roger Price and Fritz Feld. In this spoof 86 and 99 hook up with CONTROL again for a battle with KAOS.

Gautier notes: "Roger Price [Dr. Arrick in the series] was Leonard Stern's partner in Price, Stern and Sloan—they publish novelty books and children's books. Kenny Mars came on board [the reunion] to replace the Chief." (Dana Elcar had that honor in *The Nude Bomb*.)

"We couldn't find a true replacement for Ed Platt [in *The Nude Bomb*]," explains Stern, "He'd had a unique ability so we tried to get as much of an authoritative figure as we could, keeping Ed as a role model and we had two actors in mind and one got sick and so it was automatically Dana [Elcar].

"I had done a pilot that didn't sell with Kenny as the star. I had seen him first in Mel Brooks's *The Producers* and fell in love with that character and the madness of it. So, Kenny became a regular of ours."

Despite the reunion of almost the entire original cast in *Get Smart, Again!* and even though it was a cut above *The Nude Bomb*, the ambiance of the series has never been recaptured.

In a way the uniqueness of the series began in the union of Adams with his character, the bumbling spy he played so adeptly.

"Adams and Smart are getting closer and closer together," said Stern, during the series' original run. "It's like a marriage where each partner begins to resemble the other. Audiences aren't dialing *Get Smart* anymore—they're tuning into *The Don Adams Show*."

And in the end *Get Smart* did become *The Don Adams Show*. Perhaps it is for the best that he changed his name. It is doubtful that much of America would have tuned in for five seasons to watch Don Yarmy.

In the beginning there were resourceful agents John Steed and Cathy Gale (Patrick Macnee and Honor Blackman)

FIFTEEN

THE AVENGERS

(March 28, 1966—September 15, 1969)
(1962—65 in Great Britain)

"I see no point in being defensive about eroticism," says Diana Rigg of *The Avengers*. "I think it's rather good to have. I'm not ashamed of Mrs. Peel. She was ahead of her time, a new type of heroine [and quite] good for leather fetishists."

The first British television import to capture the imagination of mainstream America, the erotic and kinky *Avengers* has aired in over a hundred countries. In Spain it is called *Los Vengadores*, in Germany *Mit Schirm, Charme und Melon* (With Umbrella, Charm and Bowler), and in France *Le Chapeon Melon et Bottes De Cuir* (The Bowler Hat and Leather Boots).

"Subliminally it was quite kinky," Rigg adds. "I think I always seemed to be usually strapped to a dentist's chair with my feet in the air and the camera seemed to linger an awful lot on my high-heeled boots."

"You could show it to your maiden aunt," concurs producer Brian Clemens, "but if you had a really dirty mind there was a lot more in it. We tackled all sorts of fetishes and strange things without ever becoming offensive."

More than 350 million viewers worldwide have seen Avengers John Steed and Emma Peel outwit guest stars such as Charlotte Rampling and Donald Sutherland in "The Superlative Seven" (April 28, 1967)—in which Steed trumps an ace and Emma plays a lone hand; Christopher Lee in both "Never, Never Say Die" (March 31, 1967)—in which Steed hangs up his stocking and

Emma asks for more—and "The Interrogators" (January 20, 1969) (with Patrick Macnee and Linda Thorson); John Cleese in "Look But There Were These Two Fellers" (May 8, 1968) (with Macnee and Thorson); Peter Cushing in "The Return of the Cybernauts" (February 21, 1968)—in which Steed pulls some strings and Emma becomes a puppet; British character actor Warren Mitchell as Brodney in both "Two's a Crowd" (May 9, 1966)—in which Steed goes out of his mind and Emma is beside herself—and "The See-Through Man" (February 3, 1967)—in which Steed is singleminded and Emma sees double; and Peter Wyngarde, the British actor, in both "Epic" (April 14, 1967)—in which Steed catches a falling star and Emma makes a movie—and "A Touch of Brimstone" (February 19, 1966, in Great Britain)—in which Steed joins the Hellfire Club and Emma becomes the Queen of Sin (the latter being the sensational sadomasochistic episode which shocked censors on both sides of the Atlantic and was banned in this country).

"When we shot 'A Touch of Brimstone'" recalls Clemens, "[Diana] was whipped five times. In England we had to take out two of the whippings and in America they banned it altogether but then we found out that the people at ABC used to run it every year at their convention."

"I do remember having to wear this snake on my arm for an entire day," recalls Rigg of "A Touch of Brimstone,"'"and the snake handler was terribly sweet. He said to me, 'You know, he could pee at any moment now,' I said, 'Oh, please, no, I don't need that.'"

Another notorious *Avengers* episode, "Honey for the Prince" (March 23, 1966, in Great Britain), in which Steed joins the natives and Emma gets the evil eye, featured Rigg undercover in the harem of a Middle Eastern potentate with bejeweled belly button and all.

"I do recall I had to do a belly dance," says Rigg. "Well, I can't do a belly dance and I had to approximate a belly dance. In those days one couldn't show your navel on American TV so I had to stick a jewel in [it] and we couldn't find the right sort of glue. So the jewel kept popping out." (The daring actress would shock the western world again years later by appearing nude on stage in *Abelard and Heloise*.)

"It actually started as a live television show," says Patrick Macnee today of *The Avengers,* "with Ian Hendry." The show was originally titled *Police Surgeon,* with Macnee as John Steed and Hendry as Dr. David Keel. Honor Blackman (later Pussy Galore of *Goldfinger*) joined *The Avengers* as Steed's crime-solving cohort, Cathy Gale, (a scientist with a Ph.D. in anthropology and widow of a British rancher in Kenya), in October 1962 in the episode "Mr. Teddy Bear."

The tone for Blackman's sex-oozing allure was set in that first episode, in which a man known as Mr. Teddy Bear is hired as a killer. After he assassinates a military officer during a TV interview, One/Ten, the fictional British spy agency, orders Mrs. Gale to go undercover. This episode featured Tim Brinton, Kenneth Keeling, John Horsley, Michael Robbins, Bernard Goldman, Sarah Maxwell, and John Ruddock. It was written by Martin Woodhouse and directed by Richmond Harding.

Another episode showcasing the talent of Blackman and indicating the direction the show would take was "Build a Better Mousetrap," in which two elderly ladies invent a new type of mousetrap, only to discover that they've jammed all electrical and mechanical devices for many miles around. This episode featured Donald Webster, Nora Nicholson, Athene Seyler, Harold Goodwin, John Tate, Alison Seebohm, Allan McClelland, Marian Diamond, and David Anderson. It was written by Brian Clemens and directed by Peter Hammond.

"Honor Blackman was cast to play the man's role," says Macnee. "We were a bit confused about the characters we were to portray. Whereupon the producer turned first to me and said, 'Play it like George Sanders with a mustache.' Then he turned to Honor and said, 'You're a nymphomaniac,' and that was that. This happened to coincide with the emergence of women's lib, and Honor became a cult figure and a dramatic contrast to me—I was really playing myself. We were an unlikely couple who, for some extraordinary reason, caught the public's fancy."

"Originally *The Avengers* was written with two men," concurs producer Brian Clemens, "and one of the men left and they were then stuck with six scripts for two men and not much money and they brought in [Honor Blackman] and she played a part that had been scripted for a man."

"There was something special about those early Blackman shows," continues Macnee. "I don't know if they stand up now, but the insouciance, bohemianism, originality of approach and attitude was, in my view, never quite recaptured."

And ironically, the Macnee and Blackman record single "Kinky Boots" (a 1964 bomb) began to climb the charts in England in 1990, reaching number five.

The Avengers was sold to ABC in America in 1966 in the biggest dollar-earning TV deal to that time—$2 million for the first twenty-six episodes, rising to $45 million if the options were taken up. "In time, of course, Honor left for films—'Pussy Galore,' all that," recalls Macnee, "and she was replaced by Diana Rigg—another dazzling actress with an equally dazzling body." (Actually, the Blackman *Avenger* episodes were not initially shown in America because censors found them too kinky. Only in later years did they turn up in this country in syndication.) America first saw *The Avengers* with Mac-

Patrick Macnee as debonair John Steed and Diana Rigg as sexy Emma Peel—*The Avengers* of the mid-sixties (*photo courtesy Arts and Entertainment Network*)

nee joined by Royal Academy of Dramatic Arts graduate Rigg, as the widowed Mrs. Emma Peel (a woman ahead of her times in more ways than one).

"Diana's a versatile and she's a highly individualistic person," says Leonard Stern, who was the producer of Rigg's short-lived 1973 sitcom *Diana*. "She pursues life as she sees it and so she's not a conformist in any way. She was the kind of woman who everybody enjoyed being in her presence. She had a very great impact on people and part of her appeal may have been those erotic fantasies that were conjured up in *The Avengers*."

Though not an agent, the classy Emma Peel—who was as much at home in her posh London flat as she was behind the wheel of her Lotus Elan S2—wore sexy jumpsuits designed by T.B. Jones, Ltd. of London and dubbed Emmapeelers. They were made of Crimplene and came in eight colors.

"Quite often it's the distance between two people that's the most interesting," says Rigg today. "It's never the clinch. It's always the dialogue before the clinch or the silence before the clinch. There was never any full stop

Steed and Mrs. Peel on an *Avengers* case (*photo courtesy Arts and Entertainment Network*)

put on the relationship [with Steed] and I suppose people find that interesting and beguiling."

"Outsiders asked, 'Will they ever go to bed together?' " recalls Clemens. "[But] it wasn't a question of 'Will they?' I always said, 'Well, I think, if you ask me, they certainly have'—they've been to bed together, but will they again now that they have become really relating friends?"

But the mod Mrs. Peel was a talented amateur and the nature of her relationship with Steed was never quite ascertained.

"My physical relations with [Steed] are at times, to put it mildly, ambiguous," Rigg feels. "They're certainly not active—they might have been in the past or then again they might be in the future."

Together, Emma and Steed pursued psychopaths, robots, mad scientists, megalomaniacs, and various underworld and otherworld monsters.

"They were extremes," surmises Rigg. "Steed was the archetypal English gentleman. Emma on the other hand was a prophecy of what woman would become. She didn't mind fighting people and neither was she apologetic about her achievements."

And one thing that Mrs. Peel was not apologetic about was her physical prowess. "The fight sequences were choreographed very carefully," recalls Rigg. "They didn't want me to be biffed."

These stunts and fight scenes were choreographed by such talented experts as Cyd Child, Ray Austin, Joe Dunne, and Peter Elliot. Also lending their skills over the years were Gerry Crampton and Frank Henson. Plus Lee Crawford, Eddie Powell, Cliff Diggens, Denny Powell and Terry Richards. (And as a tribute to their expertise and Emma's skill, British songstress Betty Boo, in one of her last videos, did the Peel karate chop in the obligatory leather jumpsuit.)

"I think that [Emma] became important for women," Rigg insists, "because she arrived on the scene sort of concurrently with women's awareness that they were getting a pretty bad deal on the face of this earth, and they had to change things. And [then] suddenly on the TV was the embodiment of a woman who had done that. Women now have an extended life professionally, sexually, and socially and about time, too."

After doing a television production in the mid-sixties called *The Hot House,* Rigg joined the ranks of a dozen other actresses who auditioned for the part vacated by Honor Blackman on *The Avengers.* "It was touch and go whether I went to the audition," Rigg once told *TV Guide.* "It didn't seem to be me, somehow. In the end, though, I went, and afterward I said to one of the producers, 'This is all a waste of time, isn't it?' [and he] agreed with me."

And he was right, at least initially. Another actress was chosen but after two episodes, they reran Rigg's test, and her face had an animal quality, according to producer Julian Wintle. Though Rigg, at the time one of the most promising young actresses of the Royal Shakespeare Company, had never seen *The Avengers,* she got the part and a salary of $700 per week (no residuals rights included).

Having studied at the Royal Academy of Dramatic Art, before joining RSC in 1959, Rigg had grown restless after five years of the classics: "The trouble with staying with a classical company is that you get known as a 'lady actress.' No one ever thinks of you except for parts in long skirts and blank verse.

"I've done both—*Avengers* by day, theater performances by night," Rigg was quoted as saying in *TV Guide.* "The point is that I wanted to show I could do it. I believe that to be without money in this world is to be without anything. It's a bad comment on the world." (In 1967 she commuted between Stratford-upon-Avon where she put on Shakespearean garb for the RSC production of *Twelfth Night* and the Borehamwood Studios where she slipped into leather and played Mrs. Peel.)

"I have no blueprint of a perfect male," declared Rigg in the mid-sixties, "for my imperfect female self. Neither do I believe that there's a Mr. Right. I think that if and when I do get married it will be an enormous compromise—and the struggle starts then."

On the personal front, for eight years Rigg lived with married film and television director Philip Saville, to the astonishment of the press.

"I'm a one-man woman," she continued. "I'm faithful to the concept of marriage but not to the necessity of the sacrament itself. I'm happy and fulfilled and that's what counts."

After only two seasons Rigg departed from *The Avengers* in an episode called "The Forget-Me-Not" (March 20, 1968), featuring Patrick Kavanaugh, Jeremy Young, Alan Lake, Patrick Newell, and introducing Linda Thorson as new operative Tarra King. In this episode Mrs. Peel retires from espionage when her husband, presumed killed in a plane crash, returns to London, laying claim to sweet Emma.

"A friend once asked me," recounted Rigg at the time, "if I could ever visualize my late husband in *The Avengers,* the man whose death I was supposed to be somewhat adventurously mourning. I told him no, I couldn't visualize him at all."

And the elusive Mr. Peel finally materialized at the end of "The Forget-Me-Not," wearing a derby and carrying a brolly—the spitting image of the dapper Steed. But, was that really any surprise?

"Emma Peel is not fully emancipated," complained Rigg in *TV Guide* at the time she left the show. "Steed pats

Patrick Macnee in Steed's heyday and in the nineties (*photos courtesy Arts and Entertainment Network*)

me from time to time like a good horse. I simply had to leave the series. *The Avengers* was fun, but I had no idea when I followed Honor that it would make a name like this. I began to feel claustrophobic. I began to feel *The Avengers* was taking over. [And] the studio never liked me to give interviews. I would always try to speak the truth, you see. The degree of success *The Avengers* was getting made it more and more difficult to leave as the weeks went by. If I had stayed I would have been under pressure by forces outside myself. I knew I had to go, and why wait till I was stale if I could leave on a high note?"

One of her first projects following *The Avengers* was the 1969 period film *The Assassination Bureau,* a lark based on a Jack London story about a secret club that eliminates unworthy people until greed takes precedence over dedication. "I picked it because it was the best comedy script I had offered [to] me and it was sort of transitional from *The Avengers* since it's a fantastic story with a zeppelin about to drop a bomb on the crowned heads of Europe at a peace conference and so on."

Like her *Avengers* predecessor, Rigg also did a James Bond movie, *On Her Majesty's Secret Service* (1969), and an occasional movie since. Her stage work has been more fortuitous, ranging from *Abelard and Heloise* in 1970 to the acclaimed London production of *Follies* in the eighties.

215

Abelard and Heloise opened in this country in 1971 with as much clamor as it had in England, though in the end the general consensus was that the notorious nude scene between Rigg and Australian Keith Michell was the most tasteful love scene ever staged.

Today her attitudes about feminine sex appeal are more practical: "It's no good saying that a woman looks as good at fifty as she did at twenty-five—she may look wonderful at fifty, but she sure as hell does not look as sexy as she did at twenty-five."

In any case, in 1971 Rigg was an undisputed looker herself, showing up those who had denied her an Emmy for *The Avengers* (she was nominated during the 1967–68 season) by earning a Tony Award for *Abelard and Heloise,* before going on to star in Tom Stoppard's *Jumpers.*

She was also in Olivier's *King Lear* and PBS's *Bleak House.* And on stage in Britain she was lauded for her performances in the plays *Phaedra Britannica* and *Night and Day,* also by Stoppard.

Rigg's only TV misstep has been the ill-fated 1973 sitcom *Diana* in which she played prime time's first divorceé, a lusty thirtysomething fashion designer.

"[Diana] was always a sultry character," says its producer Leonard (*Get Smart*) Stern, "and that's what I had in mind—the ambivalence of all the people who worked for her because they found her so attractive and yet unapproachable and that dichotomy would have been very effective in *Diana.* I thought her eroticism would be a distinct advantage." And in the end Rigg's sophisticated humor and seductive demeanor were wasted in the lukewarm *Diana.*

"We were always a little ahead of ourselves," Stern adds. "Toning down the scripts was an option [of the network] and I think it was ill-founded. I regret, in retrospect, the compromise. I've had twenty-one series on the air and *Diana* is the only one that got away from us."

Despite its short life, *Diana* had its moments, as when Patrick Macnee paid a visit. This was the first time that the two had been seen together on American television since "The Forget-Me-Not" episode of *The Avengers.*

"That was one of our better episodes," stresses Stern. "[In it] her dear friend from England came over and did a play and it was terrible and she had to go backstage to tell him. You [Rigg] try to say what you're not feeling and somebody sensitive [Macnee] is able to recognize that you're giving them lipservice. And of course, he can't handle it."

And in the end the discipline of the well-trained actor rose above the ego of the well-known TV persona.

Born on July 20, 1938, in Doncaster, England, Diana Rigg was a mere toddler when she traveled with her family to Jodhpur, India, where her father was a civil engineer. A few years later her mother accompanied her back to a strict boarding school in Yorkshire, as did the mother of that other British leading lady, Vivien Leigh, years before.

Diana was schooled at Great Missenden in Buckinghamshire until her family settled in Leeds and she completed her education at Fulneck Girls' School.

Over the years Rigg has recounted how she first tapped into the power of her imagination when she was eleven and very unhappy alone at school. (She didn't see her mother for eighteen months): "I would remember images of glamour from the only film I had ever seen—*The Red Shoes*—and use them to imagine myself as a different person. I used my imagination to transport me from the distress of my environment."

Following two years at the Royal Academy, Rigg worked as a model before breaking into the legitimate theater. Eventually her theatrical break came with repertory companies in Chesterfield and York, and in 1959 she signed a five-year contract with the Royal Shakespeare Company.

In private life—post Peel—Rigg in 1973 met Menachem Gueffen, an Israeli artist, but it soon turned into a turbulent relationship. They married, only to divorce in 1974, with Rigg returning to Broadway, this time in *The Misanthrope* with Alec McCowen. Soon however, she had a new beau, Scotsman Archie Stilling, whom she didn't marry right away but with whom (at age thirty-eight) she had a daughter, Rachel Atlanta. (Rigg and Stilling were divorced a number of years later.)

Today Diana Rigg is the host of PBS's *Mystery!* series, having succeeded the aging Vincent Price, but no matter how far she's gone professionally over the years, Rigg has forever been tied to the legacy of the illusive Mrs. Peel. Perhaps this allure was best defined by *Avengers'* character Z.Z. Von Schnerck when the psychotic director (portrayed by Kenneth J. Warren in a script ["Epic"] by Brian Clemens) planned to star the reluctant Mrs. Peel in a "snuff" film.

Von Schnerck described the lovely Emma as a woman of beauty, of action, a woman who could become desperate and yet remain strong, who could become confused yet remain intelligent, who could fight back yet remain feminine—not bad for a sixties television heroine.

"I think that I'm very lucky," concludes Diana Rigg, "because an awful lot of people become famous doing things which they're subsequently ashamed of and I am not ashamed of *The Avengers.* Emma Peel did a lot for me besides making me well known over most of the world. I used to be shy about talking about myself. But I've come to realize and appreciate the interest viewers have in television people. I look back on [*The Avengers*] fondly and with much gratitude."

And what of debonair John Steed, in the person of Patrick Macnee?

Two former TV "agents"—Emma Peel and Ilya Kuryakin—together in the nineties in an episode of PBS's *Mystery!* series (*photo courtesy WGBH Boston*)

"I took the veneer of Bond for Steed without using the core," says Macnee today. "All I really had as Steed was a will to bring the enemy to book. While many of Steed's tastes and habits of speech and dress are mine, others are dream projections of the man I would like to have been had I lived in another time—an unashamed romantic buck way back in the time of King George III."

And Macnee almost got his wish in "A Sense of History" (June 20, 1966), in which Steed puts out a light and Emma takes fright, though in the end it was Mrs. Peel who was seemingly propelled back in time.

Macnee was born on February 6, 1922, into an aristocratic English family. His father was a successful racehorse trainer; his mother the lovely niece of the Earl of Huntingdon. Macnee's grandfather, Sir Daniel Macnee, was president of the Scottish Royal Academy, where his painting "The Lady in Grey" still hangs.

Young Macnee's parents divorced after his father ran off to India and his mother moved into Rooknest, an intriguing homestead in Wiltshire, run by his mother's lesbian lover, the dominating "Uncle" Evelyn. In fact, "Uncle" Evelyn paid for Macnee's Eton education, though she insisted that Patrick wear kilts at Rooknest. His mother, as it turned out, was a beautiful and eccentric yet alcoholic lesbian. Mrs. Macnee, who would later receive the British Empire Medal for the fifteen years of service she had devoted to the families of British servicemen, reformed in her eighties and was honored at the age of ninety-five on the local *This Is Your Life*.

At the age of three young Patrick had been shipped off to Summer Fields Prep School near Oxford. Macnee ultimately entered Eton College, where he excelled as campus bookie. "I went to Eton," he recalls, "overeducated. And I spent all of my boyhood practically seated on a horse. Overindulged. Extremely blueblooded, you know."

In his memoir *Blind in One Ear,* Macnee confesses that at the age of eight he had his first love affair with a boy of the same age in the bushes in the schoolyard where the duo were caught in the act by the headmaster, leading to a severe caning. Years later Macnee would remark: "You know in England, if parents don't beat their children, they send them off to be beaten by someone else. The corporal punishment on the backside was wrong and sexually dangerous because you then associate pain with sexual pleasure. I mean, the first naked girl I saw I married because I thought, 'This is great—I'm in heaven.' "

Following Eton, Macnee went on to win a scholarship to Webber Douglas Academy of Dramatic Art and got his start in show business in 1941 with a small role in a stage production of *Little Women*. He then made his film debut as an extra in *The Life and Death of Colonel Blimp*.

Macnee served as an officer in His Majesty's Royal Brittanic Navy from 1942 to 1946, after which he re-turned to the London stage. Then he helped to pioneer Canadian TV.

In the mid-fifties, he toured with the Old Vic and came to Hollywood in 1957, where he worked in films like *Les Girls* and such TV series as *Playhouse 90, Wagon Train, Rawhide,* and *Alfred Hitchcock Presents*. He returned to England in 1960 for *The Valiant Years*. Then came *The Avengers*.

"I was in Palm Springs visiting when [*The Avengers*] first came on in the States," recalls Macnee. "I saw the first show and I said, 'It's not going to make it.' At first this seemed to be true. For two months or so people seemed to think this was just another secret agent-type show."

Harry Harris of the *Philadelphia Inquirer* said (March 29, 1966): "John Steed is colorfully quirky. He wears Bat Masterson-type garb, including dapper derby and has a hankering for the old and elegant in clothes."

As for Steed, Macnee offers the dashing operative a final epitaph: "Underneath he was lethal—the dandy dressing in all those clothes, pretending he hadn't a care in the world and underneath literally saving people from the tumble." As Steed, Macnee owned forty bowler hats and thirty brollies. His trademark was the Edwardian drag—curly-brimmed bowler, braided pinstripe suits, embroidered waistcoats, cummerbunds, and a furled umbrella. And often his attire was the handiwork of Pierre Cardin.

"The umbrella was simply a symbol," Macnee notes, "not of authority but a means of concealing gadgets—which is pure Bond. If you've got an umbrella with a camera in it and a sword—you've got surprise! To carry a gun is the most dangerous thing in the world. I wouldn't carry a gun." But even without a gun, Steed was a man known to be thoroughly professional and efficient as a secret agent; an expert at murder, arson, burglary, forgery, and the use of explosives, codes and poisons—dedicated, ruthless, unscrupulous.

And just for the record, Steed, along with Mrs. Gale, Emma Peel, and later Tarra King, imbibed twenty gallons of champagne. And his favorite mode of transportation (whether for picking up ladies or chasing criminals) was a 1929 Speed Six Bentley, 1928 Green Label Bentley, 1927 Rolls Royce Silver Ghost, or maybe a 1923 Rolls Royce Phantom Tourer.

Avengers fans keep the series alive today by acquiring collectibles such as the Corgi Gift Set, which contains replicas of Steed's 1929 Bentley and Emma's Lotus Elan, and the *Avengers* jigsaw puzzle, a set of four, which was manufactured by Thomas, Hope and Sankey in 1966 and was distributed by Woolworth's. It contained scenes from "Castle Death" (May 2, 1966)—in which Steed becomes a strapping jock and Emma lays a ghost; "Death at Bargain Prices" (April 4, 1966)—in which Steed dabbles in tycoonery and Emma in chicanery; "The Master

Minds" (July 11, 1966)—in which Steed joins a secret society and Emma walks the plank; and finally (it's debatable) either "The Gravediggers" (August 4, 1966)—in which Steed seeks a wife and Emma gets buried, or "The Town of No Return" (September 1, 1966)—in which Steed flies to nowhere and Emma does her party piece.

An ongoing saga in *The Avengers*—and perhaps one of the most popular themes of true fans—was the tale of the Cybernauts. The original "Cybernauts" (in which Steed receives a deadly gift and Emma pockets it) aired March 28, 1966, and introduced Dr. Armstrong, the engineer of a fleet of killer androids known as the Cybernauts. This episode featured Michael Gough as Armstrong, Frederick Jaeger, Bernard Horsfall, Burt Kwouk, John Hollis, Ronald Leigh-Hunt, and Gordon Whiting. It was written by Philip Levene and directed by Sidney Hayers.

At the time, the *New York Times* said: "In 'The Cybernauts' it was never made clear whether the cool and clever Steed is a comparatively parochial private eye or a government agent with an international beat. It is the lack of such a fact that keeps a guy from really being able to identify. The tale was unraveled at a brisk pace and with just enough technical jargon to satisfy comic-book readers."

Steed and Mrs. Peel again battled the android assassins in "Return of the Cybernauts" (February 21, 1968). In this episode the Cybernauts become a tool of revenge with Peter Cushing as Beresford, Frederick Jaeger reprising his role as Benson, Charles Tingwell, Fulton MacKay, Roger Hammond, Anthony Dutton, Noel Coleman, Redmond Philip, and Terry Richard. It was written by Philip Levene and directed by Robert Day.

But this was not the last of the Cybernauts. "The Last of the Cybernauts" quite belatedly aired on March 9, 1979, as an episode of *The New Avengers*. One of Armstrong's assistants is released from prison and is promptly kidnapped by a burn victim who was badly disfigured in a fire while escaping from Steed and the Avengers. He wants to use the Cybernauts to exact his revenge. This final chapter in the Cybernaut saga featured Robert Lang, Oscar Quitak, Gwen Taylor, Basil Hopkins, Robert Gillespie, David Horovitch, Sally Bazely, Pearl Hackney, Eric Carte, Rocky Taylor, and Davina Taylor. It was written by Brian Clemens and directed by Sidney Hayers.

In the post-*Avengers* years, after moving on to new leading ladies, like Linda Thorson and Joanna Lumley, Macnee has been a familiar figure on television as guest star on countless series, and in the late eighties, he moved into a new persona. He has become Dr. Watson to Christopher Lee's Sherlock Holmes in a sumptuous new Holmes TV series. The first segment was "Sherlock Holmes and the Leading Lady," filmed in Luxembourg, with Christopher Lee as the great detective and Morgan

Fairchild as Irene Adler. Featured are Ronald Hines, Englebert Humperdinck, Jeremy Quayle, and Terence Beesely. The second installment, "The Incident at Victoria Falls," was filmed in Zimbabwe, and starred Richard Todd, Jenny Seagrove, and Claude Akins (as Teddy Roosevelt).

Macnee has settled in Palm Springs with Hungarian-born third wife Baba. They were wed in 1988. He was previously married to actresses Barbara Douglas and Catherine Woodville. Son Rupert, from his first marriage, is a TV producer and daughter Jenny is mother of Macnee's grandson Christopher. Macnee has also been honored by the Academy of Science Fiction, Fantasy and Horror with its Golden Scroll Award.

Today Macnee is a new man, having sworn off the drinking and womanizing that cost him his first two marriages. Long gone are the days when he ran with peers Paul Scofield, Ian Carmichael, and Richard Burton, who with Macnee, once flew a notorious eighteen-vodka flight across the Atlantic.

"I've gotten over all that chasing around," says Macnee, "At some point that kind of thing just stops."

As much a part of the success of *The Avengers* as was Rigg's allure, was the beauty of talented Linda Thorson, novice spy to veteran Steed, who, as Tarra King, tooled around in an AC Cobra 428, sometimes a Red Lotus Europa.

"When Diana left the show," recalls Macnee, "she was succeeded by Linda Thorson, a most bounteous and delightful woman."

Thorson was born Linda Robinson in Toronto on June 18, 1947, the daughter of Mr. and Mrs. Martin Robinson. She worked as a secretary after leaving Bishop Strachan School. In 1965 she entered the Royal Academy of Dramatic Arts in London. She was chosen over two hundred other actresses for the role of Tarra King, and became Patrick Macnee's sophisticated sidekick for thirty-two *Avengers* episodes during season six of the series.

And though she was subsequently honored with a Drama Desk Award for her stage appearance in *Noises Off* on Broadway and with a Theatre World Award for *Steaming,* in which she with most of her fellow actresses performed, at one time or another in the show, totally nude, Thorson is not the lady who readily comes to mind when one thinks of *The Avengers*. That honor is still held by Rigg.

There was a stunning new associate for Steed in *The New Avengers,* which aired 1978–79. Her name was Purdey and she drove a yellow MGB Drophead Sports, sometimes a yellow Triumph TR7. She was portrayed by Joanna Lumley, who some said was the hottest "Avenger" yet. Only this time around, an aging Steed had to share her with a man named Mike Gambit (Gareth Hunt), who was fond of driving a red Jaguar XJS around London. Steed, in

Linda Thorson as Tarra King, who succeeded Mrs. Peel as Steed's partner (*photo courtesy Orion Television*)

Patrick Macnee with two new partners, Joanna Lumley (as Purdey) and Gareth Hunt (as Mike Gambit),
when *The New Avengers* emerged in the late seventies (*photo courtesy Arts and Entertainment Network*)

the meanwhile, opted for the country, preferring his yellow Rover Saloon to his olive Jaguar Coupe. This was a suitable semiretirement for the agent who had frequently dazzled the likes of Emma Peel beneath the portrait of his grandfather "Stallion" Steed back in the sixties.

Purdey was described at the time as "A girl who packs ultrafemininity with a fighting style that is as effective as unique. A stockings-and-suspenders girl—a man's woman."

But actress Lumley countered in the British press: "I resent being sold as sexy. I'm certainly not a sex symbol."

The word on the new number two man in *The New Avengers* was that Gambit had served as a mercenary in the Congo and was "a man who has clawed his way up through courage, determination, and ability—he can strike as fast as a cobra."

As for Steed, he had retired to a country home, a manor aptly called Steed's Stud, where he entertained lovely ladies and bred horses—not unlike Macnee's real-life "Uncle" Evelyn.

Actually, the last time Mrs. Peel was heard of was in the final episode of *The New Avengers,* a two-parter called "K Is for Kill." It aired March 29, 1979, with a flashback to 1965 in which Steed is chasing a Russian soldier who is killed and then ages instantly. Steed phones Mrs. Peel to tell her of the incident. Twelve years later Steed is contacted by Emma to tell him of a similar incident in France. This episode featured Pierre Vernier, Maurice Marsac, Charles Millot, Paul Emile, Christine Delaroche, Sacha Pitoeff, Alberto Someno, Jacques Monet, Frank Oliver, and Eric Penrose. It was written by Brian Clemens and directed by Yvon Marie Coulais.

The "return" of Mrs. Peel was actually the resurrection of unused Rigg footage from the earlier color series and the result of clever editing.

As much a factor in the success of *The Avengers* as the performers was the compelling theme music by Laurie Johnson, who was partners with Brian Clemens and Albert Fennell in *The Avengers* and *The New Avengers*.

Johnson, born in Hampstead in 1927, studied at the Royal College of Music where he later taught. In the fifties he composed and arranged for top British bandleaders like Ted Heath, Geraldo, and Ambrose, and then began scoring movies, West End musicals (like *Lock Up Your Daughters* [with lyricist Lionel Bart], *The Four Musketeers,* and *Pieces of Eight* [with lyricist Peter Cook]), and television shows. His *Avengers* theme replaced the one by Johnny Dankworth that was used on the Honor Blackman episodes.

The Avengers was revived with great clamor on cable's Arts and Entertainment Network in 1990. A & E aired 134 episodes with Gale (Blackman) a leather-clad judo expert with a degree in anthropolgy and Peel (Rigg) a beguiling widow with a penchant for karate and kung fu, and of course with the demurely attractive King (Thorson) and Steed (Macnee). The first three years of *The Avengers* were unseen in the U.S. until January 1991, as A & E ran the Rigg episodes before the Blackman episodes.

This revival of *The Avengers* on American television found Rigg in a somewhat reflective mood, "When life has been generous to you, as it has been to me, then it's easier to avoid being 'small-minded' about anything. It's too defeating. Laugh about it, for God's sake. I could have gone on and done greater and greater things but I didn't. It's as simple as that."

Though A & E obtained the first season (1961–62) with Ian Hendry and Macnee, the channel did not plan initially to air either this first batch or *The New Avengers* (1978–79). What they did ultimately air was season two (1962), with twenty-six black and white episodes (Blackman appeared in seventeen, Julie Stevens [Venus Smith] in six, and John Rollason [Dr. Martin King] in three), and season three (1963), with twenty-six black and white episodes with Catherine Gale (Blackman) as Steed's cohort. (Only twenty-five were shown on the cable channel.)

Producers of the series over the years included Leonard White, Julian Wintle, John Bryce, Albert Fennell, and of course Brian Clemens. Fennell died in April 1988. Music was initially by Johnny Dankworth, and the episodes were scripted by Roger Marshall, Philip Levene, Tony Williamson, and Terry Nation.

Semiregulars, at one time or the other, included Douglas Muir as One/Ten (in the Honor Blackman episodes), Arthur Hewlett as One/Twelve, Patrick Newell as Mother (final season), and Ingrid Hafner as Carol Wilson.

"At the time [we first did the show] we just took it all for granted," Macnee has said. "We were working so hard we didn't think about it but now they stand up and they're damned good and I'm proud of it. Most important, I'd say, is that [we] strived for genuine wit and didn't treat the audience like cretins."

And such as it was, back in the sixties even author Ayn Rand responded philosophically, "Romantic thrillers are an exceedingly difficult job—they require such a degree of skill, ingenuity, inventiveness, imagination and logic—such a great amount of talent on the part of the producer or the director or the cast or all of them—that it is virtually impossible to fool an entire nation for a whole year."

"There were things to be found," eulogizes producer Brian Clemens, who more recently scripted *Highlander II—the Quickening* with Sean Connery, "psychological things under the surface, like Hitchcock. Hitchcock's films appeal on several levels—they're a multilayered cake. [At first] you see them as straightforward thrillers and then you realize there's all sorts of undercurrents, wonderful, nasty undercurrents."

"Regardless of conscious or subconscious motives," concluded Rand, "such thrillers, in fact, carry a message or intention of their own, implicit in their nature: to arouse people's interest in some daring adventure, to hold them in suspense by the intricacy of a battle for great stakes, to inspire them by the spectacle of human efficacy, to evoke their admiration for the hero's courage."

Such was *The Avengers*.

Macnee as Steed (*photo courtesy Arts and Entertainment Network*)

Barnabas and Elizabeth (Jonathan Frid and Joan Bennett) do some familial conspiring (*photo courtesy Dark Shadows Over Atlanta Fan Club*)

SIXTEEN

DARK SHADOWS

(June 27, 1966–April 2, 1971)

"No live organism can continue for long to exist under conditions of absolute reality; even larks and katydids are supposed, by some, to dream. Hill House, not sane, stood by itself against its hills, holding darkness within . . . silence lay steadily against the wood and stone . . . and whatever walked there, walked alone." So wrote Shirley Jackson in *The Haunting of Hill House,* and so did the manor Collinwood stand against a cliff romantically named Widows' Hill, holding within the dark shadows of its silent corridors the unspoken secrets of the Collins family.

In truth, ABC's Gothic serial *Dark Shadows,* which ran for 1,225 episodes in the late 1960s, was part *Hill House* and part *Turn of the Screw.* From regal matriarchs and naive ingenues to hunky werewolves and seductive vampires, these were the icons of America's youth.

Jonathan Frid, a Canadian born, Shakespearean-trained actor who attended Yale University Drama School and London's Royal Academy of Dramatic Arts, became an overnight sensation through his portrayal of villain-turned-hero Barnabas Collins. More sophisticated than Adam West and more cunning than Napoleon Solo, Barnabas Collins was the ultimate.

And then in early 1991 it seemed almost inconceivable that NBC would choose to revive a show known for its low-budget production, on-the-air bloopers, and bad dialogue. And this time around it was with illustrious performers such as Ben Cross as Barnabas and Jean Simmons as Elizabeth Collins Stoddard.

The new series premiered on January 13 with Robert Cobert's familiar theme music wafting through the opening credits. For many viewers it was a journey back in time to Collinsport, Maine, a place where footsteps still faintly echoed along the corridors of Collinwood.

The seed for this resurrection was actually planted in the summer of 1989 when charter cast member Kathryn Leigh Scott approached producer-director Dan Curtis about doing a television reunion movie. As fate would have it, Curtis, following on the heels of his huge success with *The Winds of War* and *War and Remembrance,* did indeed choose *Dark Shadows* as the vehicle with which to bring his television production company to NBC. But to the chagrin of Scott and her fans, the revival became a remake and the original cast members were excluded from the series.

Curtis reportedly felt that the original cast members were too old. His implication was that though most of them still looked great, particularly Lara Parker, they were still too old to reprise their roles. The bottom line, in his estimation, was that to bring back Parker and her colleagues would be disastrous.

"Dan told me that if he had gotten a run that some of us he would try to write in as new characters and put us in [the show]," says Lara Parker, who portrayed witch Angelique in the daytime version of the Gothic soap. "And I think that this would have been a good choice on his part—that it would have brought in a lot of loyal fans—it would have been a shrewd move for him."

She continues: "I thought [the new series] was wonderful. I tried to get Dan Curtis to let me write for it and I had some very strong feelings about what I thought they should do and they didn't do those things—they did other things. I thought the show got shafted by the Gulf War. It was just terrible luck. Nobody was watching anything but CNN. And then it got preempted a couple of times. Friday night was a very bad night. A lot of people watching TV on Friday night are old[er] people who don't go out. This was a show for young people.

"[And] they decided to make it romantic the way *Beauty and the Beast* was done. I thought it was a good

Jonathan Frid as Barnabas Collins and Grayson Hall as Dr. Julia Hoffman (*photo courtesy Dark Shadows Over Atlanta Fan Club*)

inventive, creative person whom I trusted. I trusted his visual judgment in directing [and] his creative judgment. Dan cannot do anything that has to do with *Dark Shadows* without being compared to [the original series]."

Nonetheless, when pressed, Millay concedes, "As far as the new series went it proved the age-old saying that technology doesn't make a better mousetrap. [By comparison] we didn't have any of the frills. We were an economy class series and we did it by tremendous devotion to each other, to the scripts, and to Dan. Our directors—we had several good ones—Lela Swift was one—[were] the tops. She was a brilliant director. She was the Ida Lupino of daytime TV."

Another excluded alumnus, Jerry Lacy (Bogey in *Play It Again, Sam*), who is presently married to actress Julia Duffy, had initially indicated that he'd be interested in playing the Reverend Trask again, but that part ultimately went to Roy Thinnes, who appears today on *One Life to Live*.

Lara Parker has her own opinion about Lacy, his talent, and the role he played in the original series: "Jerry and I

Jonathan Frid as the sixties Barnabas and Ben Cross as the nineties one (*Frid photo courtesy Dark Shadows Over Atlanta Fan Club; Cross photo courtesy Dan Curtis Productions*)

choice and I thought they did a wonderful job—it was beautiful to watch and the acting was wonderful. I loved all the actors but it missed some of the things our show had, and I admit it was inadvertent, but [our show] had a lot of humor—a lot of laughs that we didn't intend to get, but it had a wonderful feel that set it apart. Doing a romantic horror and not quite being able to bring it off because you haven't had the time to learn the lines created a certain tone that many, many times was amusing.

"And I felt that if Dan was going to recapture that," stresses Parker, reassessing her original opinion, "he was really going to have to go out on a limb and take some risks and go into some kinky things—make it kinkier—and not just straight horror."

But Diana Millay, who portrayed Laura Collins, wife of Roger (Louis Edmonds) in the 1960s soap, is quick to defend Curtis: "It was always great working with Dan Curtis. I did the very first script that he ever directed. And I know that in the [new] *Dark Shadows* they say there was some problem with Dan; maybe he's [just] older, I don't know [but] he was always—I thought—a marvelous,

Joan Bennett as Elizabeth Collins Stoddard in the sixties and Jean Simmons, who took the role in the much later version (*Bennett photo courtesy Dark Shadows Over Atlanta Fan Club; Simmons photo courtesy Dan Curtis Productions*)

were friends—he always wanted to be Bogart—that's basically what I remember about him. He was sort of stiff—I didn't really feel like he had a free, juicy talent. He was kind of resisting what he had to do and sort of faking the Trask thing—he didn't really get into it. There's a difference between playing at it and really getting into it and believing that you are this fanatic and there was this whole distance that Jerry didn't go that Thayer David [Stokes] or Johnny Karlen [Willie] would have gone.

"They would have eaten up that part. But the funny thing about *Dark Shadows* was that people's limitations would pay off as well and Jerry's limitation in a way gave Trask a hypocrisy—you didn't believe the man—you believed that he was a hypocrite. It came out of the style of Jerry's acting. You didn't believe Trask—you hated him and it worked! It gave the character the color that he had and it worked for the show."

In early 1991 another former cast member, David Selby, was less enthusiastic. He claimed to have no interest in reprising his Quentin character, encouraging Curtis to go ahead with an all-new cast.

Selby's appearance on the *Dark Shadows* scene back in the 1960s was the biggest boost to the ratings since Frid's arrival at Collinwood. As a matter of fact, the show reached its peak in the summer of 1969 when Robert Cobert's haunting "Quentin's Theme" hit the top twenty in the charts, snaring an Grammy nomination. Selby went on to play Richard Channing on *Falcon Crest*.

Curtis said in *USA Today* in December 1990: "People have been after me to do this for a long time and the timing is right. *Dark Shadows* brings back the memories of my youth—I was brash—we broke every rule in daytime because we had no experience." He went on to surmise that though people have tried to copy *Dark Shadows* over the years, " . . . they'd always failed because no one ever really seemed to understand what made the original series unique—it was not a horror show, but a Gothic romance. He explained that all of his demonic figures always had another side to them, a moment when you felt sorry for them.

"The innocence will still remain. This won't be some razzle-dazzle special effects thing. But where it was very crudely done then, now it'll be slick and classy and highly stylized. The great hall of Collinwood looks like Grand Central Station compared to that dinky little set we had for the original series." Curtis's observation was no surprise since the new series was shot at Greystone Mansion in Beverly Hills, the fifty-five-room manor of the late oil baron Edward Doheny.

Curtis promised that the new series would be grown up, an adult version of the sixties after-school classic, claiming that he would never have done *Dark Shadows* again if he'd had to come up with a whole new story line, and that he planned to tell basically the same story with certain twists. He explained that the theme would remain the same. The reluctant vampire would be released and a cure attempted by the lady doctor who falls in love with him.

The new *Dark Shadows* did, indeed, open with the vampire Barnabas coming out of the box, aided by Willie Loomis. Nothing new, no surprises. Curtis had had more than twenty-five years to look back and learn from the mistakes he'd supposedly made then.

Following the legacy of the original series, the new soap featured a flashback sequence, allowing members of the cast to play dual roles. Why the flashback sequence to begin with? In explaining this plot twist to *USA Today*, Curtis said, "I had no place else to go with the vampire story and it became the most successful portion of the show. Everyone wanted to know how Barnabas became a vampire."

Curtis today concedes that there was a time when he felt as if he had to shake the *Dark Shadows* image, though he did stay in the genre for a while with other works such as his *Dracula, Trilogy of Terror, Dr. Jekyll and Mr. Hyde,*

and *Night Stalker*. By then, as he's claimed numerous times, he never wanted to do another scary movie unless he chose to. And as luck would have it, his next career move made that possible.

After the forty-seven and a half hours of epic television based upon Herman Wouk's two World War II novels, *The Winds of War* and *War and Remembrance*, Curtis found all the networks coming to him with offers.

And though he wasn't looking to put *Dark Shadows* on the air again, he was anxious to keep his hand in television. The revamped *Dark Shadows* featured Joanna Going as governess Victoria Winters, Roy Thinnes as Roger Collins, Michael T. Weiss as Joe Haskell, Barbara Steele as Dr. Julia Hoffman, Barbara Blackburn as Carolyn Stoddard, Jim Fyfe as Willie Loomis, Veronica Lauren as Sarah, Joseph Gordon-Levitt as David Collins, Ely Pouget as Maggie Evans, and Lysette Anthony as Angelique.

Parker has her own thoughts today on the popularity of the Angelique character as well as Lysette Anthony's approach to it: "Women identified with [Angelique] because she had the courage to do what so many of them would like to have done—the courage combined with the power—the truth is she got away with deeds that other women could only fantasize about.

"Also, the thing that set her apart was that she was smarter than anyone else. She became impatient with the rest of the world but her intelligence was an intelligence of cynicism—it wasn't a spiritual intelligence [but] was sort of like street smarts in which she realized that everyone is greedy and out to get what they can get and she was better at it than any of them—not that she didn't suffer. She suffered a great deal. She suffered in a way that made her more determined that she would not suffer again. She didn't learn anything from her suffering except to be more vicious.

"I thought Lysette did a good job [but] she could have been stronger. Angelique was so ruthless. She really didn't have a choice. Lysette played it like [Angelique] chose to be mean, but she didn't choose to be mean—she just 'was.' Lysette tried to make it more rational—she chose to be mean because she was so hurt. I [on the other hand] just seemed to have this knack for playing the bad side."

Though it remains to be seen how the thirteen episodes of the *Dark Shadows* revival will affect the careers of those involved, for the cast of the 1960s version, the earlier series was a breeding ground for stars and personalities on the rise to fame, success, and in some cases, notoriety.

Roger Davis, who portrayed Jeff Clark/Peter Bradford, married and divorced miniseries queen and former Charlie's Angel Jaclyn Smith, while the equally angelic Kate

Jackson (Daphne Harridge) scored not only with *Charlie's Angels* but also with *Scarecrow and Mrs. King* and dozens of TV movies.

Parker has memories of Jackson, too: "Kate was the only actor who ever made me break up during taping. We would bait each other during rehearsal, giggling like schoolgirls in church, until the wrath came down from the control room. In the last days of the show we played sisters and . . . were given many mysteries to unravel. Our relationship offstage was so silly, and our onstage characters were so solemn, that we often suppressed fits of hysteria. I remember the director [Henry Kaplan] was very hard on Kate when she first came on the show. A lovely, natural actress with ease and intelligence, Kate had enough sense not to try to do something she couldn't do truthfully. Often her reactions would be very subtle. Henry would say, 'Kate, there is a ghost coming through the wall and if you can't scream, just imagine me coming into your dressing room after the show!' "

Today Louis Edmonds (Roger Collins) is Langley Wallingford on *All My Children,* while John Karlen (Willie Loomis) went on to recognition on *Cagney and Lacey,* winning an Emmy for his portrayal of Harvey Lacey.

"Barnabas is the one who made it happen," Karlen recalls. "It was almost live television. Unless a camera dropped in front of you or something that was a print, that was a take. It was done. You think of *Dark Shadows* you think of the vampire, you know, you don't think of the other individuals. The vampire is *Dark Shadows.*"

Chris Pennock, who was Cyrus Longworth, Jeb Hawkes, and Sebastian Shaw in different centuries on *Dark Shadows,* returned, after a seven year absence, to *Guiding Light* as Dr. Justin Marler.

The series' original ingenue Alexandra Moltke Isles (Victoria Winters) gained later notoriety as Claus von Bulow's mistress, during his sensational trials in the early 1980s for the alleged poisoning of his wife. Fans were gleeful as Isles played her greatest scene to date in a courtroom drama reminiscent of Victoria Winters's trial for witchcraft in a segment of *Dark Shadows.* This larger than fiction drama occurred in the early 1980s and involved New York's social elite and the comings and goings of the inhabitants of another expansive manor house. Ironically, the bleak house used for the exterior shots of Collinwood, patterned after a sixteenth-century French chateau and built in the late 1920s, was located in Newport, Rhode Island, as was the von Bulow House.

"I didn't think that Victoria Winters should have been as aloof as she was," Parker says. "Alexandra [Moltke] Isles had this distance, this cool, and was just ravishing. When she wanted to get off the show she stopped combing her hair and wearing makeup and she still photographed so beautifully. She didn't need to do anything. She was a socialite basically, that was her posture. She had come from a lot of money. The show was beneath her. Even in the beginning she wanted more—she did not want to be there. By the time I came on the show she wanted to get off more than anything and she finally did by getting pregnant. She didn't want to be an actress. She had thought she wanted to be an actress but it didn't do for her the things that it really does for people who really want to act. She was a very real actress but she didn't bring a lot of energy to it, but again it worked for her character because Victoria Winters was supposed to be reactive—she was the protagonist—she was the one that it was happening to.

"She was the audience's eyes. We saw it all through her eyes. She didn't have to be strong—she just had to be the bridge that carried us into the show. And her lack of energy—which drove the directors mad—didn't really do any harm because she seemed so real. The rest of us seemed larger than life but she seemed very placid [and] natural. I think she did her best at that point but she moped around like a person who had to do this and who didn't want to be there and she hated working with Roger [Davis]. I sort of always wanted to be her friend and was slightly intimidated by her wealth and her social position. Then she went on to have quite an interesting experience, larger than fiction."

Much of Isles's testimony that helped to convict Claus von Bulow during his first trial couldn't be used in the second. The judge would not allow the previous testimony to be read and ruled that the defense attorney had the right to cross examine her this time around.

Perhaps one of the most versatile of the old series veteran stars is Kathryn Leigh Scott, who continues appearing in numerous television productions, including *Dallas, Star Trek: the Next Generation, Matlock,* and *21 Jump Street.*

One of the reasons for the longevity of *Dark Shadows* is that she has kept the series alive in print for years with *My Scrapbook Memories of "Dark Shadows,"* her collection of behind-the-scenes stories, featuring eighty pages of photos and a comprehensive summary of the convoluted story line.

Despite their closeness Lara Parker has had mixed feelings about Scott's *Dark Shadows* memoirs: "Kathryn's one of my best friends. She [is] a gifted actress—she really created Josette. Kathryn was not Josette—she was closer to Maggie. She made this innocent, radiant, incredibly vulnerable person [whom] she was not and I thought she did a very good job. I used to like to watch her work. . . . She was very clean—specific in what she did: her movement, her line delivery.

"How can you resent someone who did what you could

Kathryn Ann Scott in her role as Maggie Evans (*photo courtesy Dark Shadows Over Atlanta Fan Club*)

David Selby as the brooding Quentin Collins (*photo courtesy Dark Shadows Over Atlanta Fan Club*)

have done? Kathryn has a prodigious energy. I think we all felt 'sour grapes' that her first book was all pictures of her, but so what? I've got a box of pictures of myself. If I wanted to write a book and use all pictures of myself I could. I thought it was a vanity production, but damn, she pulled it off. She was smart. She's a smart lady."

Through her own publishing company, Pomegranate Press, Scott offers several titles including *Lobby Cards: The Classic Films,* with a foreword by Joan Bennett, the original Elizabeth Stoddard.

"I really think the show had a broader audience than anyone ever suspected," says Scott. "As an afternoon soap, we were supposed to be appealing to a student audience, but we heard from just as many schoolteachers, doctors, and lawyers who hurried home from work each day so they wouldn't miss an episode."

"We had excellent writers and each wrote with a different voice. While I had no particular favorite among them, it was always easy for me to distinguish who had written a particular script. I can't imagine why, but Gordon Russell's scripts were always the easiest to learn and Sam Hall's often contained quirky phrases and subtle

bits of humor. Since no more than two or three writers were producing scripts at any given time, it was easy to distinguish their particular styles."

But Jonathan Frid begs to differ. "Sometimes I got bored silly with that show. Sometimes the writing was awful and the show would fall apart and sometimes we would have some wonderful shows. Still the show at times worked. It just didn't work often enough for my tastes."

"What we shot was exactly what you saw," Scott points out. "We never went back to fix anything. It was considered far too expensive. When we went on the air at four o'clock we had to do it. In fact they put the commercials in and everything while we were doing it. The fellow that was playing my father, David Ford, had a terrible time remembering lines so they finally made him blind so he could read the teleprompter, and then that didn't work, so they decided to kill him off, and on the last day when he was lying in the hospital room and Maggie Evans had to come in and help him on his way, camera three came through the hospital door and clattered against the bed and the teleprompter fell off and my father sat bolt upright in

worst, most pompous lines, because he was a vampire, and could say the most convoluted sentences in the world."

"Jonathan was kind and giving and completely devoted to—committed to—the show, committed to make it as good as he possibly could," contributes Parker, contradicting Frid's seeming ambivalence. "[Back then] he had not one ounce of cynicism. He was always doing everything that he could to do his best. We were not putting down what we did where today the tendency is to go, 'Oh, you know, I'm doing this piece of crap, but don't bother to watch it.' That's the way actors talk today. Nobody likes their material."

Scott is quick to elaborate on the various characters she played on the show, "Maggie, Josette, Rachel, and Kitty were all very distinct characters to me. They were of different nationalities and time periods, and they had very specific personalities and character traits. Maggie, of

Then, Jonathan Frid and Alexandra Moltke Isles as Barnabas and Victoria Winters, and later Ben Cross and Joanna Going in the same roles (*Frid and Isles photo courtesy Dark Shadows Over Atlanta Fan Club; Cross and Going photo courtesy Dan Curtis Productions*)

bed and said, 'Where is it?' and I said, 'It's okay, Pop, just let go,' and I just pushed him against the pillows and he died.

"If it didn't look like the sets were going to fall down or if dead bodies didn't move, we wouldn't have the charming show that we do."

On this point Frid concurs: "It was a very 'good looking' show—trying to create graveyards with Styrofoam tombs falling over, jingling bats, and botched lines. But the scripts weren't good enough. Finally we just ran out of gas."

Scott also recalls, "We were all so close . . . really good friends as well as coworkers"—referring to two *Dark Shadows* cast members who are now deceased. "Grayson Hall [Dr. Hoffman] and Thayer David [Professor Stokes] were close personal friends. I loved working with them, and we also got together socially. Both were colorful characters, and even now, I can hear their distinctive voices."

Frid remembers, "In spite of the fact that I could never live up to what I wanted to do each day, every once and awhile I did pull it together. But Barnabas always got the

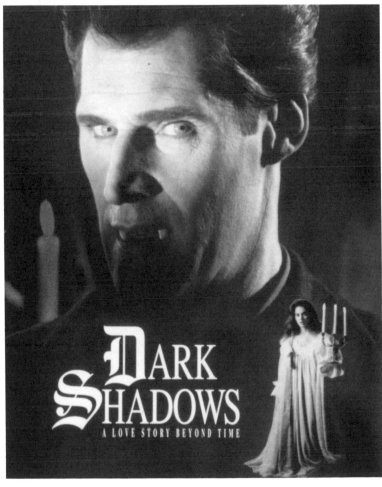

course, was closest to home for me and that role is probably my favorite. I had great respect for her feistiness and inner strength. Josette was so wonderfully romantic and I loved playing her—and the other two roles were each challenging in their own way.

"I was young and just beginning my career, so I feel all of these characters reflected my skills at the time and helped me to develop my craft."

Was it difficult for her to juggle so many roles at one time? "An actor retains a sense of self while acting," she explains, "but when one is relaxed and working well the focus is entirely on the moment being played. If an actor is well prepared and concentrating properly, the work is instinctive and genuine. When an actor really trusts his or her own instrument, there's a wonderful sense of taking flight—one does feel completely secure and comfortable living a role."

Frid has maintained his cult following, touring frequently with his one-man shows: *Fools and Fiends,* comprised of tales of the odd and macabre from the works of Edgar Allan Poe, William F. Nolan, Stephen King, James Thurber, and Irwin Shaw; *Fridiculousness,* a whimsical potpourri of Cole Porter, Dorothy Parker, Robert Benchley, and Groucho Marx; and *Shakespearean Odyssey,* containing snippets from *Richard II* and *Much Ado About Nothing* and *A Midsummer Night's Dream.* His one-man show, he concedes, was an outgrowth of what he originally did at the annual fan-produced *Dark Shadows* festivals. He told Keith Thomas of the *Atlanta Journal-Constitution* in January 1991: "I hope people who come to the show will forget about Barnabas and learn a little more about Jonathan Frid and a little more about literature. The people who come to see my one-man show expecting to see me do Barnabas Collins are in for a rude awakening. I'm not into bloodsucking anymore."

Canadian-born Frid, a native of Hamilton, Ontario, attended McMaster University before launching his acting career. In the beginning he performed with the Toronto Shakespeare Festival and then moved on to the Williamstown Theatre in Massachusetts and the American Shakespearean Festival in Stratford, Connecticut.

In the fifties Frid toured with Katharine Hepburn in *Much Ado About Nothing* and in the sixties he had roles in *Henry IV, Julius Caesar,* and the television production of *The Portrait of Dorian Gray,* before finally peaking on Broadway in *Roar Like a Dove* in 1964. There was also a brief stint on the soap *As the World Turns,* as Dr. Neil Wade.

The introduction of Barnabas, a name found on a Flushing, New York, tombstone by *Dark Shadows* producer Robert Costello, was a desperate, last-minute effort to boost sagging ratings and forestall cancellation by ABC.

"Barnabas Collins was not supposed to last," says Jim Pierson of the fan-run *Dark Shadows* Festival, "but Jonathan Frid performed the character with so much humanity and so much depth that he became what drew viewers to [the show]. The housewives, I think, related to Barnabas's yearning for happiness. They generally found the vampire a sexy hero."

Dan Curtis agrees. "No one in the world ever thought that the vampire was going to become a major star. The show was going down the tubes and my kids said to me, 'Why don't you at least make it scarier?' so I decided to see how far we could go with the spooks and I figured if we could get away with a vampire we could do anything. The housewives all loved it. I think they were hooked on the erotic vampire thing. That's what did it—they used to send [Frid] nude pictures of themselves. I was floored. So was everybody else. We had to hire a company to handle all of the mail."

Scott remembers, "I don't think that any of us were terribly pleased when we first heard that there was going to be a vampire on the show. I think that all of us had our misgivings when we realized that we were going in that direction but I think that the reason why twenty-five years later we're still seeing *Dark Shadows* [is] really because of Jonathan Frid. Barnabas saved the show from oblivion. Jonathan is the best vampire the world has ever seen."

When first approached about doing *Dark Shadows,* Frid said, "I'm going to California," and his agent replied, "Why not get a couple of weeks work and make some extra money?"

Frid relented and the casting was finally narrowed down to him and two other actors. Curtis chose the one he wanted and then forgot about it. Only when he realized that Frid had been hired did he notice that the casting agent had given the role of Barnabas to the wrong actor!

As it stood, the part was supposed to have lasted for two weeks, but not only did Frid manage to snare regular employment, he also saved the sinking show.

What was the appeal of Frid's nocturnal character? He attempted to define this allure to journalist Keith Thomas: "[He] represented something dark, mysterious and romantic. And what person hasn't dreamed of immortality? . . . There were hidden lonelinesses everywhere, going on for thousands of years. Loneliness is a terrible thing."

"Apparently it was a very important and very essential thing that this character work—it was the last hope [but] I wasn't really interested in the vampire, per se . . . I was interested in a human being with a conflict. I mean I was vulnerable, I was in love."

Though he'd never seen the original series and had no desire to do so, Ben Cross, the "new" Barnabas, had similar ideas at the time the new series premiered: "For this to be a success you have to believe that a vampire exists . . . that there's a beautiful and ugly life after

Alexandra Isles (Victoria) and Louis Edmonds (Roger Collins) at Collinwood, actually Seaview Terrace in Newport, Rhode Island (*photo courtesy Dark Shadows Over Atlanta Fan Club*)

death. I'm playing him human, sympathetic."

During his reign as daytime's vampire heartthrob receiving from two to six thousand fan letters weekly, Frid appeared on various television talk shows and also managed to juggle two jobs in 1969 while appearing on stage in *Dial M for Murder*. But life after *Dark Shadows* was not always easy. There was no work at that time except for stage roles in *Murder in the Cathedral* and *Wait Until Dark*, both in 1971.

Frid resurfaced in 1978 to appear in the Penn State University production of *The Royal Family*, but did not appear on stage again until the 1986 production of *Alpha and the Omega*. Things picked up in 1987 when he was cast opposite Jean Stapleton, first on Broadway and then nationally, in *Arsenic and Old Lace*.

Today Frid admits that the writers of *Dark Shadows* gave him an interesting role to play, adding that part of his discomfort with the show was the fact that, not being trained in television acting, he was a slow study who at times found the daily grind of daytime television almost unbearable. But when pressed about *Dark Shadows*, he becomes more reflective. "I probably wouldn't be able to

do what I'm doing without having that to draw people in. I'll tell you this one thing about [the show]. I think that probably it wasn't a very good show, generally, but every once in a while it struck me as being quite good—it coalesced into something quite unique in television and I think it was positively beautiful."

Frid's chief complaint is that people still come up to him and ask him to do the ghoul thing: "What irritated me wasn't the role, but the way the fans and the press harped on the fangs. The first time I had a little trouble—I had them in my pocket and I had to run across the studio to bite the lady [Maggie] . . . and she was in the bedroom and I came in through these French doors and . . . I got them out of my pocket. I learned that that was not the way to do it because they went in upside down. So I had to chew them . . . I didn't mind the bite, it was just the way they had me do it."

Though Jonathan Frid's memories of *Dark Shadows* may contrast with those of Kathryn Leigh Scott, the two still show up regularly at the annual *Dark Shadows* festivals in New York and Los Angeles. Ben Cross, on the other hand, has been less than accommodating. He has been quoted as saying that he cannot understand people who make clubs out of television series.

Kate Jackson as Daphne Harridge, long before *Charlie's Angels* and *Scarecrow and Mrs. King* (*photo courtesy Dark Shadows Over Atlanta Fan Club*)

Lara Parker shares some insight into the behind-the-scenes goings-on of the new *Dark Shadows:* "Lysette Anthony is a delightful person—exquisite looking—very bright. She's a very talented actress but she had problems with Ben Cross. She said that he was a cold fish and that was not true of Jonathan."

And with perhaps a better understanding and appreciation of fan loyalty and cast camaraderie than Cross, Frid penned a foreword to Scott's latest book, *The "Dark Shadows" Companion.*

Those very fans who attend the *Dark Shadows* festivals and who purchase all of Scott's books are quite well versed in such trivia as the fact that she made her major motion picture debut back in 1970, starring opposite Frid in *House of Dark Shadows,* a full-length feature which marked Joan Bennett's last significant American film appearance.

Parker fondly recalls *Dark Shadows*'s resident star: "Joan was our star and she was really used to being pampered and there's no pampering on soap operas—I mean—they gave her her own dressing room and some beautiful dresses to wear but she had to go through the same rigorous schedule in terms of preparation. It's very hard to do a half-hour show with only three rehearsals. You have that awful feeling in your head that the way you're doing this line right now [you] hate but there's nothing you can do about it. It was very hard on her. She had to remember whole scenes and she was really shaking during taping—she was scared. I remember being sort of amazed that with all of her experience, I was being calmer that she was and I think this gave her a kind of one dimension—she played one mood—she always played [it] stiff, uptight. It was a difficult situation for someone with her background. And yet she was a grand lady and she brought to the show major Hollywood stardom and elegance and that kind of radiance that only movie stars have. Never an unkind word, always genuinely interested in other people, considerate, a real lady, a well-bred person, she had a sense of the way a person should conduct themselves in the work place. Everyone adored her. Everyone was very, very fond of her."

Born in Palisades, New Jersey, Joan Bennett had grown up in the Park Hill section of Yonkers and was educated at St. Margaret's School in Waterbury and L'Hermitage in Versailles. She debuted on Broadway in 1928 in *Jarnegan,* which also starred her father, Richard Bennett. The youngest daughter of a show biz family—her mother, Adrienne Morrison, and sisters Constance and Barbara were actresses also—Joan eventually abandoned the stage to appear in over seventy films beginning in 1929.

Although a mousey youngster who considered herself an ugly duckling, Bennett blossomed into a beauty in her teens, as her personal life became as turbulent as some of her steamy movie roles.

A bizarre twist in *Dark Shadows*'s story line explained matriarch Elizabeth Collins Stoddard's uptight stiffness as the result of the tragic, violent death of husband Paul Stoddard many years before. This was ironic, as in 1951, in the parking lot of the Beverly Hills City Hall, Joan Bennett's real-life husband number three, producer Walter Wanger, shot and wounded her agent Jennings Lang, accusing her of infidelity. She said that Wanger was depressed over financial losses. Wanger pleaded not guilty to a reduced charge and served a one hundred day-prison sentence. He bounced back and Lang recovered, but Bennett's career did not. For all practical purposes, at the age of forty-one she found her film career finished.

Bennett and Wanger (who had wed in 1940) had been separated for five years when she made her move to New York in 1961, though they would not be divorced until 1965. Wanger went on to produce *Cleopatra.*

Finally Bennett's agent talked her into doing *Dark Shadows.* She had just turned down three plays and couldn't find an appropriate stage vehicle, so she made the leap to television. However, as with Frid, she was stunned by the daily routine and had to make adjustments. Gone were the days when she'd make twenty-two takes on a single scene, as she once did portraying Amy in *Little Women* in the thirties. Now, she would often have to learn twenty-four pages of dialogue for one episode of *Dark Shadows,* once commenting that "there's no time on [the show] for errors. You do it once and that's it."

The noted actress died of cardiac arrest on December 7, 1990, at her Scarsdale, New York, home, survived by her fourth husband, David Wilde, a former newspaper critic and publisher whom she'd married in 1973.

Following in Bennett's footsteps, Jean Simmons was more lighthearted about her chance to portray the Collins family matriarch. She said at the time the new series premiered that she and her children had watched Bennett on the original program daily back in the sixties. It was common, according to Simmons, for her kids to come in after school, and before homework (or before anything, for that matter), they'd all sit down and watch the show. She claimed that because she and her family had been great fans of Bennett, she thought that the new series would be fun to do.

Herself a Hollywood legend, Simmons described the production period prior to the premiere of the new series as a great experience, made pleasant by a professional cast and crew.

"If it appealed to viewers at one time, it should appeal to them again," said Dan Curtis of the new *Dark Shadows.* But this was not to be the case. Though NBC bet an estimated $20 million that the show could thrive in its Friday night time slot, low ratings foreshadowed the cancellation of the series, which ran only six episodes.

On Wednesday, May 8, 1991, fans across the nation proclaimed "Save *Dark Shadows* Day," as support rallies were held in front of NBC affiliate stations.

"I resisted a lot in the beginning," says Parker on the subject of the *Dark Shadows* festivals. "I thought it was sort of like Sally Field in *Soapdish* when she goes to the mall so she can get some strokes. It felt like I was trying to take advantage of something that was over but now it's just one of those things that I do. It's like going to see your family once a year.

"I go to see the people that like *Dark Shadows* once a year. Jim Pierson—who runs [the festival]—definitely makes it worthwhile—he's such a nice person. Jim gave [Lysette and me] an hour on the last festival program. They showed clips and fans asked [us] questions and it was really fun. Scenes I had learned the night before and rehearsed three times, they'd play [those]—for instance that scene where I cursed Barnabas and turned him into a vampire, and then they'd play Lysette's rendition of the scene which took a week to shoot and was done on film and was edited and was just dynamite in comparison, and it was really good for laughs because of how superior [today's] production values are and what wonderful things Lysette got to do and all the things we couldn't do. So completely different but we were saying the same lines.

"[Back then] we just had to stand there on our marks and say the words. And then they'd show a scene of mine that was particularly good and I'd turn to Lysette and say, 'Eat your heart out.' And she'd laugh and then they'd show one of her [scenes] that was particularly good and she'd say 'Match that!' And so we had this sort of fun rivalry on the stage but she's a delightful person—exquisite looking, very bright."

"One of the reasons for the success of *Dark Shadows* was the friendship and closeness of the cast which was a very tight, close-knit little group," Diana Millay says, "and the interesting thing is that the tremendous love and affection that the fans have given us through the years, [which] is why we go to the festivals, has done the most amazing thing—it has kept us together—in touch—seeing one another, calling one another."

On the subject of former child actor David Henesey, who portrayed her TV son, David Collins, Millay responds, "I tried so hard to get David to come with me [to the festivals] so I could walk out on stage with him and say, 'Oh, I have a surprise.' Jim Pierson had asked me if I would just bring David down [one year] and David said yes and as the time got closer he just couldn't do it—it was a real problem for him. He became paranoid about it.

Lara Parker as the original Angelique and Lysette Anthony in the nineties reincarnation (*Parker photo courtesy Dark Shadows Over Atlanta Fan Club; Anthony photo courtesy Dan Curtis Productions*)

Lara Parker, contemporary author (*photo courtesy Lara Parker*)

"He is married and he has babies—he doesn't want anyone to know where he is. The hatred [for the show] ran deep. It's very sad. He's a perfectly normal and well-adjusted husband and father [now], but he had a mother hang-up. He was a child actor who was forced to something he didn't want to do. He was the most obnoxious little brat at times but I would say, 'Alright, David, that's enough!' and we got along very well. We've remained very close friends over the years. David is a wonderful father and he has done a beautiful job in the restaurant business [in New York] but [back then he] was not a happy actor on the show."

Millay also admits, "*Dark Shadows* has kept us together for twenty-five years which never would have happened if it hadn't been for the fans. We were great friends in those [early] days but now it's a more adult, mature closeness. I speak to Lara all the time. We all speak to Jonathan and to Kathryn. We love seeing Roger [Davis]. We love seeing Louis [Edmonds]. I gave a party in my home [because of] the fans bringing me [back] to my old friends. We gave something to the fans and they gave it back to us again by keeping us in touch with each other which is an incredible thing."

Lara Parker has had a few fan-related experiences that were a bit less pleasant than those of Millay: "When the show was on the air I had one girl [fan] threaten to kill herself. My worst fan—I think that she's dead now—weighed about three hundred pounds. I used to walk to the subway and she was right by the door every day. She wasn't scary, she was just annoying.

Roger Davis as Jeff Clark and Thayer David as Professor Stokes in the feature *House of Dark Shadows* (*photo courtesy Dark Shadows Over Atlanta Fan Club*)

"She walked with me all the way to the subway and I'd walk very fast. She was so fat it was hard for her to walk fast. She was a drag. She used to call me all the time and tell me all her problems but I tend to be soft-hearted and I put up with [it]. I got some phone threats but nobody ever actually carried them through. People get confused. They think I'm really Angelique and Jonathan is really Barnabas and they get confused."

But in the final analysis, as for redoing *Dark Shadows*, perhaps when brunette Joanna Going was cast as Victoria Winters, Curtis should have heeded the ominous warning in young Sarah Collins's diary: "You must stop your plans for the young girl with the dark hair."

Or perhaps when the Trask character was entombed behind a wall, Curtis should have listened to actor Roy Thinnes's muffled cries, "I beg you—I implore you. Don't do this!"

In any case, Curtis did do it and it failed dismally. The bad scripts, the jingling bats, the Styrofoam tombstones, and the botched lines, and yes, even the cast that Curtis had labeled as "over the hill," were the magical ingredients that made the show work the first time around. The charm of the original series was in all that fumbling around, in all the subplots that didn't work, in all the uncertainty as to what kind of show it was going to be.

"It was humiliating," remembers Parker. "It was very embarrassing because often there were forgotten lines or missed cues or flubbed words. We were all painfully aware that it looked rough and it seemed rough."

And despite Curtis's good intentions and for all the talent of a commendable new cast, there was the mistake of tampering with something that had become classic because of the very imperfections he sought to correct.

"[Dan] had to do what he had to do," stresses Parker, who insists that she feels no resentment. "The old story required young actors. I don't think we could have played our old parts—I think that would have been ridiculous. I don't take anything that happens in Hollywood personally because I know how hard all those choices are. Those choices were very hard for Dan. He had to decide—he had to make decisions about what he was going to do and he had to make choices and then he had to go with them and commit to them and not go back."

But one wonders if Parker, whose career has never regained the momentum experienced during the original run of *Dark Shadows* is not, in defending Curtis's choices, defending her own as well.

"What I wanted as a young actress and what they gave me to do was in conflict," she says. "I thought of *Dark Shadows* as only the first step up the ladder of success. When the show went off the air, I went to California, so that I could become a movie star. Although I played many wonderful parts and had many lovely opportunities, years later I realized that *Dark Shadows* had been my most

Diana Millay, the Laura Collins of *Dark Shadows*
(*photo: Sy Tomashoff. Courtesy Diana Millay*)

exciting job. It was great and we're all glad we did it and it's behind us. To a certain extent all of us wish that it wasn't our only claim to fame.

"I thought *Dark Shadows* was just the beginning but now I look back and realize it was my best job and that's a little hard because I thought it was just a step up the ladder. I didn't realize at the time that it was probably the one good thing I was ever going to get."

"I was in New York where my husband was, so that was why I did *Dark Shadows*," stresses Millay, who has given up acting.

"That's why I carried on and did *Secret Storm* and did soaps for ten years and then just sort of drifted out of the business. By that time I didn't want to do any more plays because you had to go there every night. [But] I'm very sorry that after I did *Dark Shadows* for the length of time I did it nobody really wanted me. Everybody so identified with the character of Laura on [that show].

"I was referred to recently in a press clipping as a cult luminary—and I must say that I've had rave reviews in

New York—but the thing that means the most is for someone to say that I'm a cult luminary—I just love it. I love it so much because after all the wonderful things and the rave notices—I realize that [those] things didn't matter. What matters is I did something that was important to millions of people."

"Jonathan's said many times that in one afternoon we appeared before more [viewers]," Parker interjects, "than we would have before audiences in a theater in a lifetime and that always gave him a buzz. But people do get older and they go on with their lives and this is what I keep telling the fans—we've all gone on with our lives and done other things."

"[Back then] everywhere I went in New York I was recognized. Even my own children asked me not to pick them up after school. They were embarrassed. Their friends would go, 'Oh, your mommy's in that dumb TV show.' They'd ask me if I'd please wait a block away and they'd walk and meet me. We'd go to the skating rink or ball game and it was constant recognition and it lasted even after the show went off the air."

"Even now I am amazed when I see clips [of] myself doing things I don't remember," Parker exclaims. "It seems like another person. And then I see myself doing something kind of neat and I go, 'Oh, I see why they all liked me,' but it's completely over, all gone."

"The reason that *Dark Shadows* has a cult following," Millay feels, "is this—people want, of course, to be taken outside of themselves—that goes without saying, but what *Dark Shadows* did was [to] show that there was more than life as we see it—there is something to be amazed about. Miracles do happen. There is something beyond [this] life. And we showed them—even in the most amateurish manner, we showed people that there is the possibility that you may live many lives and that you perfect yourself in each life coming back to do it better again and again. It's not all over when you die. We gave people another chance to see, to believe, if they chose, that they can come back and do it right and do it again and again until they get it perfect.

"Nothing is wasted. All of our mistakes are lessons. People have said to me at festivals, 'You know you [Laura] were such a bad person,' and I always say, 'I wasn't—I was a wonderful person because I thought I was a wonderful mother and a wonderful person.' And people identified not with the character but with the ability of the character.

"We gave people the power to be something more and in life we have to give ourselves the power to do more than we believed could be accomplished. This is the reason we [the cast] still get this tremendous attention."

And indeed *Dark Shadows* continues receiving attention in many different arenas. Innovations has a new line of *Dark Shadows,* which Lara Parker has been writing

with Dave Campiti. MPI Home Video periodically releases episodic installments of the *Dark Shadows* collection, which debuted on January 31, 1990, with a thirty-minute compilation for $9.98, followed by *The Resurrection of Barnabas Collins* (a two-hour overview of the first year, plus Barnabas's first five episodes, for $29.95). Episodes six through twenty were issued next in a multicassette package for $79.98.

"We have a whole new generation who watch us on [the MPI] video tapes," says Parker. "Now people say, 'Weren't you on *Dark Shadows*?' or 'Aren't you Angelique?' and it's sort of flattering. . . . They say, 'This is my son, this is my daughter, and I used to watch you when I was fourteen and now they watch you.'"

Other tape compilations include *Scariest Moments from "Dark Shadows," The Best of Barnabas, The Best of "Dark Shadows,"* and *"Dark Shadows": 1840 Flashback.* Only the middle three years of the five-year run were initially released. 245 cassettes, forming the entire collection, would add up to a personal investment of $7,300. Also available on video are the MGM features *House of Dark Shadows* and the 1971 sequel *Night of*

Dan Curtis, creator and director of Dark Shadows (both series) and the two feature movies (*photo courtesy Dan Curtis Productions*)

A Story of Blood Relations

house of Dark Shadows

Come see how the vampires do it.

Metro-Goldwyn-Mayer presents "House of Dark Shadows" starring Jonathan Frid Also starring Grayson Hall
with Kathryn Leigh Scott Roger Davis Nancy Barrett
John Karlen Louis Edmonds Donald Briscoe and Joan Bennett as "Elizabeth Collins Stoddard" Screenplay by Sam Hall and Gordon Russell Produced and Directed by Dan Curtis Metrocolor MGM

Most of the original cast reunited for the 1970 feature film and some even turned up in the 1971 follow-up, *Night of Dark Shadows* (*photo courtesy Dark Shadows Over Atlanta Fan Club*)

Dark Shadows, starring Parker, Selby, Jackson, and Millay.

"What Dan did in *Night of Dark Shadows* was something totally different," Millay recalls today, "but I trusted him. It was not the old character [of Laura] exactly, but I couldn't play a bigger part in the film because I was doing a running part on *Secret Storm* at the time and he [had] said, 'Diana, you can't not be in this picture. You have to come [back] for old time's sake. I'll write something in and you'll come and do three or four days work or whatever.' It ended up being a week—I was able to get ten days off of *Secret Storm*."

According to Millay, before the cancellation of *Dark Shadows* they had even asked her to come back as a regular on the series. "I said, 'fine,'" she remembers. "I had a weekly contract with *Secret Storm* and I had let Dan know I had done enough of [it] and was ready to come back and he said, 'Fine, I want you back.' I had great respect for him."

Kathryn Scott's latest production is the audio book version of *The "Dark Shadows" Companion,* in which she reunites with Jonathan Frid and Roger Davis, recreating their original characters. There is also a special section called "Out of Angelique's Shadow," with Lara Parker, who is indeed, as Curtis said, still as lovely today as she was then. At least he got that right.

ORDER NOW!
Citadel Film Books

If you like this book, you'll love the award-winning Citadel Film Series. Each volume is packed with photos and behind-the-scenes insight about your favorite stars--from James Stewart to Moe Howard and The Three Stooges, Woody Allen to John Wayne. The Citadel Film Series is America's largest and oldest film book library.

With more than 150 titles--and more on the way!--Citadel Film Books make perfect gifts for a loved one, a friend, or best of all, yourself!

A complete listing of the Citadel Film Series appears below.
If you know what books you want, why not order now!
It's easy! Just call 1-800-447-BOOK and have your MasterCard or Visa ready.

STARS
Alan Ladd
Barbra Streisand: First Decade
Barbra Streisand: Second Decade
Bela Lugosi
Bette Davis
Boris Karloff
The Bowery Boys
Buster Keaton
Carole Lombard
Cary Grant
Charles Bronson
Charlie Chaplin
Clark Gable
Clint Eastwood
Curly
Dustin Hoffman
Edward G. Robinson
Elizabeth Taylor
Elvis Presley
Errol Flynn
Frank Sinatra
Gary Cooper
Gene Kelly
Gina Lollobrigida
Gloria Swanson
Gregory Peck
Greta Garbo
Henry Fonda
Humphrey Bogart
Ingrid Bergman
Jack Lemmon
Jack Nicholson
James Cagney
James Dean: Behind the Scene
Jane Fonda
Jeanette MacDonald & Nelson
  Eddy
Joan Crawford
John Wayne
John Wayne Reference Book

John Wayne Scrapbook
Judy Garland
Katharine Hepburn
Kirk Douglas
Laurel & Hardy
Lauren Bacall
Laurence Olivier
Mae West
Marilyn Monroe
Marlene Dietrich
Marlon Brando
Marx Brothers
Moe Howard & the Three Stooges
Norma Shearer
Olivia de Havilland
Orson Welles
Paul Newman
Peter Lorre
Rita Hayworth
Robert De Niro
Robert Redford
Sean Connery
Sexbomb: Jayne Mansfield
Shirley MacLaine
Shirley Temple
The Sinatra Scrapbook
Spencer Tracy
Steve McQueen
Three Stooges Scrapbook
Warren Beatty
W.C. Fields
William Holden
William Powell
A Wonderful Life: James Stewart
DIRECTORS
Alfred Hitchcock
Cecil B. DeMille
Federico Fellini
Frank Capra
John Huston

Western Films of John Ford
Woody Allen
GENRE
Bad Guys
Black Hollywood
Black Hollywood: From 1970
  to Today
Classics of the Gangster Film
Classics of the Horror Film
Cliffhanger
Comic Support
Divine Images: Jesus on Screen
Early Classics of Foreign Film
Martial Arts Movies
Great Adventure Films
Great French Films
Great German Films
Great Romantic Films
Great Science Fiction Films
Great Spy Films
Harry Warren & the Hollywood
  Musical
Hispanic Hollywood: The Latins
  in Motion Pictures (English &
  Spanish editions available)
The Hollywood Western
The Incredible World of 007
The Jewish Image in American
  Film
The Lavender Screen: The Gay
  and Lesbian Films
The Modern Horror Film
More Classics of the Horror Film
Movie Psychos & Madmen
The Pictorial History of Science
  Fiction Films
Second Feature: "B" Films
They Sang! They Danced! They
  Romanced!: Hollywood
  Musicals

Thrillers
The West That Never Was
Words and Shadows: Literature on
  the Screen
DECADE
Classics of the Silent Screen
Films of the Twenties
Films of the Thirties
More Films of the 30's
Films of the Forties
Films of the Fifties
Lost Films of the 50's
Films of the Sixties
Films of the Seventies
Films of the Eighties
SPECIAL INTEREST
America on the Rerun
Bugsy (Illustrated screenplay)
Dick Tracy
Favorite Families of TV
Film Flubs
Film Flubs: The Sequel
First Films
Forgotten Films to Remember
Gilligan, Maynard & Me
Hollywood Cheesecake
Hollywood's Hollywood
Howard Hughes in Hollywood
More Character People
The Nightmare Never Ends:
  Freddy Krueger & "A Night-
  mare on Elm Street"
The "Quantum Leap" Book
Sex In the Movies
Sherlock Holmes
Son of Film Flubs
They Had Faces Then
Those Glorious Glamour Years
Who Is That?: Familiar Faces and
  Forgotten Names
"You Ain't Heard Nothin' Yet!"

For a free full-color brochure describing the Citadel Film Series in depth, call 1-800-447-BOOK; or send your name and address to Citadel Film Books, Distribution Center 1409, 120 Enterprise Ave., Secaucus, NJ 07094.